THE IMPERILED UNION

THE
IMPERILED UNION

*Essays on the
Background of the Civil War*

Kenneth M. Stampp

New York   Oxford
OXFORD UNIVERSITY PRESS
1980 ✓

Copyright © 1980 by Oxford University Press, Inc.

Library of Congress Cataloging in Publication Data

Stampp, Kenneth Milton.
   The imperiled union.

   Includes index.
   1.   United States—History—Civil War, 1861-
1865—Causes—Addresses, essays, lectures.
2.   United States—History—Civil War, 1861-1865—
Historiography—Addresses, essays, lectures.
I.   Title.
E458.S825   973.7′1   79-20276
ISBN 0-19-502681-0

Printed in the United States of America

For
Sara, Michèle, and Jennifer

Preface

Though I wrote each of the essays in this book to stand by itself, they do fall into a chronological order, and they all relate to a common historical theme: the American sectional conflict. They deal with the constitutional debate over the nature of the Union, some recent interpretations of southern slavery, the political crisis of the 1850s, the perennial problem of Civil War causation, and the controversial question of why the Confederate States of America lost the war. Some of the essays are in part historiographical; all advance interpretations that evolved during many years of teaching and research in what was once called the Middle Period of American history. Several of my interpretations are quite different from those I found convincing in earlier years—for example, my view of the causes of the Civil War has changed drastically since graduate-school days when I thought that Charles A. Beard was the most reliable authority on that subject. These interpretive permutations have resulted from my own research, from the writings of other historians, from debates and discussions with my students in Berkeley, and, no doubt, from my changing perceptions of human behavior and perspectives of the past.

Two of the essays, Chapters IV and VII, have not been

published before, and all but two of the remaining six have undergone substantial revision and rewriting. Two were first written as public lectures, two for delivery at historical meetings, two for inclusion in volumes of essays, and one as a contribution to a historical journal. Because of the different audiences for which they were originally prepared, some are more heavily documented than others. In order to preserve the substantial documentation that I think necessary in some chapters, the notes have been placed at the end of the book rather than at the bottom of the page. This will be an inconvenience to some readers, but it is a necessary concession to the realities of publishing today.

Chapter I, "The Concept of a Perpetual Union," my presidential address before the Organization of American Historians in 1978, was first published in the *Journal of American History*, LXV (June 1978), pp. 5-33. It is republished here with minor revisions by permission of the editor. The essay had its inception in a question that occurred to me a few years ago: When and under what circumstances was a full and systematic argument first developed to uphold the Union's perpetuity? The question proved to be more difficult than I had anticipated, because, as far as I have been able to discover, a substantial case for a perpetual Union was not devised until several decades after the adoption of the Constitution. Meanwhile, those who, at one time or another, had espoused the principle of state sovereignty had fashioned an impressive argument to defend the right of a state to nullify an act of Congress or to dissolve its connection with the Union. This may help to explain why the nationalists ultimately were unable to prevail without a resort to military force.

Chapter II, "Rebels and Sambos: The Search for the Negro's Personality in Slavery," was read at the annual convention of the Southern Historical Association in 1970 and published in the *Journal of Southern History*, XXXVII (August 1971), pp. 367-92. (Copyright 1971 by the Southern Historical Association.) With some revisions and added material on the problem of slave sources, it is republished with the permission of the Managing Editor. Most of my discussion of slave sources was part of a paper I read at a conference on slavery at the University of Mississippi in 1975; it was subsequently published in Harry P. Owens, ed., *Perspectives and Irony in American Slavery* (Jackson, Mississippi, 1976), pp. 153-70. Extracts from pp. 165-70 are reprinted with the permission of the University Press of Mississippi. I trust that my essay in its present form emphasizes sufficiently the difficulty of arriving at conclusions about the personalities of slaves from the sources available to historians, and the need to be somewhat tentative in making generalizations. I have raised doubts about the validity of the Sambo personality that Stanley Elkins described as typical of plantation slaves, but I should note that the interpretation I have presented here revises somewhat the earlier interpretation in my own study of slavery. I was, of course, the beneficiary of recent writings about slavery when I undertook the revision of this essay.

Chapter III, *"Time on the Cross:* A Humanistic Perspective,"* was originally published as an introduction to Paul A. David, Herbert G. Gutman, Richard Sutch, Peter Temin, and Gavin Wright, *Reckoning with Slavery* (New York, 1976), pp. 1-30. It has been revised to the extent necessary for publication as an independent essay and is included in this volume with the permission of Oxford University Press. Robert W. Fogel and Stanley L. Engerman, in their book, *Time on the Cross* (Boston, 1974), came down rather hard on my earlier book, *The Peculiar Institution: Slavery in the Ante-Bellum South* (New York, 1956). Tempting though it was to respond to their criticism, I have tried to address myself entirely to their interpretations and to some of their rather sensational claims. Moreover, I have left the technical criticism to other "cliometric" historians and focused on those aspects of Fogel and Engerman's book that can be dealt with competently by a historian familiar with the literary sources upon which many of their generalizations are based.

Chapter IV, "Race, Slavery, and the Republican Party of of the 1850s," was delivered in 1978 as the first Arthur Petit Memorial Lecture at Colorado College and is published here for the first time in a revised and expanded form. In recent years some historians have viewed the alleged commitment of Free-Soilers and Republicans to antislavery and racial justice with a critical eye and found good cause for considerable skepticism. Others have thought that the criticism of these political movements had gone too far and that the genuine element of idealistic antislavery needed to be reemphasized. My essay is an attempt to evaluate the arguments in this historiographical dispute and to reach some tentative conclusions from an analysis of the Lincoln-Douglas debates.

Chapter V, "The Republican National Convention of 1860," was originally a contribution to J. Jeffery Auer, ed., *Antislavery and Disunion, 1858-1861: Studies in the Rhetoric of Compromise and Conflict* (New York, 1963), pp. 193-211. It is reprinted here in revised form with the permission of the publishers, Harper & Row. Prepared under the auspices of the Speech Association of America, the book was designed to integrate rhetorical criticism and historical analysis. My essay on the Republican convention of 1860, therefore, focuses on the speeches and public discussions on the convention floor in order, first, to evaluate the kind of public image that Republicans tried to create for their party, and, second, to determine the degree to which public discussion affected the decisions of the delegates.

Chapter VI, "Lincoln and the Crisis at Fort Sumter," was first published in the *Journal of Southern History*, IX (August 1945), pp. 297-323, under the title, "Lincoln and the Strategy of Defense in the Crisis of 1861." (Copyright 1945 by the Southern Historical Association.) With the permission of the Managing Editor it is republished with revisions and additional material. Though I wrote this essay thirty-five years ago, I am still convinced that my argument is sound. However, David M. Potter raised some questions about it in the Preface to the paperback edition of his book, *Lincoln and His Party in the Secession Crisis* (New Haven, 1962). I responded to his criticism briefly in a Preface to the paperback edition of my book, *And the War Came: The North and the Secession Crisis, 1860-1861* (Baton Rouge, 1970). Excerpts from pages xiv-xvi have been integrated into my essay with the permission of Louisiana State University Press. Because I contended that Lincoln's principal goal during the secession crisis was not the preservation of peace, this essay has sometimes been interpreted as an attack upon him on ethical grounds. However, it was not written in such a spirit; rather, it was an attempt to understand how Lincoln viewed the crisis and how he responded to the problem of Fort Sumter which confronted him as soon as he became President. I found consistency between his clear determination to preserve the Union by force if necessary and his decision to send supplies to Fort Sumter—a decision that made the outbreak of hostilities extremely likely, but in a manner most favorable to him.

Chapter VII, "The Irrepressible Conflict," was written expressly for this book and has not appeared in print before. Sooner or later a historian with my teaching and research interests is bound to try his hand at explaining what *really* caused the Civil War, and this essay presents my view of the problem at this time. It is based on my reading of both the sources and the works of past and present-day historians. I trust that my discussion of the historiography of Civil War causation will make it clear that many historians disagree sharply with my point of view. On the other hand, my interpretation is far from a total break with recent historical writing on the problem. Though I do not accept the conclusions of the economic determinists, or of the school known as revisionist, or of those who stress profound cultural and ideological differences between North and South, my interpretation is in part a synthesis of other strains of thought about the causes of the Civil War.

The final chapter, "The Southern Road to Appomattox," was first delivered in 1968 at the University of Texas, El Paso, and later that year, in a revised form, at the annual convention of the American Historical Association. It was published originally as Cotton Memorial Papers No. 4 (U.S. copyright Texas Western Press, The University of Texas at El Paso, 1969), and it is republished with further revisions by permission of Texas Western Press. This essay won something less than universal acceptance in its earlier forms, and it will no doubt continue to be controversial as it is presented here. However, after seriously considering various objections to its argument, I remain stubbornly convinced of its plausibility as a partial explanation of Confederate defeat. My argument is based, first, on a conviction that the cultural differences between North and South were not in themselves sufficiently great to cause a prolonged sectional conflict and a civil war; second, on a belief, based on my reading of slaveholders' letters, diaries, and other writings, that many were severely troubled about the morality of slavery and that the proslavery argument was not sufficient to quiet their doubts. This, in my opinion, explains what appeared to have been a lack of deep commitment to the Confederate cause among a significant number of the southern people.

Though I alone am responsible for the interpretations (and errors), I am grateful to friends and colleagues for advice and critical readings of various chapters at one or another stage in their development. Chapter I was read by James H. Kettner and Robert Middlekauff; Chapter II by the late Richard Hofstadter; Chapter III by Paul A. David; Chapter VI, long ago, by Richard N. Current, who also discussed the Fort Sumter problem with me on numerous occasions; Chapter VII by

Robert Middlekauff; and Chapter VIII by George M. Fredrickson, Henry F. May, and the late David M. Potter. Sheldon Meyer and Leona Capeless improved the manuscript with their perceptive editing. Two exceptionally able research assistants, William Gienapp and Kerby Miller, gave me invaluable aid on Chapter I. Dorothy Shannon, while typing the manuscript, much of it more than once, contributed some discreet editing as well. My wife Isabel read and listened to it all several times; her gentle criticism and prodding—and patience—have been more crucial than she knows. Finally, I am indebted to the University of California, Berkeley, for research support, and to All Souls College, Oxford, for a Visiting Fellowship that enabled me to finish this book.

Berkeley   Kenneth M. Stampp
August 1979

Contents

Unum aut Plures?

I

The Concept of a Perpetual Union

The American Civil War, whatever else it may have been, was unquestionably America's most acute constitutional crisis. Viewed from this perspective, the fundamental issue of the war was the locus of sovereignty in the political structure that the Constitution of 1787 had formed. Did this document create a Union of sovereign states, each of which retained the right to secede at its own discretion? Or did it create a Union from which no state, once having joined, could escape except by an extra-constitutional act of revolution? In a Constitution remarkable for its ambiguity on many substantive matters, none was more fateful than its silence on this crucial question. Even the Articles of Confederation, which the nationalists despised, were unequivocal in defining the Union of the states. Their title was "Articles of Confederation and Perpetual Union," and Article XIII stipulated that their provisions "shall be inviolably observed by every state, and the Union shall be perpetual. . . ." Whether the incorporation of these words in the Constitution of 1787 would have been sufficient to prevent the crisis of 1861-65 is problematic, but at the very least we would have been spared the prolix and convoluted debate over the legality of secession.

In returning to the old controversy about the nature of the Union, I am not, of course, exploring one of the neglected problems of American history. The evolution of the doctrine of state sovereignty, from the protests against Alexander Hamilton's economic program to the southern movement for secession, has been thoroughly examined.[1] The growth of American nationalism in the nineteenth century has also been the subject of numerous studies.[2] However, one aspect of nationalist thought—the origin of the concept of a perpetual Union and of the complex argument that supported it—has received surprisingly little critical analysis and is not, I think, very well understood. Since the Union's perpetuity was rather firmly established at Appomattox and has rarely been disputed since, this antebellum topic of debate lacks the urgency of a still relevant political issue. Nevertheless, it is worth noting that the Unionist case was sufficiently flawed to make it uncertain whether in 1865 reason and logic were on the side of the victors—indeed, whether, in the tangled web of claims and counterclaims, they were indisputably on either side.

Lacking an explicit clause in the Constitution with which to establish the Union's perpetuity, the nationalists made their case, first, with a unique interpretation of the history of the country prior to the Philadelphia Convention; second, with inferences drawn from certain passages of the Constitution; and, third, with careful selections from the speeches and writings of the Founding Fathers. The historical case begins with the postulate that the Union is older than the states. It quotes the reference in the Declaration of Independence to "these united colonies," contends that the Second Continental Congress actually called the states into being, notes the provision for a perpetual Union in the Articles of Confederation, and ends with the reminder that the preamble to the new Constitution gives as one of its purposes the formation of "a more perfect Union." In 1869, when the Supreme Court, in *Texas* v. *White*, finally rejected as untenable the case for a constitutional right of secession, it stressed this historical argument. The Union, the Court said, "never was a purely artificial and arbitrary relation." Rather, "It began among the Colonies. . . . It was confirmed and strengthened by the necessities of war, and received definite form, and character, and sanction from the Articles of Confederation."[3] Abraham Lincoln, in his first inaugural address, summarized this part of the Unionist case most succinctly:

> [We] find the proposition that, in legal contemplation, the Union is perpetual, confirmed by the history of the Union itself. The Union is much older than the Constitution. It was formed in fact, by the Articles of Association in 1774. It was matured and continued by the Declaration of Independence in 1776. It was further matured and the faith of all the then thirteen States expressly plighted and engaged that it should be perpetual, by the Articles of Confederation of 1778. And finally, in 1787, one of the declared objects for ordaining and establishing the Constitution, was *"to form a more perfect union."*[4]

In the secessionists' interpretation of history, the states are older than the Union—in fact, they created the Union, but without yielding any part of their sovereignty. According to South Carolina's secession convention, the colonies in 1776 had declared "that they are, and of right ought to be, FREE AND INDEPENDENT STATES." The quotation is inaccurate, of course, for it substitutes "they" for "these united colonies." Similarly, the South Carolina convention ignored the reference in the Articles of Confederation to a perpetual Union, but it made the most of Article II: "each State retains its sovereignty, freedom and independence, and every power, jurisdiction and right which is not . . . expressly delegated. . . ."[5] Both Lincoln and the Supreme Court left this article unexplained.

As a matter of logic, however, the long debate over the state of the Union prior to 1787 was rather pointless, because the action of the Constitutional Convention made it irrelevant to any convincing case for or against a perpetual Union. When the Confederation Congress agreed that the states should send delegates to the Philadelphia Convention, it stipulated that the "sole and express purpose" was to revise the Articles of Confederation. The revisions, or amendments, were to be submitted to the state legislatures for ratification, each requiring unanimous consent. But the delegates ignored their instructions, wrote an entirely new Constitution, and specified ratification by specially elected state conventions rather than by the legislatures. Most important, they abandoned the requirement that ratification be unanimous. Instead, when nine states had approved, the Constitution would at once become operative for them, leaving any states that declined to ratify outside and independent.

By these acts, the Philadelphia Convention made the historical argument for perpetuity invalid, because the Convention and the ratifying states destroyed the existing Union. Every state had the option of *not* ratifying, and as many as four might have remained independent (as two did for a time) while the other nine entered a new Union.[6] The result of this dismantling of the "perpetual" Union created by the Articles of Confederation was a break in historical continuity. The preamble to the Constitution, be it noted, does not propose to make the old Union more perfect but to "*form* a more perfect Union"—that is, to create a new and better one.

That the old Union would be dissolved was acknowledged occasionally at the Philadelphia Convention, in the state ratifying conventions, and during the public debates. James Madison, in one of his contributions to *The Federalist,* agreed that if some states refused to ratify, "no political relation can subsist between the assenting and dissenting States," but he hoped for "a speedy triumph over the obstacles to *re-union.*"[7] In Philadelphia, Elbridge Gerry of Massachusetts, stressing the disunion implicit in requiring ratification by only nine states,

"urged the indecency and pernicious tendency of dissolving
. . . the solemn obligations of the articles of confederation."
He warned that if nine of the thirteen states could abolish the
old Union, six of the nine might just as easily abolish the new.[8]
At the North Carolina ratifying convention, William Lenoir
accused the authors of the Constitution of dissolving the
Union and foresaw the possibility that at some future time "it
may be thought proper, by a few designing persons to destroy
[the new Union] . . . in the same manner that the old system is laid aside."[9] In Pennsylvania, Antifederalist Robert
Whitehill objected that "it never was in the contemplation of
any man" that the delegates to Philadelphia "were authorized
to dissolve the present union."[10] However, George Clymer, a
Federalist, insisted that the Confederation Congress could not
prevent the states from entering the new Union "separately
and independently" if they wished.[11] Indeed, Thomas Fitz-
simons believed that the proposed Constitution "presupposes
. . . that no Confederation exists."[12]

Some Federalists, attempting to escape responsibility for de-
stroying the old Union, claimed that it already had been destroyed by the failure of certain states to respect their obligations under the Articles of Confederation. Madison charged
that state violations of the Articles "had been numerous and
notorious." Considering the Union as "analogous . . . to the
conventions among individual states," he believed "that a
breach of any one article, by any one party, leaves all the
other parties at liberty to consider the whole convention as
dissolved. . . ."[13] In the South Carolina legislature, Charles
Cotesworth Pinckney argued that the old compact "had been
repeatedly broken by every state in the Union; and . . .
when the parties to a treaty violate it, it is no longer binding.
This was the case with the old Confederation; it was virtually
dissolved. . . ."[14] James Iredell of North Carolina asserted
that the failure of several states to comply with the requisi-
tions of Congress meant that the "Articles of Confederation

are no longer binding."[15] John Jay contended that no Union in fact existed and that none would exist until the Constitution was ratified. Meanwhile, the states were not only without money or credit but also "without Union, without Government."[16]

Arguments such as these might have relieved the Philadelphia Convention of responsibility for abolishing the old Union; but those who advanced these arguments were playing a dangerous game, for they were explaining to posterity how even a perpetual Union might be dissolved. As a matter of fact, the secessionists of 1860-61 used precisely this logic to justify their action. Oliver Ellsworth of Connecticut, concerned about the consequences, told the delegates at Philadelphia that he "could not admit the doctrine that a breach of (any of) the federal articles could dissolve the whole. It would be highly dangerous not to consider the Confederation as still subsisting."[17] But in avoiding that trap, Ellsworth, in effect, placed the onus of terminating the old Union on his fellow delegates. Either way, the break in historical continuity undermines the case for a perpetual Union based on the country's political condition before 1787. Hence, the only relevant arguments are those derived from the language of the Constitution and from the statements of the Founding Fathers about their intentions.

When they turned to the Constitution for supporting evidence, the nationalists were confronted with the problem of ambiguity. At one point during the Philadelphia Convention, a Committee of Detail had before it a number of draft resolutions, one of which, written by Charles Pinckney of South Carolina, contained the provision of the Articles of Confederation that "the Union shall be perpetual." However, the subject was never brought before the general body for discussion. This fact is all the more remarkable because, as Max Farrand noted long ago, the drafting committee took a number of provisions directly—sometimes word for word—from the Articles.[18] Apparently the Articles, which guaranteed the states their sovereignty and independence, could speak boldly of perpetuity; but the Philadelphia delegates, who endowed the federal government with substantial power, thought such language too risky. Perhaps they also found it slightly embarrassing to declare their intention to build a new perpetual Union on the wreckage of the old.

Eventually those who developed the case for perpetuity claimed that the equivalent of the wording in the Articles had been incorporated in the preamble of the Constitution—that is, in its stated aim "to form a more perfect Union." As Lincoln argued in his first inaugural address, "if destruction of the Union, by one, or by a part only, of the States, be lawfully possible, the Union is *less* perfect than before the Constitution, having lost the vital element of perpetuity."[19] The Supreme Court found the preamble decisive on this point: "It is difficult to convey the idea of indissoluble unity more clearly than by these words. What can be indissoluble if a perpetual Union, made more perfect, is not?"[20] But Lincoln and the Court, by linking the Articles and the preamble, were again assuming continuity, and my contention is that there was no continuity—that the aim announced in the preamble is not to strengthen the old Union but to form a new, "more perfect Union." Therefore, a valid case for perpetuity cannot lean on the terms of the Articles but must demonstrate that it is clearly articulated in the Constitution itself.

Taken alone, the language of the preamble fails to solve the problem of ambiguity, for the phrase "a more perfect Union" does not inescapably evoke the idea of a perpetual Union. It is more than a mere metaphysical quibble to question whether, in a political system, perpetuity is a necessary attribute of perfection. Before 1861, many thoughtful people in all sections understood a perfect Union to be one to which the citizens of each state belong by their own consent, and they regarded a Union held together by military force as decidedly less than

perfect. In 1814, Joseph Lyman of Massachusetts contended
that a "Union founded upon submission is the Union of
slaves."[21] Years later, a southern editor opined that the term
union "implies voluntary association" and that "a compulsory
compact . . . would cease to be a Union, and would become
a despotism."[22] As late as 1861, this alternative concept of perfection still troubled some northern Unionists.

Apart from the preamble, the body of the Constitution contains its own ambiguities. Clearly, some delegates to the Philadelphia Convention wanted to take from the states every
vestige of sovereignty and create a consolidated national government. The Virginia Plan would have denied the states equal
representation in either branch of Congress, endowed Congress with power to veto the acts of state legislatures, and
authorized federal military coercion of any state that failed to
fulfill its duties. A few delegates would have gone further and
either abolished the states or converted them into mere administrative districts. But these were the very issues on which the
nationalists suffered their most severe defeats. The rejection
of the veto power in the Virginia Plan and the provision for
equal representation of all states in the Senate, together with
the subsequent adoption of the Tenth Amendment, preserved
the principle of state sovereignty to some indeterminate degree. Thus, as Alpheus T. Mason observed, the nationalists had
failed "to stave off what they thought would vitiate the nationalizing features of the new system." They had protested
that equal representation "would infect the new government
with the same disease that plagued the Articles," for it "would
make the states a constituent part of the national government,"
thus permeating it with "the very infirmity which the new
system was designed to correct. . . ."[23]

In the end, "We the People," in whose name the Constitution was framed, created a Union of states—to be sure, a union
with the powers of the federal government significantly aug-
mented and the powers of the states curtailed, but a Union

rather than a consolidated nation nonetheless. Only uncertainty about which states would ratify prevented the delegates from writing the preamble to read "We the People of the States of New Hampshire, Massachusetts, Rhode Island," etc., rather than "We the People of the United States."[24] Moreover, Article VII declares that "The Ratification of the Conventions of nine States, shall be sufficient for the Establishment of this Constitution between the States [not the people of the states] so ratifying the Same." Following this article, a concluding statement compounds the ambiguity: "Done in Convention by the Unanimous Consent of the States present. . . ."

Needless to say, the defenders of state sovereignty suffered their own damaging defeats. They lost equal state representation in the House of Representatives. The portentous "supreme law of the land," "necessary and proper," and treason clauses, as well as the requirement that state officers take an oath of allegiance to the federal Constitution, were powerful weapons in the hands of nationalists in subsequent years. But none of these provisions is fatal to the logic of the case for state sovereignty. For example, secessionists could argue that the Constitution is the "supreme law" and that state officers take an oath of allegiance only so long as their state chooses to remain in the Union. Nationalists made much of the fact that popularly elected state conventions, not the legislatures, ratified the Constitution, but secessionists could contend that what the sovereign people of a state had done they could also undo. To quote Alpheus T. Mason again, "What emerged from this often ambiguous interplay was a document no less ambiguous. The Constitution reflects the conflicting influences and drives of latter-day Federalists and Antifederalists alike."[25]

In truth, the wording of the Constitution gives neither the believers in the right of secession nor the advocates of a perpetual Union a case so decisive that all reasonable persons are bound to accept it. Lincoln, in his first inaugural address, offered the most persuasive constitutional argument for perpe-

tuity ever devised, but at the same time he virtually conceded
that the language of the document is not conclusive. "Perpetuity," he said, "is *implied*, if not expressed, in the fundamental
law of all national governments. It is safe to assert that no
government proper, ever had a provision in its organic law for
its own termination." Lincoln then tried to place the burden
of proof on the secessionists, claiming that they could not destroy the Union "except by some action not provided for in
the instrument itself."[26] Unfortunately, the secessionists could
argue with equal plausibility that Lincoln could not preserve
the Union except by some action whose constitutionality
would also be in doubt.

Because of the ambiguities of the Constitution, those who
built the case for perpetuity eventually turned to the debates
at the Philadelphia Convention for explanations and amplifica-
tion. Instead, they found baffling inconsistencies and obscuri-
ties. The delegates never engaged in a discussion that produced
a clear consensus that the Union formed by the Constitution
was to have perpetual life; nor did they arrive at an understanding about the related matter of federal options if one or
more states should attempt secession. To be sure, Madison
later recalled that "It appeared to be the sincere and unanimous wish of the Convention to cherish and preserve the
Union of the States."[27] But that was merely a pious wish
shared by Federalists and Antifederalists alike, not an interpretation of agreements reached in formal debates. Some delegates did hint at the idea of a perpetual Union circuitously—for
example, when they agreed that the government was to oper-
ate on the people directly rather than through the states, and
when they decided to circumvent the state legislatures and
secure ratification "by the supreme authority of the people
themselves."[28] Occasionally a delegate expressed a general purpose, unrelated to any specific clause in the Constitution, that
might give comfort to future nationalists. Thus, Elbridge
Gerry of Massachusetts asserted that "we never were inde-

pendent States, were not such now, and never could be.
. . . The States and the advocates for them were intoxicated
with the idea of their *sovereignty*."[29] George Read of Delaware called for a national government that would be strong
enough to obliterate the states, one that would "soon of necessity swallow all of them up."[30]

However, sentiments such as these usually were expressed in
support of proposals that were rejected and therefore do not
elucidate the Constitution as adopted. For example, Madison
favored a congressional veto of state legislation in order to
"controul the centrifugal tendency of the States; which, without it, will continually fly out of their proper orbits. . . ."
He also urged strong federal authority over the state militias,
because "the greatest danger is that of disunion of the States."[31]
Neither power was granted. At the same time, Madison spoke
eloquently against the alternative of federal military coercion
of a state, which he feared would "be considered by the party
attacked as a dissolution of all previous compacts by which it
might be bound."[32] This was not the only occasion when
Madison seemed to give comfort to both perpetualists and
secessionists.

During the Philadelphia debates, several delegates viewed
the prospect of secession quite philosophically, offering neither
a federal remedy nor a doctrine of perpetuity. Rufus King,
speculating about circumstances that might cause the southern
states to secede, concluded that they would always be in a
position to say, "do us justice or we will separate."[33] Because
the country was so large, Nathaniel Gorham of Massachusetts
doubted that it would "150 years hence remain one nation."[34]
William Blount of North Carolina predicted privately that in
"not many Years" the states would be "distinct Governments
perfectly independent of each other."[35]

Most arresting is the contribution that George Mason inad-
vertently made to the mechanics of secession, should it ever
be attempted. Mason opposed referring the Constitution to

state legislatures for ratification, "because succeeding Legislatures having equal authority could undo the acts of their predecessors; and the National Govt. would stand in each State on the weak and tottering foundation of an Act of Assembly."[36] For this reason, he favored ratification by the people through state conventions. Of course, the logic of this argument could easily lead to the conclusion that succeeding state conventions, having equal authority, could undo the work of their predecessors—precisely what the secessionists of 1860-61 believed. Thus, delegates to the Philadelphia Convention, in effect, explained both what proved to be the principal justification for secession (violations of the compact) and the method by which it might be accomplished (through a state convention).

The debates over ratification in the state conventions and in the press merely heightened the uncertainty about whether secession was a reserved right of the states. In a general evaluation of the debates, Alpheus T. Mason noted that "strategic considerations drove the contestants on both sides to minimize and exaggerate. To quiet the fears of opponents, advocates of ratification said things which, in later years, proved embarrassing to themselves and misleading to scholars."[37] Some Federalists stated clearly and openly their belief that the Union was to be perpetual and that the federal government would have sufficient power to prevent secession. Jay, in *The Federalist*, affirmed that "the great object" of the Convention was to "preserve and perpetuate" the Union.[38] In the Massachusetts convention, several delegates maintained that the federal government would be able to protect the Union from the acts of "designing and refractory states."[39] In South Carolina, Federalist Charles Cotesworth Pinckney urged his countrymen to "consider all attempts to weaken this Union, by maintaining that each state is separately and individually independent, as a species of political heresy. . . ."[40] Samuel Johnson told the North Carolina convention that "The Constitution must be the supreme law of the land; otherwise, it would be in the power of any one state to counteract the other states, and withdraw itself from the Union."[41]

However, most Federalists cautiously confined such opinions to their private correspondence or evaded the issue altogether. Blunt assertions that ratification was a perpetual commitment were hardly calculated to convert the doubtful and might even lose some supporters; hence, the Federalists were decidedly more intent on giving assurances that the states would retain their sovereignty. The declaration by John Dickinson of Delaware that the Union would be "a confederacy of republics . . . in which, the sovereignty of each state was equally represented," was by no means uncommon.[42] In their formal resolutions of ratification, the state conventions merely agreed to "assent to, and ratify" the Constitution; none acknowledged that it was entering a perpetual Union. Seven states demanded a constitutional amendment explicitly declaring, in the words of the Massachusetts resolution, "that all Powers not expressly delegated . . . are reserved to the several States, to be by them exercised." Virginia's convention affirmed "that the powers granted under the Constitution being derived from the People of the United States may be resumed by them whensoever the same shall be perverted to their injury or oppression. . . ."[43] The New York and Rhode Island conventions, attempting to reassure those with lingering doubts, adopted a similar resolution.

Several prominent Federalists made substantial contributions to *both* sides of the debate between nationalists and advocates of state sovereignty. At the Pennsylvania ratifying convention, even so rugged a nationalist as James Wilson, having one day affirmed that "the bonds of our Union ought . . . to be indissolubly strong," could another day assure the timid that "those who can ordain and establish may certainly repeal or annul the work of the government. . . ."[44]

Madison urged the delegates to the Philadelphia Convention

to give the federal government sufficient power to prevent a dissolution of the Union. When he learned that the New York convention might reserve the right to withdraw from the Union if certain constitutional amendments were not adopted, his private advice to Hamilton was unequivocal: "My opinion is that a reservation of a right to withdraw . . . is a *conditional* ratification, that it does not make N. York a member of the New Union. . . . The Constitution requires an adoption *in toto,* and *for ever.* . . . In short any *condition* whatever must viciate [*sic*] the ratification."[45]

In contrast, Madison's contributions to *The Federalist* sounded no such warning of a perpetual commitment; rather, they dwelt on the theme that the states would retain much of their sovereignty. Ratification, he explained, "is to be given by the people, not as individuals composing one entire nation; but as composing the distinct and independent States to which they respectively belong. . . . Each State . . . is considered as a sovereign body independent of all others, and only to be bound by its own voluntary act. In this relation then the new Constitution will . . . be a *federal* and not a *national* Constitution." The powers delegated to the federal government, Madison added, "are few and defined. Those which are to remain to the State Government are numerous and indefinite."[46] At the Virginia ratifying convention he asked: "Who are the parties to . . . [the Constitution]? The people—but not the people as composing one great body; but the people as composing thirteen sovereignties."[47] The contest in Virginia was close, and Madison's comforting description of the new political order was important in carrying the day for the Federalists.

Hamilton's course during the debates over ratification indicated a readiness to say almost anything that would assure Federalist success. At the Philadelphia Convention, no proposal to curb the power of the states had been too drastic for him—even federally appointed state governors with power to veto acts of the legislatures. The federal government, he said, must have full sovereignty, for "the states will be dangerous . . . and ought to be extinguished . . . or reduced to a smaller scale."[48] The finished Constitution disappointed Hamilton, and he feared that a dissolution of the Union would be "the most likely result." His only hope was that a "good administration" might "triumph altogether over the state governments and reduce them to intire [sic] subordination, dividing the larger states into smaller districts."[49]

However, while there was danger that New York might not ratify, Hamilton suppressed his true feelings and courted those who were wavering with beguiling expressions of respect for the states. To be sure, in *The Federalist*, he hinted at an "indissoluble" Union, but in an ambiguous context which left it unclear whether he was merely expressing a hope or stating what he considered to be a fact. He also observed that the federal government would have power to enforce its laws without state assistance, but he said nothing about federal authority over states that tried to secede.[50] Beyond these ambiguities, which were characteristic of Federalist rhetoric, Hamilton made two rather astonishing comments. First, in *Federalist* 33, he declared with sweet innocence that the Constitution's "necessary and proper" clause, which he would use with great effect as Secretary of the Treasury, "may be chargeable with tautology or redundancy, [but it] is at least perfectly harmless."[51] Second, in *Federalist* 28, he suggested forms of protective state action against a threat of federal tyranny:

> It may safely be received as an axiom in our political system, that the state governments will in all possible contingencies afford complete security against invasions of the public liberty by the national authority. . . . The Legislatures . . . can discover the danger at a distance; and possessing all the organs of civil power and the confidence of the people, they can at once adopt a regular

plan of opposition, in which they can combine all the resources of the community. They can readily communi-
cate with each other in the different states; and unite
their common forces for the protection of their common
liberty.

Thus, Hamilton concluded, the people would be able,
"through the medium of their state governments, to take measures for their own defence with all the celerity, regularity
and system of independent nations. . . ."[52] This, I think, is a
fair description of both the justification and the method of
nullification and secession when they were attempted in later
years.

While the Federalists quieted the fears of the doubtful with
equivocations and comforting promises that state sovereignty
would survive ratification, the Antifederalists, ironically,
warned that the Constitution would in fact create a perpetual
Union. Latter-day nationalists might have taken much comfort from descriptions of the new Union provided by the opponents of ratification. Only occasionally did Antifederalists
agree with John Smilie of Pennsylvania that if the people
changed their minds, "they will still have a right to assemble
another body . . . to abrogate this Federal work so ratified."[53] More commonly, they spoke of ratification as a binding commitment that could not be annulled. Luther Martin
cautioned that if a Bill of Rights were not adopted later, "you
cannot free yourselves from the yoke you will have placed on
your necks."[54] A Pennsylvania Antifederalist asserted that the
question of ratification "involves in it not only your fate, but
that of your posterity for ages to come. . . . Consider then
duly before you leap, for after the Rubicon is once passed,
there will be no retreat."[55] No nationalist ever stated the essence of his case more succinctly than the New York Antifederalist, Robert Yates. The proposed Constitution, he said,
"will not be a compact entered into by states, in their cor-

porate capacities, but an agreement of the people of the United States, as one great body politic. . . ."[56]

The key word in the Antifederalist attack was "consolidation," which in its application meant the reduction of the states to impotence in a perpetual Union. According to Richard Henry Lee, "The plan of government now proposed is evidently calculated totally to change, in time, our condition as a people. Instead of being thirteen republics, under a federal head, it is clearly designed to make us one consolidated government."[57] Whitehill of Pennsylvania complained that the phrase "We the People of the United States" meant that "the old foundation of the Union is destroyed, the principle of confederation excluded, and a new and unwieldy system of consolidated empire is set up upon the ruins of the present compact between the States."[58]

The Antifederalists, not the Federalists, occasionally declared bluntly that the remedy of secession would not be available to a state whose citizens found the new Union despotic. Smilie, on further reflection, decided that the federal government "must be too formidable for any single State, or even for a combination of the States, should an attempt be made to break and destroy the yoke of domination and tyranny. . . ."[59] Martin foresaw a time when a state might be driven to resist federal oppression. But, he noted, the proposed Constitution provides that a citizen who supports his state would be "guilty of a direct act of treason; reducing, by this provision, the different states to this alternative,—that they must tamely and passively yield to despotism, or their citizens must oppose it at the hazard of the halter, if unsuccessful. . . ."[60] Thus, a few Antifederalists, to advance their cause, tried to force a clarification of federal-state relations; but the Federalists, appreciating the value of ambiguity, were usually too cautious to respond.

The consequence was that, in 1789, when the present Union

came into existence, the question whether a member state
could secede at will remained unresolved. In spite of the occasional oblique hints of the Federalists and warnings of the
Antifederalists, the debates over ratification had been remarkably unenlightening. No state convention made the right of
secession the subject of extended inquiry; not one of *The
Federalist* papers was devoted to the matter; nor was it aired
in the press or in the flood of pamphlets written by the friends
and foes of the Constitution. In short, the Founding Fathers,
hoping for the best, left the question of perpetuity to posterity.

Perhaps it was inevitable that in the young republic a decisive resolution of this crucial matter should have been long
delayed. What is surprising is that even a theoretical argument for a perpetual Union—at least one that can be described
as systematic and comprehensive—failed to materialize for
many years. Such an argument is not to be found in the writings of Hamilton or, as far as I have seen, in the writings of
any other early nationalist. The Supreme Court, as we know,
did not confront the issue directly until after the Civil War.
Indeed, though threats of secession were common and were
soon supported by an elaborate case for state sovereignty,
some forty years elapsed before a comparable counterargu-
ment for perpetuity bolstered the Union cause.

Meanwhile, the most common perception of the Union was
as an experiment whose future was uncertain at best. The
Union was valued less for its own sake than as a means to certain desirable ends, especially the protection of the people's
liberties and the defense of the country from enemies abroad.
Not many were inclined to challenge John Randolph when
he declared in 1814 that the Union was "the *means* of securing
the safety, liberty, and welfare of the confederacy and not
itself an end to which these should be sacrificed."[61] Apparently almost everyone, even the most ardent believers in state
sovereignty, thought of disunion as a calamity. "Among the
upright and intelligent," wrote Edmund Randolph, "few can

read without emotion the future fate of the States if severed from each other." The Antifederalist Richard Henry Lee agreed that "our greater strength, safety, and happiness, depends on our union. . . ."[62] But there were few signs of the kind of American national identity from which might grow a concept of a perpetual union as an end in itself. As William T. Hutchinson observed, "The weakness of [the people's] nationalism is not surprising. If their loyalty to Great Britain, centuries-old in the background of many of them, could not outlast a decade of discontent charged against their mother country, it could hardly be transformed overnight into a heartfelt allegiance to a newly-born United States of America."[63]

Almost from the start, anxiety about the future of the Union centered on the prospect of a separation along sectional lines. In 1792, both Thomas Jefferson and Hamilton warned President Washington of this danger. According to Jefferson, disunion was possible because "the division and interest happens unfortunately to be so geographical." Hamilton reported that, in both North and South, "there are respectable men who talk of separation, as a thing dictated by the different geniusses [sic] and different prejudices of the parts."[64] A few years later, a Boston writer also perceived the potential of disunion in the "coincidence which happens to exist between the *political differences*, and the *geographical divisions* of the United States."[65] Hamilton's own fiscal policies contributed significantly to the earliest stirrings of sectional unrest. In 1790, the Virginia General Assembly denounced federal assumption of state debts as repugnant to the Constitution and proclaimed its members "the guardians . . . of the rights and interests" of the people, the "sentinels placed by them over the ministers of the federal government."[66] Hamilton, after countenancing in *The Federalist* the very role that Virginia was playing, now wrote in alarm that her action was "the first symptom of a spirit which must either be killed or kill the constitution of the United States."[67]

Distressed by the signs of sectional tension, Washington devoted much of his Farewell Address to stressing the value of
the Union. He urged his countrymen to reject "whatever may
suggest even a suspicion that it can in any event be abandoned" and to rebuke "every attempt to alienate any portion
of our country from the rest." Above all, he resorted to what
was at that time the most persuasive appeal: "Is there doubt
whether a common government can embrace so large a
sphere? Let experience solve it. . . . It is well worth a fair
and full experiment."[68] Thus, Washington rested his case on
the prevalent idea of a political experiment, not on a concept
of a perpetual Union.

Soon after Washington's appeal, Madison and Jefferson formulated an ingenious doctrine of state sovereignty that stood
for many years as a formidable challenge to any notion that
the Union's permanence was underwritten by the Constitution
itself. Their Virginia and Kentucky Resolutions of 1798-99
held that the Constitution is a compact to which "each State
acceded as a State"; that the states had reserved the right to
judge when the federal government exceeds its powers; that
such measures are "unauthoritative, void, and of no force";
that states can "interpose" their authority to arrest the evil of
unconstitutional federal acts; and that nullification is a "right-
ful remedy" in such cases. These resolutions, especially Jefferson's, adopted only a decade after the ratification of the Constitution, contained the essential ingredients of the case not
only for nullification but for secession as well.

Yet even their passage evoked no detailed Unionist rebuttal.
Nine states, all controlled by the Federalists, responded with
assertions that the federal judiciary was the proper judge of
the constitutionality of acts of Congress. Several of them denounced Madison's and Jefferson's resolutions as "inflammatory and pernicious" or "dangerous in their tendency." The
Massachusetts legislature affirmed that the states were united
"by a common interest, which ought to render their Union

indissoluble." The most forceful reaction came from the New Hampshire legislature, which resolved to defend the Union "against every aggression, either foreign or domestic" and to "support the government of the United States in all measures warranted by the [Constitution]."[69] Though these hostile responses to the Virginia and Kentucky Resolutions indicated the need for a well-reasoned counter-argument, the Federalist legislatures, like the Federalist press, left the need unfilled.

However, the public reaction did include one early, fragmentary statement of the case for a perpetual Union—not from a political body or public meeting but, ironically, in a pamphlet by another Virginian, the staunch Federalist Henry Lee. "In point of right," Lee argued, "no state can withdraw itself from the Union. In point of policy, no state ought to be permitted to do so." The burden of his case rested on the premise that the federal government "was created by, and is entirely dependent on, the people." The state governments "are not parties to the . . . [Constitution], they did not form or adopt it, nor did they create or regulate its powers. . . . The people, and the people only, were competent to those important objects." The Constitution, he concluded, "was proposed not to the different state governments, but to the people for their consideration and adoption. The language of the instrument is no longer the language of the states. . . . It was sanctioned by the people themselves, assembled in their different states in convention."[70] This single, relatively brief, formulation of a case against state sovereignty and the right of secession is the only one that I have discovered in the Federalist period. If there were others, they were rare, for even the Virginia and Kentucky Resolutions more commonly elicited sentimental Unionist appeals, doleful descriptions of the tragic effects of disunion, and admonishments to give the "experiment" a chance to prove itself.

During the Republican era, the Louisiana Purchase, the embargo, and the War of 1812 provoked northeastern Federalists to take a turn at calculating the value of the Union. An address prepared by the minority in the House of Representatives who had voted against war in June 1812 claimed that the Union was based on "a form of government in no small degree experimental, composed of *powerful* and independent sovereignties. . . ."[71] Timothy Pickering of Massachusetts found "no magic in the sound of Union. If the great objects of union are utterly abandoned . . . let the Union be severed. Such a severance presents no Terrors for me."[72] Threats of this kind usually educed the same mild responses as those evoked in the Federalist era. Jefferson loved the Union, but to him it was always a means rather than an end in itself; and in his mind the question of secession centered on its wisdom, not its constitutionality. He had toyed with a threat of secession when he wrote the Kentucky Resolutions, and he had discussed it with John Taylor purely in terms of its expediency. During his presidency, Jefferson viewed with equanimity the prospect of an eventual separation of the eastern and western states: "God bless them both and keep them in the union if it be for their good, but separate them if it be better."[73] Even young John Quincy Adams could see no alternative to acquiescing in secession if it were attempted. "I love the Union as I love my wife," he wrote. "But if my wife should ask for and insist upon a separation, she should have it though it broke my heart."[74]

The consensus in all sections still seemed to be that the future of the Union was uncertain and largely dependent on the practical value of its survival. In 1815, Joseph Story urged that useful public works be undertaken in order that "the United States will be endeared to the people. . . . Let us prevent the possibility of a division, by creating great national interests which shall bind us in an indissoluble chain."[75] Samuel H. Smith, in a Fourth of July oration, pinned his hopes for perpetuity not on the wording of the Constitution but on a mystical belief that the Union was "the emanation of Divine Beneficence" and therefore "stamped with the seal of Heaven."[76] Occasionally, especially during the War of 1812, these by now traditional appeals were punctuated with sharp denials that the states were completely sovereign. "There is no inherent power left in any state, without the consent of congress, to recede," asserted one nationalist. "Massachusetts cannot prevent [its] agents from being *hanged by the neck* for the *first* overt act they commit against the confederation of the Union," warned another.[77] But neither advanced an argument to offset the well-developed case for the sovereignty of the states.

Once again, as during the Federalist period, the only impressive, though still fragmentary, presentation of a case for a perpetual Union that I have found came from a Virginian— Thomas Ritchie, editor of the Richmond *Enquirer*. During the War of 1812, in a series of editorials, Ritchie denounced the allegedly disloyal elements in New England who wished "to dash to pieces the holy ark of the Union of our country."[78] These editorials culminated in one that accused the delegates to the Hartford Convention of plotting secession and warned that "the first act of resistance to the law is *treason* to the U.S." The editorial concluded thus:

> No man, no association of men, no state or set of states *has a right* to withdraw itself from this Union, of its own accord. The same power which knit us together, can only unknit. The same formality which forged the links of the Union, is necessary to dissolve it. The *majority of States* which form the Union must consent to the withdrawal of *any one* branch of it. Until *that* consent has been obtained, any attempt to dissolve the *Union*, or obstruct the efficacy of its constitutional laws, is Treason— Treason to all intents and purposes. . . . This illustrious Union, which has been cemented by the blood of our forefathers, the pride of America and the wonder of the world must not be tamely sacrificed to the heated brains

or the aspiring hearts of a few malcontents. The Union
must be saved, when any one shall dare to assail it.[79]

Ritchie's rhetoric, to be sure, was more passionate assertion
than reasoned argument, but it was as far as the case for a
perpetual Union had developed even at the end of the War
of 1812.

For more than another decade, the idea of the states irrevo-
cably united by unbreakable constitutional commitments and,
to the extent necessary, by federal force, was seldom voiced.
Thus, in 1815, a long oration entitled "Permanency of the
American Union," delivered by an unidentified speaker before
the Literary and Philosophical Society of Charleston, still described a voluntary Union bound by tradition, affection, and
practical interests. The thought that the Union is temporary,
he said, "would chill the hope of every patriot." However,
"we think we see by the lights of history, that the American
union is permanent," because "time is preparing new cords to
encircle and bind us more closely and more firmly." Commerce unites the nation in mutual dependence; the press helps
to "effect uniformity of opinion and of conduct"; and the
"anticipation of the future grandeur of united America . . .
will never allow the sentiment of Union to be cold." Hence,
he concluded, from the adoption of the Constitution, "wealth
and happiness, the fruit of union, have confirmed our determination to remain forever one people. . . . [The] union is the
result of *reason*, sympathy and general interest, not (like the
nations of Europe) of compulsion. In the retrospect we see
every thing to revive and animate *affection*, nothing that can
irritate the pride or provoke the anger of *any one* of its members."[80] In short, the experiment was a success, and, because
the Union had proved its value, love for it had grown apace.
But, until then, love for the Union had not generated a compelling case for perpetuity.

The debate over Missouri's application for admission as a

slave state provoked an unprecedented outburst of secession threats. According to Daniel P. Cook, an Illinois congressman, "The sound of disunion . . . has been uttered so often . . . and has become so familiar, that it is high time . . . to express our solemn disapprobation. . . ." Secession, wrote an editor, "has been spoken of publicly and privately—on the floor of congress and in private coteries . . . and [is] regarded as an event likely to happen.'[81] The threats did not emanate from Southerners alone. Senator Walter Lowrie of Pennsylvania warned that if the choice were between a dissolution of the Union and the extension of slavery, "I, for one, will choose the former." John Quincy Adams wrote in his diary, "If the Union must be dissolved, slavery is precisely the question upon which it ought to break."[82] Both Jefferson and John Adams feared that the Union would not survive, and even the young nationalist, Henry Clay, told John Quincy Adams that "he had not a doubt that within five years from this time the Union would be divided. . . ."[83]

The Missouri crisis did produce a number of brief, dogmatic assertions of federal supremacy. For example, Representative Joshua Cushman of Massachusetts declared that "sovereignty resides, not in minute portions or States, but in the whole people whose will, expressed in their Constitutional organs, is the law, and must be obeyed." The people of the United States gave the federal government "ample powers, competent not only to ordinary, but to extraordinary exigencies. Hence we may hope for the durability and perpetuity of our Republic." Cushman urged that "the proud and aspiring States . . . be taught to know their distance, to lower their lofty crests, to revolve in their humble orbs around the National Government. . . ."[84] But this outburst, and others like it, did not supply the still missing articulation of a concept of a perpetual Union. As in the past, the characteristic response to secession talk was an appeal to both sentimental and practical motives for keeping the country united. William Plumer, Jr., of New

Hampshire, reminded the malcontents that "our Confederacy is not so easily destroyed; it is cemented by the mutual interests of all its members; and the understandings, the affections, and the hearts, of the people are knit together in one common bond of indissoluble union."[85] Thus, even Republican nationalists, in the heat of the Missouri controversy, failed to challenge the firmly established and much-used case for state sovereignty with a full-blown Unionist case of their own.

During the years of uncertainty about the nature and future of the Union, the United States Supreme Court delivered some of the most impressive challenges to the state sovereignty school. Although the Court under Chief Justice John Marshall never gave an explicit opinion on the right of secession—and was never asked to—it repeatedly emphasized the supremacy of the federal government in the exercise of its constitutional powers.[86] In *Fletcher* v. *Peck*, Marshall ruled that a state "is part of a large empire; . . . a member of the American union; and that union has a constitution the supremacy of which all acknowledge, and which imposes limits to the legislatures of the several states. . . ."[87] In *McCulloch* v. *Maryland*, he stressed the "supreme law of the land" clause and affirmed that the federal government, "on those subjects on which it can act, must necessarily bind its component parts."[88] In *Gibbons* v. *Ogden*, Marshall reiterated this point, adding that in 1787, when the sovereign states "converted their league into a government, . . . the whole character in which the States appear, underwent a change. . . ."[89]

By far the sharpest of Marshall's decisions relevant to the nature of the Union—that in the case of *Cohens* v. *Virginia*—appears to have been shaped in part by the Missouri crisis that immediately preceded it. In the most forceful language he ever used on the question of state sovereignty, Marshall wrote:

> That the United States form, for many, and for most important purposes, a single nation, has not yet been de-

nied. In war, we are one people. In making peace, we are one people. In all commercial regulations, we are one and the same people. . . . America has chosen to be, in many respects, and to many purposes, a nation; and for all these purposes, her government is complete; to all these objects, it is competent. The people have declared, that in the exercise of all the powers given for these objects, it is supreme. . . . The constitution and laws of a State, so far as they are repugnant to the constitution and laws of the United States, are absolutely void. These States are constituent parts of the United States. They are members of one great empire—for some purposes sovereign, for some purposes subordinate.

Marshall concluded that the people who had made the Constitution can unmake it, but this supreme power "resides only in the whole body of the people; not in any sub-division of them. The attempt of any of the parts to exercise it is usurpation, and ought to be repelled by those to whom the people have delegated their power of repelling it."[90] Thus, Marshall clearly affirmed the power of the federal government to resist an attempt by a state or "a section of the nation" to unmake, or overthrow, the Constitution of the United States. What he still left unsettled was whether a state had the right not to unmake the Constitution but peacefully to separate from the Union it had created. That, of course, was the crucial question of 1861-65.

By the end of the 1820s, after the government under the federal Constitution had been in operation for forty years, the prevailing view of the Union in the political rhetoric of the time still remained that of an experiment, albeit one that had already shown much promise of success. Though secession had been threatened repeatedly and the idea of secession as a constitutional right of the sovereign states was fully developed, the secessionist argument still lacked a comprehensive and effective rebuttal. More than that, the language of state sovereignty had become deeply embedded in the American vocabulary. Almost everyone spoke of the Union as "our confederacy," of the Constitution as a "compact." The term "sovereign" was associated with the states far more than with the federal government; and state legislatures took for granted their right to "instruct" their United States senators on how to vote on important legislation. Meanwhile, formulations of the idea of a perpetual Union remained rare, brief, and incomplete.

Of course, this does not mean that, during the four decades following ratification of the Constitution, the state of the Union had not changed. It had, after all, survived, and with each passing year an attempt to dissolve it was bound to become an increasingly serious and formidable undertaking. Love for the Union had become well-nigh universal, secession a disaster dreaded by all—even by those who believed it to be a constitutional remedy for unbearable grievances. Forty years had afforded time for the emergence of numerous interest groups possessing practical reasons for wishing to preserve the Union, especially those involved directly or indirectly in interstate commerce. Indeed, hardly any group existed that would not be in some degree adversely affected by disunion. These interests, together with the sense of nationhood and pride in American citizenship that had developed during and immediately after the War of 1812, made almost inevitable the eventual construction of a case for a perpetual Union.[91] The Western world was entering an era of romantic nationalism, and the United States was much affected by its impelling force.

The spark that finally set off what can only be described as an explosion of Unionist rhetoric was the nullification controversy in South Carolina. Between 1830 and 1833, all of the ideas that formed the core of the case for a perpetual union were embodied in the speeches or writings of at least a half dozen major politicians and constitutional scholars. Among these, Daniel Webster's reply to Robert Y. Hayne, while the most famous and certainly the most eloquent, was by no means the most penetrating or comprehensive. Webster presented much of what became the classic unionist argument and denied that a state can protect secessionists from the penalties for treason, but the heart of his response was a traditional, sentimental appeal for the Union as a blessing to mankind. He rejoiced "in whatever tends to strengthen the bond that unites us, and encourages the hope that our Union may be perpetual."[92]

Soon after Webster had finished, Senator Edward Livingston of Louisiana delivered a less glittering but far more trenchant speech against nullification and the alleged constitutional right of secession. His key assertion was that in all the "attributes of sovereignty, which, by the federal compact, were transferred to the General Government, that government is sovereign and supreme; the States have abandoned, and can never reclaim them." They had, by the Constitution, "unequivocally surrendered every constitutional right of impeding or resisting the execution of any decree or judgment of the Supreme Court. . . ." A state, he agreed, might elect in an extreme case to attempt secession, but such action "is not a right derived from the constitution." Rather, it is an extralegal right, and "whenever resorted to, it must be at the risk of all the penalties attached to an unsuccessful resistance to established authority."[93]

In 1831, in a Fourth of July oration, John Quincy Adams presented a case for perpetuity that was notable for its emphasis on the Union's historical origins. The states, he claimed, were the offspring of the Union, whose existence was announced in the Declaration of Independence. By that Declaration, the people of the united colonies "had bound themselves, before God, to a primitive social compact of union, freedom and independence." Thereafter, "no one of the States whose people were parties to it, could, without violation of that

primitive compact, secede or separate from the rest." Nullification, he said, was a virtual attempt to dissolve the Union, "to
organize an insurrection against the laws of the United States;
to interpose the arm of State sovereignty between rebellion
and the halter, and to rescue the traitor from the gibbet." In
short, nullification "would, however colored, and however
varnished, be neither more nor less than treason, skulking
under the shelter of despotism."[94]

Story, in his *Commentaries on the Constitution,* published
in 1833, amplified the historical argument and culled passages
from *The Federalist* and the ratification debates that bolstered
the case against state sovereignty. From his rather selective
reading of this literature, he concluded that the Federalists
had always emphasized the Constitution's "character as a permanent form of government, as a fundamental law, as a supreme rule, which no State was at liberty to disregard, suspend, or annul. . . ." In an exhaustive examination of the
nature of compacts, Story found no basis for the contention
that the Constitution was a mere compact between sovereign
states. He thought it significant that at the ratifying conventions no state reserved the right "to dissolve its connection,
. . . or to suspend the operation of the Constitution, as to itself." Therefore, he concluded, the Constitution was "framed
for the general good and designed for perpetuity."[95]

Of the many writers who joined the attack on the South
Carolina nullifiers, James Madison was no doubt the most pro-
lific. Until his death in 1836, he devoted much of his time to
refuting those who claimed that his Virginia Resolutions and
Jefferson's Kentucky Resolutions of 1798-99 justified nullification or secession. Numerous efforts, he often complained,
"are made to stamp my political career with discrediting inconsistencies."[96] He responded with a flood of letters, essays,
and memoranda asserting that what South Carolina now
claimed the right to do was not what he and Jefferson had had

in mind thirty years earlier. The Virginia Resolutions, Madison insisted, gave "not a shadow of countenance to the doctrine of nullification."[97] His defense was not altogether convincing, but in developing it he made a significant contribution to the emerging nationalist case for a perpetual Union. There is a great difference, he wrote, between "the claim to secede at will" and the right to secede "from intolerable oppression." The first is "a violation, without cause, of a faith solemnly pledged. The latter is another name only for revolution, about which there is no theoretic controversy."[98] For ordinary disputes over the powers and jurisdiction of the federal government, the Constitution recognizes the Supreme Court, not the individual states, as the final arbiter. Madison branded state nullification as a "preposterous and anarchical pretension" to which the Constitution gives not the slightest support.[99] Collectively, these writings of his last years constitute something approaching a revised version of his contributions to *The Federalist*, with the new emphasis decidedly more on the national features of the Constitution and less on the surviving aspects of state sovereignty. Most important, he was now open and explicit in denying the constitutional right of secession by individual states.[100]

Among the numerous formulations of the concept of a perpetual Union that appeared during the nullification crisis, one stands above the rest for its incisiveness, coherence, and comprehensiveness: President Andrew Jackson's Proclamation on Nullification of December 10, 1832. This document, prepared for Jackson by Secretary of State Edward Livingston, comes close to being the definitive statement of the case for perpetuity. It is so complete that even the Supreme Court, in *Texas v. White*, could find no additional argument of any significance. The proclamation embraces the crucial nationalist assumption that the Union is older than the states: "Under the royal Government we had no separate character; our opposition to its oppressions began as *united Colonies*. We were the United States under the Confederation, and the name was perpetuated and the Union rendered more perfect by the Federal Constitution." How was it possible, then, "that the most perfect of these several modes of union should now be considered as a mere league that may be dissolved at pleasure?"

The notion of a right of secession, Jackson claimed, grew out of the mistaken belief that the Constitution is only a compact between states whose sovereignty was not diminished by the act of ratification. Yet the Constitution was not framed by the states but by the people, "acting through state legislatures when they made the compact . . . and acting in separate conventions when they ratified those provisions." Thus, they formed "a *government*, not a league. . . . It is a Government in which all the people are represented, which operates directly on the people individually, not upon the States." The individual states did not retain all their sovereignty, for their citizens transferred their allegiance to the government of the United States and became American citizens. "How, then, can that State be said to be sovereign and independent whose citizens owe obedience to laws not made by it . . . ?" Showing a respect for the Supreme Court that had been less evident in the past, Jackson proclaimed it, rather than the states, the proper authority to settle disputes arising under the Constitution and laws of the United States. He denied that the right to secede was a constitutional remedy reserved to the states, for such action "does not break a league, but destroys the unity of a nation." Secession is an act of revolution, which "may be morally justified by the extremity of oppression; but to call it a constitutional right is confounding the meaning of terms. . . ."

Jackson's conclusion appears to be the model from which Lincoln drew inspiration for some critical statements in his first inaugural address. Jackson warned the people of South

Carolina that he would fulfill the obligation imposed on him by the Constitution "to take care that the laws be faithfully executed." In this he had no discretionary power, for "my duty is emphatically pronounced in the Constitution." There- fore, if an attempt at disunion should lead to "the shedding of brother's blood," that result could not be attributed to "any offensive act on the part of the United States." Having urged South Carolinians to consider the dangers they risked, Jackson closed on a softer note with an appeal to their love for the Union.[101]

Before the enactment of the tariff compromise of 1833, the concept of a perpetual Union had achieved its full develop- ment, and a President of the United States had pledged himself to use all the power of the federal government to uphold it. Yet, even after the nullification controversy, when the theo- retical justification for the use of force stood ready to be in- voked in a national crisis, most Americans still dreaded such a remedy, as did Jackson himself. During the sectional conflicts of the 1840s and 1850s, they continued to cherish the hope that love for the Union, together with the Union's obvious benefits, would suffice to hold it together. Even so, by 1833, to the nationalists the Union had become an absolute, an end in itself; and, in retrospect, it seems clear that by then the time had passed when the people of a state might resort to the rem- edy of secession without confronting the coercive authority of the federal government. The arguments for perpetuity of Webster, Livingston, John Quincy Adams, Story, Madison, and Jackson, among others, had brought the days of our po- litical innocence to an end.

Nevertheless, an adequate explanation of the events of 1861 must take into account the fact that the case for state sover- eignty and the constitutional right of secession had flourished for forty years before a comparable case for a perpetual Union had been devised. Because that case came so late, because the logic behind it was far from perfect, because the Constitution and the debates over ratification were fraught with ambiguity, the pessimistic premonition of John Quincy Adams, expressed in a letter of 1831, was tragically fulfilled. "It is the odious nature of the question," he wrote, "that it can be settled only at the cannon's mouth."[102]

Two Controversies over Slavery

II

Rebels and Sambos:
The Search for the Negro's Personality
in Slavery

I think it is safe to say that no historical scholar has ever been altogether satisfied with his sources. Whatever the subject of investigation, whether it concerns the remote or recent past, the available records never tell all the historian would like to know—never permit more than a partial reconstruction and tentative explanation of any historical event. Under the best of circumstances the historian is obliged to write about men and women he has never known from scattered, fragmentary, and often censored records that leave many crucial questions unanswered.

Historians who investigate the subject of slavery in the antebellum South confront this problem in one of its more exasperating forms; and they find it most acute when they inquire, as some have done in recent years, about the interior life of slaves—what slaves felt and thought about bondage, how they related to the master class, what their religious experiences meant to them, how their family life affected them, and, most difficult of all, what kinds of personalities they developed. Most of the conventional literary sources for information of this kind simply do not exist. The slaves had no

organizations, no literary or political spokesmen, and no newspapers; they kept no diaries and rarely wrote letters. We are
indebted to Robert S. Starobin for collecting and publishing
the few letters from slaves that survive; but since most of them
were written to white masters and mistresses, they do not help
us penetrate very deeply into the mind of the slave.[1] No congressional committee investigated the conditions of American
slavery or permitted slaves to give their own testimony. No
antebellum oral history project collected data through the
systematic interviewing of slaves. The evidence from white
slaveholders about the lives of slaves is immense—some of it of
great value—but the evidence from the slaves themselves is but
a small trickle.[2]

Slave evidence in twentieth-century historical writings
comes chiefly in three forms—the autobiographies of fugitives
and freedmen, slave narratives based on oral interviews undertaken in the 1920s and 1930s, and postbellum collections of
slave songs and folklore. These sources have been exploited
extensively—too often uncritically, as if they were the long-
lost keys to a full understanding of the slave's mind, feelings,
and personality. I do not mean to suggest that they have no
value, but I do think that their extensive use merely illustrates
the scarcity of good source material and the desperation of
historians who strive to understand slave life.[3] In evaluating
the quality of this material, we should remember that slaveholders also wrote autobiographies; but historians use them
cautiously and sparingly, because the diaries, letters, and other
contemporary writings of slaveholders are plentiful and vastly
superior as sources. For the same reason, no one in the 1930s
belatedly proposed a program to interview former slaveholders.

Slave autobiographies and narratives hardly inspire confidence in their reliability when they are subjected to the tests
that should be used in evaluating all forms of historical evidence. For example, historians, like courts of law, are highly

skeptical of second-hand or hearsay evidence. Therefore it is important to know that most of the autobiographies of former slaves were actually written by white amanuenses. In an autobiography of this kind we never hear directly from the former slave; instead we read what a white author tells us in *his* words a former slave told him. I do not propose that we reject altogether this hearsay evidence—we cannot be quite as rigid as courts of law—only that we use it with extreme caution and with a clear understanding of what it is.

Historians, again like courts of law, agree that the best evidence is not only first-hand but recorded soon after an event has occurred. This rule is especially relevant to the evaluation of slave narratives compiled in the 1920s and 1930s.[4] These narratives were given to us by people who were, on the average, more than eighty-five years old, who were born in the 1850s, and who were children when the Civil War began. For the slave experience all we can obtain from most of them are the memories of childhood after the passage of more than seventy years.

Finally, the historian must always consider the circumstances which produced a body of evidence and the motives of those who provided it. We properly discount as special pleading the public defenses of slavery written by slaveholders and their political and intellectual apologists, but we must also take account of the extremely subjective influences that helped to shape the autobiographies and narratives of former slaves. It is not enough merely to say that *all* sources are biased, or that historians have methods for dealing with the problem of bias, for these autobiographies and narratives present some rather special problems. In addition to the common shortcomings of autobiographies—special pleading, the author's desire to make himself look heroic or long-suffering, and, above all, his fallible and selective memory—the autobiographies of former slaves were usually tailored to the tastes of a northern antislavery audience. Even some of the best of them, including the autobiography of Frederick Douglass written by himself, were in part abolitionist tracts.

The slave narratives of the 1930s were gathered by predominantly white interviewers at a time when race relations in the rural South hardly encouraged candor. The narrators were not only very old but characteristically very poor and economically dependent on whites. Many of them seemed to believe that the interview might have some bearing on their chances of receiving a rumored federal pension. The importance of these subjective influences can be illustrated by the following facts: slavery was remembered as a harsh institution by 7 percent of the narrators interviewed by whites and by 25 percent of those interviewed by blacks, by 16 percent of the narrators living in the South and by 38 percent of those living in the North, by 3 percent of the narrators clearly dependent on white support and by 23 percent of those who seemed to be financially independent. Comparing the nineteenth-century autobiographies of former slaves with the narratives of the 1930s, the autobiographies describe life in bondage less favorably than the narratives. Given the very different external pressures on the autobiographers and narrators, this result is hardly surprising.[5]

Another source of direct evidence concerning the minds and personalities of slaves may prove to be the most valuable of all. This is the evidence provided by freedmen in the years immediately following their liberation, perhaps until the end of the 1860s. The time of emancipation was a crucial point in the history of black people in America—a "moment of truth," as Eugene Genovese calls it. When four million slaves were transformed into freedmen they found opportunities that had never existed before to explain in their own words who they were and what they thought. Their behavior in the presence of whites, though still far from uninhibited, derived its motivating force from within more often than in slavery days, when so much of it had to conform to the norms set by white masters. In short, the 1860s was a time of self-revelation, a time when the testimony of those who had lived in slavery first became a significant part of the historical record.

Of course, all freedmen did not suddenly find voices or begin an orgy of letter-writing and diary-keeping—after all, well over 90 percent of them were illiterate. Nevertheless they did speak in unprecedented numbers. They expressed their opinions to members of freedmen's aid societies and to agents of the Freedmen's Bureau; some of them even testified before congressional committees. Very soon black newspapers appeared in the South, and their editors began to get some input from the freedmen themselves. Leaders emerged from their ranks to speak for them; within a few years some served in constitutional conventions, in state legislatures, and a small handful in Congress. More than ever before, blacks moved about freely, consulted their own wishes and interests, and made their own decisions. For the first time those who had been slaves could come together in religious and secular organizations which they controlled. The crucial fact about all these developments is that they occurred when it was still possible to study the freedmen in action with the minds and personalities that had been formed in slavery days. Thus, compared with the limited testimony available from earlier years, we have during the 1860s a veritable explosion of firsthand testimony from those who so very recently had been slaves. Here, surely, is some of the best evidence historians can hope to find to answer the questions they have been asking about the culture, personalities, and minds of black people in bondage.[6]

These, then, are the black sources for nearly all that we are able to learn directly about the slave. They tell us much, though far less than we would like to know—and too often pretend to know. However, for the *external* behavior of slaves, from which historians can draw inferences, speculate, and hypothesize about the slave mind and personality, three kinds of white sources exist which I think are at least as valuable as the available black sources. These consist of the diaries of slaveholders, the essays written by slaveholders on the management of slaves, and the advertisements for fugitive slaves. I am not suggesting that they can tell us anything directly about what slaves thought or felt; but as sources for the behavior of slaves, I do think that they pass the tests for the evaluation of historical evidence remarkably well. First, all of them provide large quantities of first-hand rather than hearsay evidence; second, they record events soon after they occurred; last, external pressures for distortion were minimal, while internal pressures to report accurately were substantial. Slaveholders kept diaries for their own private use, not for public consumption. Although we must be aware of the unconscious censorship that may affect the contents of even a private diary, historians justly prize these documents as among the most candid sources available to them. Slaveholders' essays on slave management were published in southern agricultural periodicals that circulated mostly among the slaveholders themselves. Their purpose was not propagandistic but to offer professional advice. We must, of course, make allowances for the inclination of the writers to establish a good image among their peers; but my impression of these essays is that they are, by and large, remarkably candid about the problems of managing slaves and are rich in illustrative detail. In the advertisements for fugitive slaves, which deserve more attention than they have received, the major exception to their descriptive reliability is the frequent insistence of the master that his slave ran away for "no cause." But to misrepresent the appearance or characteristic behavior of a fugitive would obviously defeat the purpose of advertising. Therefore, historians interested in slave culture and in what can be inferred about the slave's mind and personality from his behavior should not overlook the evidence available in these white sources.[7]

Still, all of this adds up to making the best of a bad situation. The fact remains that in the case of most available sources the ubiquitous white man, as master, editor, traveler, reporter, amanuensis, and interviewer, stands forever between slave and historian, telling the historian how the slave was treated, how he behaved, what he thought, and what sort of personality he had. However imaginative the historian may be, he will always have trouble breaking through this barrier, and he will always be handicapped by the paucity of first-hand testimony from the slave himself.

Given the problem of sources, it is hardly surprising that historians who have studied the behavior and personality of the Negro in slavery have failed to agree on the meaning of the evidence and have left many problems unsolved. Indeed, two of the books that addressed themselves most directly and explicitly to this problem—Herbert Aptheker's *American Negro Slave Revolts*[8] and Stanley M. Elkins's *Slavery*[9]— arrived at opposite conclusions. Aptheker, whose purpose was to depict "in realistic terms the response of the American Negro to his bondage," found "that discontent and rebelliousness were not only exceedingly common, but, indeed, characteristic of American Negro slaves."[10] Elkins, focusing more narrowly on plantation field hands, suggested that characteristically they were not rebels but Sambos, with personalities very much as they were described in southern lore:

> Sambo, the typical plantation slave, was docile but irresponsible, loyal but lazy, humble but chronically given to lying and stealing; his behavior was full of infantile silliness and his talk inflated with childish exaggeration. His relationship with his master was one of utter dependence and childlike attachment: it was indeed this childlike quality that was the very key to his being.[11]

These two portraits of the southern slave, one as the discontented rebel, the other as the passive Sambo, are worth examining, because together they define the two extremes—the outer limits—of possible slave behavior.

Of the two portraits, Aptheker's is the easier to evaluate. From his empirical research, mostly in newspapers and government documents, he claimed to have uncovered approximately 250 revolts and conspiracies, each involving a minimum of ten slaves and having the winning of freedom as its apparent goal.[12] He made no attempt to explain slave behavior with any personality theory; but implicit throughout the book is an assumption that when a mass of people is as brutally exploited as the southern slaves, discontent and rebelliousness against the ruling class are bound to be endemic.

We are indebted to Aptheker for providing a useful corrective to the view, still prevalent when his book was published in 1943, that the slaves were almost uniformly contented. He presented detailed accounts of a few rebellions and of a number of authentic conspiracies; but above all he showed how persistent the *fear* of rebellion was among white Southerners and how frequently insurrection panics drove them to near hysteria. However, the book has three major shortcomings. First, it fails to use sources critically; second, it argues beyond the evidence; and, third, it does not distinguish between slave discontent, which was probably widespread, and slave rebelliousness, which was only sporadic and always local. A more accurate title for this book would be "American Negro Slave Revolts, Conspiracies, and Rumors of Conspiracies," for it is the last of these things that most of the book is really about.

An example of Aptheker's misinterpretation of his data can be found in the twelve pages devoted to the years 1835-42, which follow a chapter on the Nat Turner Rebellion. He begins by declaring: "The year 1835 witnessed the reopening of this never-long interrupted drama of the organized struggle

of an enslaved people to throw off their yoke." Then, presenting his evidence year by year, he tells us of rumors that "began to fly around," of plots that "were overheard," of reports of "what appears to have been a bona fide conspiracy," and of whisperings of "large-scale conspiracies." Aptheker then relates that after 1842 the "remainder of the forties were relatively quiet years." But his own evidence indicates that in the history of slave insurrections, except for the usual budget of rumors and alarms, the years 1835-42 were also quiet ones.[13] Clearly, though revealing much about the anxieties of white masters, he failed to establish his thesis that rebelliousness was characteristic of American Negro slaves.

Elkins, in a decidedly more influential counter-hypothesis, presented the placid and contented Sambo as the typical plantation slave. He was concerned almost entirely with describing and explaining Sambo's personality and behavior rather than with offering convincing evidence of Sambo's existence. He disposed of the problem of evidence in two sentences: "The picture [of Sambo] has far too many circumstantial details, its hues have been stroked in by too many different brushes, for it to be denounced as counterfeit. Too much folk-knowledge, too much plantation literature, too much of the Negro's own lore, have gone into its making to entitle one in good conscience to condemn it as 'conspiracy.' " Beyond this, at several points, Elkins simply told his readers that the widespread existence of Sambo "will be assumed," or will be "taken for granted," and then proceeded to his explanation.[14]

Since the Elkins thesis is familiar, I will only summarize the three chief points of his strategy, which are 1. his use of comparative history, 2. his use of personality theory, and 3. his use of analogy. Elkins argued, first, that the Negro with a Sambo-type personality was not a universal product of slavery in the Americas but, because of certain unique conditions, a peculiar product of slavery in the United States. The principal differences between North American and Latin American slavery, he believed, were the latter's relatively greater flexibility and openness, the far greater opportunities it gave the Negro to escape into free society, and the presence of not one but several centers of authority: church and state as well as master. In the antebellum South, slavery grew unchecked by church or state; its form was dictated by the needs of the planter capitalists; and state laws treated the slave essentially as property, thus depriving him of his identity as a human being. Southern slavery operated as a "closed system" in which the slave had only limited contacts with free society and little hope of becoming part of it. It was this closed system that produced Sambo.[15]

Second, to explain how southern slavery had so devastating an effect on the Negro, Elkins utilized some of the literature on personality theory. Using Freud, he pointed to the impossibility of a "meaningful relationship between fathers and sons" and to the difficulty of becoming a man without "acceptable male models to pattern yourself after."[16] But he relied chiefly on a blend of certain aspects of the interpersonal theory of Harry Stack Sullivan and of role psychology. Sullivan maintained that personality can be studied only as it manifests itself in interpersonal relations,[17] and he stressed the manner in which personality is formed in relationships with so-called "significant others"—that is, with those in positions of authority or otherwise capable of enhancing or endangering one's security. Out of anxiety concerning the attitudes of significant others a person learns to behave in ways that meet their expectations. Eventually, some of this behavior is internalized and becomes part of the personality. Role psychology emphasizes the roles, or models of behavior, that are extended to individuals throughout their lives by organizations, by groups, and by society at large.[18] There are rewards for playing the expected role well and penalties for playing it badly or not at all. How well an individual plays a role de-

pends in part on his skill, on his motivation, on his "role knowledge," and on "role clarity," the last requiring a condition of general agreement about proper behavior. The more clearly a role is defined the better it is likely to be performed, and the greater its impact is likely to be on the personality of the performer. Thus, it may be argued that to some degree one's personality consists of the roles one plays.

Applying these ideas to southern plantation slaves, the Elkins hypothesis runs something like this: In a closed system from which there was virtually no escape, the master, whose authority was absolute, who dispensed rewards and punishments, was the only significant other in the slave's life. The master defined the slave's role, provided him with a clear and simple script, judged his performance, and rewarded him according to its quality. The result was Sambo, the perpetually dependent, irresponsible child. Elkins did not claim that Sambo was the universal slave personality, for he recognized that there was "a great profusion of individual types." A "significant number," including house servants, skilled craftsmen, slaves who hired their own time, slave foremen, and those who lived in single families on small farms, managed "to escape the full impact of the system and its coercions upon personality." For these slaves "there was a margin of space denied to the majority," and few of them took on the character of Sambo. But of the mass of field hands on large and small plantations, though Elkins conceded that some did not fit the classic Sambo type, it was clearly his intention to suggest that Sambo embraced the majority.[19]

Finally, to illuminate certain aspects of southern slavery, Elkins resorted to the analogy of the Nazi concentration camp. He warned that an analogy must not be taken literally, for things that are analogous are not identical. His purpose was to examine two situations which, in spite of their "vast dissimilarities," contain "mechanisms that are metaphorically comparable and analytically interchangeable." In this analogy

the mechanism was "the infantilizing tendencies of absolute power."[20] Elkins saw a rough similarity between the Sambo produced by slavery on the southern plantation and the human product of the concentration camp, whose experiences often led to personality disintegration, infantilization, and even a tendency to look on SS guards in a childlike way as father figures.

According to Elkins, both the master of the plantation and the commander of the concentration camp were the only significant others in the lives of the people under their control. Both could mete out punishment or grant protection, while the slaves and inmates were reduced to complete dependence. "A working adjustment to either system," Elkins concluded, "required a childlike conformity"; the crucial factor

> was the simple "closedness" of the system, in which all lines of authority descended from the master. . . . The individual, consequently, for his very psychic security, had to picture his master in some way as the "good father," even when, as in the concentration camp, it made no sense at all. But why should it not have made sense for many a simple plantation Negro whose master did exhibit, in all the ways that could be expected, the features of the good father who was really "good"? If the concentration camp could produce in two or three years the result that it did, one wonders how much more pervasive must have been those attitudes, expectations, and values which had, certainly, their benevolent side and which were accepted and transmitted over generations.[21]

It is no small tribute to Elkins's achievement that his essay should have provided the focus for virtually all scholarly discussion of slave personality for more than a decade and that it elicited a volume of commentary, with a response from Elkins.[22] I doubt that any future historian of slavery will fail to recognize Sambo as an authentic personality type among the

slaves on southern plantations. More generally, Elkins contributed much to arousing interest in the problem of slave
personality and to making historians aware of the possibility
of dealing with the problem through an interdisciplinary approach. On the other hand, I believe that the discussion was
for a time rather too much preoccupied with his hypothesis.
Elkins, after all, intended his essay to be the start of a new approach, suggestive rather than definitive; and, accordingly, he
left plenty of work for others to do. Moreover, his essay contains a number of flaws, some of which recent investigations
have clearly exposed.

Because of their fascination with the essay's methodology
and conceptualization, many scholars seemed to have overlooked its lack of empirical evidence—its bland assumption
that the prevalence of Sambo on the plantations could be
taken for granted. The concentration-camp analogy, of
course, proved nothing; at most, Elkins could argue that *if*
the typical plantation slave was a Sambo, the literature on the
camps might suggest an explanation of *why* he was a Sambo.[23]
Elkins, as I have noted, took Sambo for granted because
Sambo appeared so prominently in antebellum plantation literature. But most of this literature was written by white men,
much of it in defense of slavery. To accept it at face value
would be only slightly more justifiable than to accept at face
value a body of literature on the concentration camps written
not by former inmates and competent scholars, such as Bruno
Bettelheim, but by the SS guards. Moreover, the public testimony of white witnesses did not by any means invariably
support the Elkins hypothesis, for contemporary writers
often spoke of the resourcefulness and guile of Negroes, and
numerous essays on the governing of slaves warned masters
never to trust them.[24] Elkins was certainly mistaken when he
asserted that the prevalence of Sambo was part of the Negro's
own lore. Neither the slave narratives nor the Negro's oral

tradition gave validity to Sambo as the typical plantation
slave; rather, both emphasized the slave dissemblers and the
ways in which they deceived their masters.

In an essay on sources, Elkins explained why he did not use
manuscript plantation records, which constitute the private
testimony of the white slaveholders. Manuscripts, he wrote,
"are useful principally on questions of health and maintenance, and they have already been worked over with great
care and thoroughness by eminent scholars."[25] But the plantation manuscripts are in fact quite valuable for the study of
slave personality, and even information on maintenance and
health (including mental health) is decidedly relevant. If the
manuscripts had been worked over by other scholars, that was
really of little help to Elkins, because no one had used them
for precisely his purpose and with his hypothesis in mind. He
offered no explanation for his failure to examine other
sources, especially newspapers, with their extremely revealing
fugitive-slave advertisements, and contemporary periodicals,
with their countless essays on the management of slaves and
their descriptions of slave behavior. As a result, Elkins was
obliged in the end to offer corroborating testimony from
sources such as John Pendleton Kennedy's *Swallow Barn*
(1832), where we learn that the slave had "the helplessness of
a child—without foresight, without faculty of contrivance,
without thrift of any kind"; and from Edward Pollard's *Black
Diamonds Gathered in the Darkey Homes of the South*
(1859), which assures us that "The Negro . . . in his true
nature, is always a boy, let him be ever so old." "Few Southern writers," Elkins concluded, "failed to describe with obvious fondness . . . the perpetual good humor that seemed
to mark the Negro character, the good humor of an everlasting childhood."[26]

David C. McClelland, one of Elkins's authorities, devoted
two chapters of his book on personality to the problems of
collecting and interpreting data. In one of these chapters, Mc-

Clelland observed that an individual's personality may change "as he changes or as the scientist's insights improve."[27] This is an important point, for the accumulation of an ample supply of data is often the beginning of improved insight. Eugene D. Genovese, after paying tribute to Elkins's achievement, reminded us "that all psychological models may only be used suggestively for flashes of insight or as aids in forming hypotheses and that they cannot substitute for empirical investigation."[28]

The remaining shortcomings of the Elkins essay concern its conceptual and methodological strategies and its apparent misunderstanding of the life of plantation slaves. Several critics have questioned Elkins's comparative approach, particularly his exaggerated notion of the success of church and state in Latin America in protecting the humanity of slaves. They have also demonstrated that Sambo was not a unique product of North American slavery, for he appeared in Brazil, in the French colonies, and in Spanish America as well. "On close inspection," wrote Genovese, "the Sambo personality turns out to be neither more nor less than the slavish personality; wherever slavery has existed, Sambo has also."[29] Since Sambo was not a unique product of the antebellum South, the explanation for him may be sought not there alone but everywhere in the western world.

Elkins's concentration-camp analogy, as I will try to demonstrate, may help to illuminate the condition of one small group of plantation slaves, but it is of little value as an aid to understanding Sambo. He would have been quite justified in using his analogy for limited purposes, provided, first, that he could have established a controlling mechanism that was in truth "analytically interchangeable," and, second, that the obvious and admitted elements of dissimilarity between slavery and the concentration camps did not themselves have an important bearing on the formation of personality. To Elkins, the "shock and detachment" experience of adult camp inmates—an experience that slaves born into the system did not endure—was less crucial to personality than adjusting to "the requirements of a 'closed system' of absolute authority."[30]

However, Elkins dismissed far too easily certain vital elements of dissimilarity that did have a profound impact on adult personality, and first among them was the systematic policy of terror and brutality in the concentration camps. Slaves were rarely treated as cruelly as camp inmates. The realities of slavery dawned on them gradually over a period of years, while the realities of the concentration camp hit the inmates more suddenly, often with one stunning and disintegrating blow. Moreover, plantation slavery was a rational institution; it had a logic and purpose that was utterly missing in the camps, where life, with its total unpredictability, had about it a nightmarish quality. The extermination policy eventually adopted in the camps destroyed all belief in the value of human life. Everybody in the camps, as Bettelheim observed, "was convinced that his chances for survival were very slim; therefore to preserve himself as an individual seemed pointless."[31] It was this hopelessness, rather than the absolute authority of one significant other, that explained the phenomenon of inmates walking without resistance to the gas chambers. Slavery, though its influence on personality was severe, still afforded its victims something a good deal closer to normal life, and therefore it did not ordinarily have anything like as shattering an impact on personality as did the concentration camps.

The most momentous difference between the two institutions was evident in the fact that only about 700,000 out of nearly eight million inmates survived the camps. Elkins declared that he was necessarily concerned only with the survivors, but among those he thus eliminated from consideration were nearly all who in some manner resisted the system and many whose personalities were not crushed by it.[32] To establish a comparable situation in slavery, one would have to

imagine that the system had become vastly more brutal in the 1850s and that, in consequence, only 400,000 rather than four million slaves were alive in 1860, the rest having been murdered by their masters for resistance or rules infractions, or in medical experiments, or as victims of a Negro extermination policy. One could hardly argue seriously that such a profound change in the nature of slavery—in terms of the slave's expectations of survival—would have had no significant impact on personality. Nor would one then want to limit a study of slave personality to the cringing 400,000 survivors. It would appear, therefore, that absolute power was not the controlling mechanism as much as the manner in which the power was used.

In turning finally to the theoretical foundation of the Elkins essay, the important question is whether personality theory, when applied to the available data, points unmistakably to Sambo as the typical plantation slave. This does not seem to be the case, for there are important aspects of the theories that Elkins used, together with much data, that suggest other plausible hypotheses.[33] In addition, personality theory contains more than a few ambiguities. For example, role psychology does not provide a clear answer to the question of whether the Sambo role played by many plantation slaves was internalized and became part of their personalities, or whether it was a form of conscious hypocrisy, a mere accommodation to the system. David McClelland asserted that the roles an individual plays are part of his knowledge "and therefore part of his personality."[34] But Ralph Linton thought that playing a role proves nothing about an individual's personality, "except that he has normal learning ability." The psychologist, he argued, must be able "to penetrate behind the façade of social conformity and cultural uniformity to reach the authentic individual."[35] Similarly, Erving Goffman contended that role performance "serves mainly to express the characteristics of the task that is performed and not the characteristics of the performer."[36] Two recent writers on role theory, Theodore R. Sarbin and Vernon L. Allen, illustrating a new trend, hardly touched on the matter of role and personality. They were far more interested in the interaction between role and social identity, and they stated explicitly that they "are not using 'social identity' and 'self' as synonyms. Selfhood . . . embodies more residuals of behavior than those generated through role enactment."[37]

At times Elkins approached this problem warily, suggesting only that the roles an individual plays are internalized to "an extent," or that "deliberate" role-playing and "natural" role-playing grade into each other "with considerable subtlety." Returning to the problem in an appendix, Elkins again refused to generalize: "The main thing I would settle for would be the existence of a broad belt of indeterminacy between 'mere acting' and the 'true self' "; to the extent that they "grade into one another" it seems "permissible to speak of Sambo as a personality 'type.' "[38]

These cautious statements are hardly disputable, but they do not represent the tone of the essay as a whole. The clear inference to be drawn from Elkins's comparison of North American and Latin American slavery, from his introduction of the concentration-camp analogy, and from his use of personality theory is that Sambo was not a dissembler but a distinct personality type and the typical plantation slave. Indeed, in one footnote, Elkins explicitly rejected the possibility that the Sambo role was only a form of conscious accommodation. Not until after emancipation, he insisted, did the Negro's "moral and psychological orientation" permit the development of "the essentially intermediate technique of accommodation . . . as a protective device beneath which a more independent personality might develop."[39]

Yet the theory of role psychology, when applied to the information we have concerning the life and behavior of plantation slaves, provides plenty of room for personalities other than Sambo. This theory, which stresses the importance of "role clarity," holds that adequate role performance will be unlikely if there is uncertainty concerning the nature of an appropriate role. In addition, role conflict occurs when a person finds himself occupying more than one status at a given time, each requiring different behavior, or when there is more than one source of advice about how a role is properly played. Conflicting obligations or conflicting expectations may lead to a personal crisis and to difficulty in playing any role successfully.[40] Moreover, as Goffman has shown, an individual may play a role with no deep involvement in it—"with detachment, shame or resentment." In such a case there is "a wedge between the individual and his role, between doing and being," and the individual denies "not the role but the virtual self that is implied in the role for all accepting performers."[41] These were problems that troubled plantation slaves in their daily lives—problems whose psychic strains they resolved in ways that varied with their individual natures and experiences.

Harry Stack Sullivan's model of interpersonal relationships, when fully utilized, also provides theoretical support for a variety of plantation slave personalities. Sullivan described a highly complex and subtle interplay between an individual and the significant others in his life. One side of it—the side that Elkins explored—is the anxiety that helps to mold an individual's personality as he behaves in certain ways to meet the expectations of authority figures. But there is another side, which involves the conscious manipulation of significant others to the individual's own advantage. By the time a child is ready for school, Sullivan observed, he has "evolved techniques" for handling his parents "with only a modicum of pain"; he now encounters other adults "who have to be managed."[42] In addition to manipulation, there is still another and less fortunate way that a person deals with tendencies in his personality that are strongly disapproved by his significant others. These tendencies are neither lost nor resolved but simply "dissociated from personal awareness." In the process of dissociation they are "excluded from the self" and become part of the unconscious, or "extra-self." But the tendencies still remain an integral part of the personality, manifesting "themselves in actions, activities, of which the person himself remains quite unaware."[43]

Sullivan's concept of dissociation describes a condition which, at a certain point, may lead to serious psychic problems. Generally speaking, he believed that the "healthy development of personality is inversely proportionate to the amount, to the number, of tendencies which have come to exist in dissociation."[44] In Elkins's conceptualization we encounter the significant other of Sullivan's interpersonal theory but not the phenomena of manipulation and dissociation; yet all three concepts are integral parts of Sullivan's theory and are relevant to the problem of slave personality.

I believe that a historian utilizing the available evidence concerning slave behavior and master-slave relationships and taking account of all aspects of the personality theories used by Elkins will be forced to abandon his hypothesis that Sambo was the typical plantation slave. Several historians have already suggested other possibilities.[45] The following is my own sketch of an alternative to the Elkins hypothesis.

I would begin by accepting Elkins's description of southern slavery as a closed system from which few escaped and in which the slaves had only limited contacts with free society; his emphasis on the dehumanizing tendencies of slavery (though not in North America alone); his belief that the system had built into it powerful pressures toward dependent, infantilized, emasculated personalities;[46] and his conception of the master as a formidable significant other in the life of nearly every slave—partly an object of fear, partly a Freudian father figure. But I would reject his assertions that a master's power was absolute; that he was the only significant other in the lives of his slaves; that he was the sole author of the role, or roles, they played; and that southern slaves were almost totally dehumanized. Finally, I would suggest that plantation slaves encountered significant others in their own families and communities; that dissembling, manipulation, dissociation, role conflict, and lack of role clarity were important ingredients of slave behavior; and that plantation life enabled most slaves to develop independent personalities—indeed, provided room for the development of a considerable range of personality types.

In his concentration-camp analogy Elkins observed that a small minority of the inmates, who held minor administrative jobs, was able to escape the full impact of the system on personality. This minority could engage in petty underground activities, such as stealing blankets, getting medicines from the camp hospital, and negotiating black-market arrangements with the guards. These activities turned out to be crucial for the fortunate prisoner's psychological balance. For him the SS was not the only significant other, and the role of the child was not the only one open to him—he was able to do things that had meaning in adult terms.[47]

If these trivial activities could preserve the psychic balance of camp inmates, then the plantations offered the great mass of field hands infinitely greater opportunities to preserve theirs. Though plantation slaves were exposed to influences that encouraged childlike dependency and produced emasculated personalities, the system nevertheless permitted them a degree of semi-autonomous community life and the opportunity to do many things that had meaning in adult terms. They lived in their own separate quarters where they could escape the constant scrutiny of their masters. Unlike the slaves on the sugar and coffee plantations of Brazil and Cuba, where men outnumbered women by as many as three to one, those on the plantations of the Old South could experience something like a normal sex life, because the sexes were usually

evenly divided. Though slave marriages had no legal support
and families were ever in danger of being broken by sales,
southern slaves nevertheless lived in family groups more often
than those on the commercialized plantations of Latin America.[48] A survey of the slave narratives of the 1930s indicates
that, while 39 percent of the slave children lived with their
mothers alone, slightly more than half lived in families with
both mothers and fathers.[49]

Slave families, because of their relative lack of economic
significance, their instability, and the father's severely restricted role, may well have been no more important in the
lives of slaves than the broader plantation slave communities.
The latter provided opportunities for self-expression in their
celebrations of holidays, in their music and folklore, and in
other aspects of community life. Historians have perhaps
viewed religion among plantation slaves too much in terms of
the nonreligious uses to which it was put. We know that
masters used religious indoctrination as a means of control
and that slaves found in their religious services subtle ways of
protesting their condition. But there were other and deeper
ways in which religion served them. It provided a system of
beliefs that comforted and sustained them in their bondage
and assured them of their individual worth, and it afforded
additional means of self-expression that helped them retain
their psychic balance.[50] I do not believe that a truly autono-
mous Afro-American subculture developed in slavery days,
but some of the ingredients for one were certainly there.

According to Goffman, "it is a basic assumption of role
analysis that each individual will be involved in more than
one system or pattern and, therefore, perform more than one
role. Each individual will, therefore, have several selves, providing us with the interesting problem of how these selves
are related."[51] Both the family and the community provided
plantation slaves with roles other than that defined by the
master. For the very young child the mother, not the master,

was the significant other in the sense that Sullivan used this concept. Though the near impossibility of the father acting as a true authority figure was of great psychic importance, a meaningful relationship did sometimes exist between father and son. As the child grew, the master's role as a significant other became increasingly vital, but he was always in competition with significant others in the slave community: with husbands, wives, fathers, and mothers; with religious leaders; with strong male models, some of whom may even on occasion have served as substitute father figures;[52] with slaves believed to possess mystical powers; and with those whose wisdom was respected. Few planters had any illusions about being the only authority figures on their estates; as one of them noted, there were always slaves who held "a kind of magical sway over the minds and opinions of the rest."[53]

In his community, in the presence of these significant others, the slave could play roles decidedly different from the one prescribed by his master. As Goffman explained, while playing one role the individual is able "to hold in abeyance his involvement in other patterns, thus sustaining one or more dormant roles that are enacted roles on other occasions." This works well enough as long as the audiences are segregated, thereby allowing the individual to play contradictory roles and "to possess contradictory qualities." However, when the audiences are mixed the psychologically important problem of role conflict arises.[54] An obvious illustration is the dilemma of a slave being questioned by his master, in the presence of other slaves, concerning the whereabouts of a fugitive. Here the rules of proper conduct that the master tried to instill in him came in conflict with the values of his community. If we can trust the testimony of the masters themselves, community values usually triumphed, even though punishment might be the consequence.

Was there any sense in which the master's power was really absolute? Only in the sense that if a master killed a

slave by overwork, or by cruel punishment, or in a fit of
rage, it was nearly impossible to convict him in a court of
law. But southern state laws did not themselves give a master
absolute power over his slaves, for the laws recognized their
humanity and attempted to control the degree of punishment
that might be inflicted, the amount of labor that could be required, and the care that was to be provided. Where the laws
failed, a master might be restrained by his own moral standards or by those of the white community. If law and custom
were not enough, he was still confronted by the fact that,
unlike the inmates of a concentration camp, his slaves had
monetary value and a clear purpose—to toil in his fields—and
therefore bargaining power. The master got work out of his
slaves by coercion, by threats, by promises of rewards, by
flattery, and by other devices he knew of. But if he were pru-
dent, he knew that it was not wise to push slaves too far—to
work them too long, punish them too severely or too often,
or make too many threats. Slaves had their own standards of
fair play and their own ways of enforcing them.[55] The relationship between master and slave was not one in which absolute power rested on one side and total helplessness on the
other; rather, the relationship was one of everlasting tensions,
punctuated by occasional conflicts between combatants using
different weapons.

   If a master had *de facto* the power of life and death over
his slaves, the slaves knew that he was most unlikely to use it.
They knew that rules infractions and certain forms of resistance did not ordinarily lead to death but to milder and
often quite bearable forms of punishment, or to sale to another master, or, on occasion, to no penalty at all. In the conflicts between masters and slaves, the masters or their overseers sometimes suffered defeat, and the resulting collapse of
discipline led inflexibly to economic disaster. To read the essays "On the Management of Negroes" that frequently ap-

peared in southern periodicals is to appreciate the practical limits of the master's power. Clearly, for the slave, as he responded to the problems of his existence, the choices open to him were a good deal more varied than a simple one between life and death.

Role psychology, as those who have written on the subject observed, tempts one to view the whole problem metaphorically as drama.[56] But in slavery the theatrical situation was seldom one in which the master wrote the script and the slaves played their roles and read their lines precisely as their master had written them. The instructions masters gave to their overseers, which described the qualities they hoped to develop in their slaves, suggested something quite different. Significantly, the model slave described in these instructions was not Sambo but a personality far more complicated. Masters wanted their slaves, like Sambo, to be docile, humble, and dependent; but they also wanted them to be diligent, responsible, and resourceful—in short, as Earle E. Thorpe has noted, "to give a very efficient and adult-like performance."[57] The slaves in turn had to find ways to resolve the obviously incongruent role expectations of their masters, and many of them responded as persons troubled with this or other forms of role conflict often do. They resorted to lying and deceit.

Eugene Genovese, in an otherwise valuable essay on slave personality, was not very perceptive when he argued that slaves who tricked their masters, rather than coping with problems of role conflict and role definition, were merely playing a game which the masters enjoyed and had themselves written into the script.[58] True, a master might occasionally be amused when a house servant outwitted him, but there is scant evidence that he enjoyed the "game" when played by field hands. This was certainly not in the script, and masters frequently expressed their anger or perplexity at the "untrustworthiness" of Negroes. Their appreciation of the slave trickster was confined mostly to their public defenses of slavery and to sentimental plantation literature. In private they were seldom amused.

Plantation field hands, finding no escape from slavery but plenty of elbow room within it, usually managed to preserve their individuality and therefore revealed a considerable variety of personality types. Among the types, there were, to be sure, genuine Sambos who seemed to have internalized much of the role, for some slaves simply lacked the psychic strength to withstand the infantilizing pressures of the system. They looked on the master as a father figure, accepted his values, identified with him, and perhaps even viewed themselves through his eyes.

We may assume that the slave who internalized the Sambo role did accept his master as his only significant other and that he was relatively untroubled by the problem of role conflict. But he must have been sorely disturbed by the psychic process of dissociation—that is, exclusion from the self of disapproved personality tendencies, which then become part of what Sullivan called the "extra-self." Such dissociated tendencies, we must remember, still remain part of the personality; and, therefore, Sambo was Sambo only up to a point—in Genovese's words, "up to the moment that the psychological balance was jarred from within or without."[59] Plantation records often reveal the astonishment of masters when slaves, who had long given evidence of Sambo personalities, suddenly behaved in disturbingly un-Sambo ways.

Another personality type was evident on certain large plantations, especially on those of absentee owners in new areas of the Southwest, where labor was sometimes exploited ruthlessly and punishments were brutal. This type displayed none of the silliness of Sambo, none of his childlike attachment to master or overseer; rather, he was profoundly apathetic, full of depression and gloom, and seemingly less hostile than indifferent toward the white man who controlled him. One slaveholder observed that slaves subjected to overwork and cruel punishments were likely to fall "into a state of impassivity" and to become "insensible and indifferent to punishment, or even to life."[60] These brutalized slaves had their counterparts on Latin American plantations, where extreme cruelty produced in some a state of psychic shock manifested in apathy and depression. In colonial Brazil this condition was sufficiently common to be given a special term: *banzo*.[61] It is this condition that seems to be analogous to the concentration camps, where life had lost its meaning, and to prisons and asylums, where "situational withdrawal" is a form of institutional adaptation.[62]

More numerous among plantation personalities were the men and women with sufficient strength of character to escape the emasculating tendencies of the system, a group whose size Elkins seriously underestimates. These slaves not only were not Sambos, but they did not *act* like Sambos—their behavior was in no respect infantile. Though observing all the niceties of interracial etiquette, they maintained considerable dignity even in their relations with their masters. To judge from plantation diaries, masters often treated slaves of this kind with genuine respect and seldom made the mistake of regarding them as children. Slaves such as these were not troublemakers; they were rarely intransigent as long as what was asked of them and provided for them was reasonable by their standards. They worked well and efficiently and showed considerable initiative and self-reliance. They tended to be fatalistic about their lot, expected little of life, and found their satisfaction in the religious and social activities of the slave communities. No doubt their psychic balance and their relative tranquillity were sometimes disturbed by a certain amount of role conflict; and they could hardly have escaped the phenomenon of dissociation described by Sullivan.

Herbert Aptheker's rebels must also be included among those whose personalities were far removed from the traditional Sambo. I would not limit these to the organizers of or participants in rebellions, for their number was very small.[63] Rather, I would include all who were never reconciled to the system and engaged in various acts of resistance: running away, arson, the damaging of crops and tools, and sometimes even assaults on masters, overseers, or other whites. Needless to say, it is often impossible to distinguish conscious resistance from the unconscious carelessness and indifference of slaves, but the evidence of genuine resistance is clear enough in some cases.[64] Genovese argued that the slaves did not develop a genuine revolutionary tradition, that their acts of resistance were usually nihilistic, and that at best they came out of slavery with a tradition of recalcitrance—"of undirected, misdirected or naively directed violence." George M. Fredrickson and Christopher Lasch objected even to calling the acts of slave rebels "resistance" and insisted that it was only "intransigence." They defined the former as organized, purposeful political action, the latter as mere "personal strategy of survival" which could easily lead to "futile and even self-destructive acts of defiance."[65] Surely, little that was done by the rebels could form the basis for a revolutionary tradition or satisfy so narrow a definition of resistance; but these were rebels, nonetheless, who never internalized the masters' standards of good conduct and never dissociated from their conscious selves all the disapproved tendencies of their personalities.

All of these slave types, with myriad individual variations, were recognizable on the plantations. But I believe that the personalities of most slaves are less easily classified, because their behavior when observed by whites was usually that of conscious accommodators. They played the role of Sambo with varying degrees of skill and consistency,[66] but, in contrast to the authentic Sambos, most characteristics of the role did not become part of their true personalities. For them the Sambo routine was a form of "ritual acting"—that is, they went through the motions of the role, but with a rather low degree of personal involvement.[67]

Several aspects of role theory support this hypothesis. One assumption of this theory, as we have seen, is that the average normal person plays not one but several roles, and often two or more simultaneously. To think of the slave as playing but one role—that of Sambo—is to assume that he responded to a single social situation, which was clearly not the case. Moreover, when a role performance is demanded primarily in terms of the pains and penalties for nonperformance, as it was on the typical plantation supervised by an overseer and run as a business enterprise, the role is likely to be enacted with little conviction and minimal personal involvement. The Sambo role doubtless was performed more convincingly and with more feeling in a paternalistic situation. Finally, the extent to which a given role makes an impact on the self depends on its "preemptiveness"—on how much of a person's time is spent playing the role.[68] Therefore, one must ask how preemptive the Sambo role actually was. During the week the plantation field hand spent most of his waking hours as an agricultural worker, planting, cultivating, or harvesting, and the demand on him was for a responsible adult performance. He spent evenings and holidays in the slave community playing a variety of roles, only occasionally being observed by master or overseer. The one occasion that might evoke the Sambo role was that of a direct contact with a member of the white race, when the Negro was forced to acknowledge in some way not only that he was a slave but that he belonged to a degraded caste. However, for the average field hand such contacts were brief and relatively infrequent; therefore the pressures on him most of the time were to play roles other than Sambo.

In short, most plantation slaves avoided the internalization of Sambo, first, because they were able to play different roles in their communities; second, because the Sambo role was not unduly preemptive; third, because masters were not the only significant others in the lives of slaves; fourth, because slaves found abundant opportunities to behave in ways that had meaning in adult terms; and, last, because conditions on the average plantation were not so brutal that slaves were destroyed as human beings. In consequence, slaves could use the essentially external Sambo role, in Elkins's words, "as a protective device beneath which a more independent personality might develop."[69] Those who consciously and purposefully acted the part of Sambo, thereby reducing sources of friction and putting limits on what would normally be expected of them, were in no sense being childish or infantile; rather, their behavior was rational, meaningful, and mature.

In an essay based on studies of other total institutions, George Fredrickson and Christopher Lasch suggested that conditions in prisons and asylums are more analogous to slavery than conditions in concentration camps. They noted that inmates of prisons and asylums do not usually internalize a sense of obligation to obey their rules and accept their values. In the case of slavery, they concluded, "a system that rigorously defined the Negro slave not merely as an inferior but as an alien, a separate order of being," could hardly have instilled in him "the sense of belonging on which internalized obedience necessarily has to rest."[70]

However, I think there is a better approach to understanding the personalities of plantation slaves than that provided by either of these analogies. Much more can be learned from a study of ex-slaves and their descendants in the rural South in the decades after Reconstruction, when, for all practical purposes, the system was still a closed one from which few escaped, and when powerful forces again generated tendencies toward emasculated personalities. Now their humanity was assaulted and their race denigrated by the most extreme forms of prejudice, segregation, and discrimination; and they felt strong pressures, both subtle and crude, to internalize the white man's opinion of them. After emancipation there was still a white landlord to serve as a counterpart to the slaveholder as a significant other. More important, the whole white community now became, collectively, a significant other, imposing a subservient and dependent role on the Negro and enforcing an etiquette of race relations with sanctions equal to those available to masters in slavery days. Yet, most Negroes, as in slavery days, found ways of maintaining a degree of psychic balance. Through their churches, their music, and a great variety of organized social activities, they gradually developed a semi-autonomous Afro-American subculture; in their communities and families they responded to their own significant others; and in their mature years they had a variety of adult roles to play, even though whites persisted in calling black men boys and black women girls.

In circumstances whose psychic impact had many parallels to slavery, Negroes once more resorted to conscious accommodation. The investigations of twentieth-century social scientists provide much evidence that most post-Reconstruction Negroes did not internalize the Sambo role they played before the white community. For example, in the 1930s, John Dollard observed that the southern Negro played two roles:

> one that he is forced to play with white people and one the "real Negro" as he appears in his dealings with his own people. What the white southern people see who "know their Negroes" is the role that they have forced the Negro to accept, his caste role. . . . It is perhaps this fact which often makes Negroes seem so deceptive to white people; apparently our white caste wishes the Negro to have only one social personality, his caste role, and to *be* this with utter completeness.[71]

The testimony of post-Reconstruction Negroes themselves, especially in their music and folklore, also suggests a prevalent pattern of conscious accommodation.[72]

Similarly, slaves, in their scattered records, and masters, in their private papers and published essays on the management of Negroes, indicate that conscious accommodation was a widespread behavior pattern on the antebellum plantations. Whatever masters may have said about the loyal, childlike "darkies" in their public defenses of slavery, dissembling pseudo-Sambos were the most common realities that confronted them in their daily lives. As one planter wrote: "The most general defect in the character of the Negro, is hypocrisy; and this hypocrisy frequently makes him pretend to more ignorance than he possesses; and if the master treats him as a fool, he will be sure to act the fool's part. This is a very convenient trait, as it frequently serves as an apology for awkwardness and neglect of duty."[73]

However, the fact that some masters saw through the Sambo act, as this one did, suggests that slave accommodators may often have missed their lines. Playing this intricate role could never have been easy, and it may have caused even the most skilled of them serious psychic problems, especially if there was a basic incongruence between the self and the role.[74] I suspect that many had profound difficulties with role conflict, as the weaker characters who internalized the Sambo role suffered from dissociation. Those who study slave personality would be well advised to watch for signs of character disorders in these seemingly gay dissemblers. I want to point again, as I did in *The Peculiar Institution*, to the astonishing frequency of speech problems among slaves. Time after time, owners advertising for runaways reported that a slave "stutters very much," "stammers very much," "speaks quickly and with an anxious expression of countenance," or is "easily confused when spoken to."[75] Such data are open to several interpretations, but one respectable theory suggests that speech impediments are symptomatic of buried hostility. Dr. Murry Snyder of the Speech Rehabilitation Institute of New York City believes that "Underneath the cloak of inhibition and

lously weighed and finely measured data, both numerical and literary, must be subjectively interpreted by the historian, for historical facts do not speak for themselves. Rather, as Edward H. Carr observed, "The facts speak only when the historian calls on them: it is he who decides to which facts to give the floor, and in what order or context."[2] How the historian decides these matters depends in part upon his own experiences and his perception of the world in which he lives. Between past and present, Marc Bloch reminded us, "the lines of connection work both ways. . . . In the last analysis, whether consciously or no, it is always by borrowing from our daily experiences and by shading them, where necessary, with new tints that we derive the elements which help us to restore the past."[3]

Historians react to this reality in different ways. Some simply get on with their research, adapt their procedures to the problem at hand, and refuse to be distracted by philosophical questions concerning the nature and meaning of history. Others, more keenly aware of the limitations of even the best historical work, still accept their mortality without despair, and are content to offer such revisionist insights as they have with full knowledge that one day a new revisionism will overtake them. Eugene Genovese, in a recent evaluation of slave culture, offered his reading of the sources "as one historian's considered judgment," warning nonspecialists "that all the sources are treacherous and that no 'definitive' study has been or ever will be written," for "the writing of history is a process of constant revision and debate."[4]

However, a few historians dream of immortality. Lee Benson, for one, deplored the "recurrent cycles of wheel-spinning revisionism" and insisted that a more durable history can be written by replacing the "established historiographic system" with the analytical tools of modern social science. Thanks to data banks and computers, he argued, history can now be studied scientifically, and historians should be concerned with "discovering and developing general laws of human behavior."[5] Douglass C. North, for another, believed that history can be "something more than a subjective reordering of the facts of the past as man's perspective changes with each generation." He, too, found in the social sciences and in the methods of scientific research the tools for "a basic restructuring of historical inquiry." North suggested that the New Economic History, with its "well articulated body of theory and . . . abundance of relevant quantitative data," is the discipline best equipped to accomplish the restructuring he thought was needed.[6]

Fogel and Engerman are prominent practitioners of the New Economic History, often called cliometrics, and *Time on the Cross* was an attempt at the kind of methodological restructuring for which present-day believers in the scientific study of history have called. Nowhere, Fogel and Engerman believed, had "the passion for numbers been more vigorously pursued than in the study of the economics of slavery." Cliometricians, they claimed, in searching for quantifiable material, had ransacked "every conceivable source of information bearing on the operation of the slave system," including the manuscript census returns of 1850 and 1860, the family papers and business records of numerous planters, and the wills, probate records, and other legal documents deposited in county courthouses and now available on microfilm. As a result, "the cliometricians have amassed a more complete body of information on the operation of the slave system than has been available to anyone interested in the subject either during the antebellum era or since then."

According to Fogel and Engerman, great masses of quantifiable data were beyond the reach of "traditional" historians, because they lacked mathematical and statistical training and were therefore limited to the impressionistic use of "fragmentary" literary sources. The exploitation of the new data had to await the appearance of historians and economists "trained in the application of quantitative methods to historical problems." After World War II "a series of rapid advances in economics, statistics, and applied mathematics, together with the availability of high-speed computers, put information long locked in obscure archives at the disposal of a new generation of scholars."[7]

What had been the result? A long-established "traditional interpretation" of slavery, incorporated in a "vast literature" written by "hundreds of historians" and "taught in most high school and college classes across the nation," had been contradicted in many of its essential aspects. "As significant as the correction of past errors," Fogel and Engerman reported, was "the new information brought to light on the conditions of black bondage."

> Some of the discoveries [they explained] were at one time as unbelievable to the cliometricians as they will be to the readers of [*Time on the Cross*]. Indeed, many of the findings . . . were initially discounted, even rejected out of hand. But when persistent efforts to contradict the unexpected discoveries failed, these scholars were forced into a wide-ranging and radical reinterpretation of American slavery.

Accordingly, Fogel and Engerman warned their readers that *Time on the Cross* would be "a disturbing book" and asked them to show forbearance and to recognize that the book represented "the honest efforts of scholars whose central aim has been the discovery of what really happened."[8] The authors assured readers that forbearance would be rewarded, and, in explaining how, they executed a sudden and rather startling transition from cliometrics to presentist polemics: "For the findings we discuss not only expose many myths that have served to corrode and poison relations between the races, but also help to put into a new perspective some of the most urgent issues of our day."[9]

This polemical style appeared frequently in the text and supplement and became quite strident in the Epilogue, where the purveyors of the traditional interpretation of slavery were castigated for their "perversion of the history of blacks." Here Fogel and Engerman made clear the full significance of their title, *Time on the Cross*—an unlikely title for an ordinary work of cliometrics. In their rich metaphor, the spikes that still hold blacks on the cross after three hundred and fifty years "are fashioned of myths [about slavery] that turned diligent and efficient workers into lazy loafers and bunglers, that turned love of family into a disregard for it, that turned those who struggled for self-improvement in the only way they could into 'Uncle Toms.' . . . It's time to reveal not only to blacks but to whites as well, that part of American history which has been kept from them—the record of black achievement under adversity."[10] So ended the book that, in the opening pages of the Prologue, was soberly introduced as "part of a more ambitious effort to reconstruct the entire history of American economic development on a sound quantitative basis."[11]

Time on the Cross was clearly a blend of several ingredients. One consisted of findings based on "systematic data," defined as quantifiable data that lend themselves to "systematic statistical tests." Another consisted of findings based on "fragmentary, impressionistic evidence" from literary sources, which Fogel and Engerman regarded as "on a relatively low level of reliability." For example, they reported that systematic data on the quality of slave family life are lacking, and that "it has been impossible thus far, to devise a meaningful index of the effect of slavery on the personality or psychology of blacks." They based four of their ten "principal corrections" of the traditional interpretation of slavery wholly or in large part on evidence that, by their definition, is fragmentary and impressionistic. The third ingredient consisted of interpretation, which often turned rather polemical and which was sometimes based on fragmentary data (literary or numerical) or on "assumptions which, though they are plausible, cannot be verified at present."[12]

In commenting on *Time on the Cross* after publication, Fogel explained that in attempting "to weave the findings of the cliometricians into a wide-ranging reinterpretation of the slave economy we passed over from social science to traditional history. Appendix B [in the supplement] is social science; volume I is not. Volume I is traditional history." Fogel did not claim that *Time on the Cross* was "more scientific" than earlier works on slavery—only that it drew more heavily "on the findings of social science." Yet, when Fogel and Engerman asked "how those who framed the traditional interpretation of the slave system could have been so wrong," and, presumably, why Fogel and Engerman have been able to make their "radical reinterpretation," their explanation was entirely cliometrical. The differences hinged "on the role of mathematics and statistics in historical analysis," often on "technical mathematical points," and on "thousands" of computer hours.[13]

Fogel and Engerman are well-known American cliometricians, and *Time on the Cross* must be judged, above all, as a product of their methodology. But the combination of several sometimes incongruous approaches—cliometrics, traditional history, and a blend of speculation, interpretation, and polemics—leaves readers somewhat uncertain about what they are reading. Large parts of the book hardly conform to Benson's and North's model for the scientific study of history; its structural eccentricities, on the other hand, will puzzle traditional historians who have been trained to expect a great deal less.

However, about the general thrust of *Time on the Cross* there is no ambiguity. Fogel and Engerman rejected an alleged traditional view that plantation agriculture was inefficient and that slavery was "so cruel, the exploitation so severe, the repression so complete, that blacks were thoroughly demoralized by it." In a flight of hyperbole (the handmaiden of polemics) they expressed their scorn for traditional notions, "contained in many current histories of the antebellum South," that black slaves were "cultural ciphers," lazy and careless workers, undernourished "if not starved," capable of only "routine tasks," sexually promiscuous, indifferent to family ties, and typically Sambos in their personalities. In short, their purpose was to disprove a tradition in which "masters and slaves are painted as degraded brutes. Masters are vile because they are the perpetrators of unbridled exploitation; slaves are vile because they are the victims of it."[14]

In the historiography of antebellum southern slavery, *Time on the Cross* now stands unchallenged as the most favorable assessment of the impact of slavery on the southern economy, and the most cheerful portrayal of virtually all aspects of slave life, including income, conditions of labor, occupational mobility, marriage and child-rearing, family life, cultural advancement, master-slave relationships, and, inferentially, the psychological impact of bondage on black people. Before the publication of this book, Ulrich B. Phillips, a Southerner noted for his sentimental view of life on antebellum plantations (though critical of their efficiency), had written the classic account of slavery as a benign institution.[15] Fogel and Engerman were not sentimental about slavery or about planter entrepreneurs, and they were by no means members of the Phillips "school." Nevertheless, as to the conditions of life among slaves, Phillips in some respects portrayed the system as slightly less benign than they, and he acknowledged more fully and explicitly its harsher side. As one reviewer, an economist, observed, Fogel and Engerman "are rather like prosecuting attorneys with a fine case who are . . . unwilling to cloud the jurors' minds with ambiguity."[16] Without qualification, slavery as an economic institution was efficient;

only after checking and rechecking their data is not supported by a reading of their sources, which they have in fact used carelessly.[23]

Fogel and Engerman suggested, erroneously I believe, that some absolute measure exists by which a historian can distinguish qualitatively between the two kinds of evidence they claimed to have used: "systematic evidence subject to rigorous statistical tests" and "informal and fragmentary evidence." At the risk of ignoring the technical meaning of these terms, I suggest that, for certain purposes, "systematic evidence," such as census returns, can be fragmentary, and that for many purposes the census returns of 1850 and 1860 are unreliable. On the other hand, literary evidence, which Fogel and Engerman classified as "informal and fragmentary," can be quite "formal"—when, for example, it consists of a systematic government report based on public hearings. Nor is it necessarily fragmentary: it may consist of every speech and official letter written by a public officeholder. For the public career of this person the literary evidence may be complete and, in some aspects, even quantifiable. It is therefore misleading to pretend that "systematic evidence" is for all purposes and in every respect superior to, or more reliable than, evidence that Fogel and Engerman labeled as "informal and fragmentary." One needs only to read the essay on the shortcomings of the Seventh Census, written by Superintendent J. B. D. DeBow as an appendix to the printed returns, to grasp the weakness of their claim. No statistical procedures for the processing of "biased" data can remedy the defects in systematic evidence accumulated by untrained, negligent, or incompetent census takers.

To turn from the problem of evidence to the argument of *Time on the Cross*, a common complaint of reviewers was that the authors were engaged much of the time in battles with straw men: they distorted the work of other scholars through exaggeration or by quoting out of context, they refuted myths discredited long ago, and they attacked misconceptions of which no responsible scholar was ever guilty, thus encouraging readers unfamiliar with the literature to think that their book was far more revolutionary than in fact it was. Moreover, with disturbing frequency they failed to acknowledge the contributions of earlier historians, or referred to them so unspecifically as to amount to no acknowledgment at all. Commenting on practices such as these in a broader context, Charlotte Erickson protested that "to play this game in academic literature . . . may indeed rob students of insights into the way in which scholars build upon each other's work in extending knowledge even with the most exciting new techniques."[24]

According to Fogel and Engerman, the "traditional interpretation" of slavery consists of five fundamental generalizations: 1. that, except on new land, capital investments in slaves were generally unprofitable, unless the owner supplied surplus slaves to the interstate slave trade; 2. that slavery in the late antebellum period was a dying institution; 3. that slave labor and the agricultural economy that exploited it were "economically inefficient"; 4. that slavery produced a stagnant, or retarded, southern economy; and 5. "that slavery provided extremely harsh material conditions of life for the typical slave."[25] Though an occasional "conventional" historian may have rejected one or another of these generalizations, the burden of the argument of *Time on the Cross* was that all five of them are demonstrably incorrect.

In their Prologue, Fogel and Engerman listed ten "principal corrections" of the traditional interpretation of the southern slave economy: 1. Slavery was a rational labor system that survived because it was profitable. The return on investments in slaves compared favorably with the return on other available forms of investment. 2. On the eve of the Civil War, slavery was still flourishing and gave no indication of an imminent collapse for economic reasons. 3. During the 1850s slaveholders were optimistic about the future of their labor system and anticipated continued economic prosperity. 4. Slave agriculture was efficient—indeed, 35 percent more efficient than the family farms of the North. 5. The slave field hand was typically a diligent laborer—"harder working and more efficient than his white counterpart." 6. Slave labor was adaptable to an industrial economy, and the demand for slaves was rising more rapidly in southern cities than in rural, agricultural areas. 7. The slave family was not undermined by the interstate slave trade or by sexual exploitation; rather, the family was "the basic unit of social organization." Slaveholders encouraged stable family life, because it was to their economic advantage to do so. 8. The standard of living of southern slaves "compared favorably with [that] . . . of free industrial workers." 9. "Over the course of his lifetime, the typical slave field hand received about 90 percent of the income he produced." 10. Between 1840 and 1860 the southern economy was characterized by rapid growth and by an increase in per capita income that exceeded the rate of increase in the rest of the country. "By 1860 the South attained a level of per capita income which was high by the standards of the time."[26]

Among the straw men who marched through the pages of *Time on the Cross*, the most imposing was the "traditional interpretation of slavery," which Fogel and Engerman themselves created and which they failed to identify with any twentieth-century historian. Most historians of the southern economy accepted long ago the first four of Fogel and Engerman's ten "principal corrections." Here the only innovation was the assertion that southern slave agriculture was 35 percent *more* efficient than northern family farms, an assertion whose validity other economic historians have questioned.[27] (The third of their "corrections," concerning the sanguinity of slaveholders, was a rather exaggerated statement based on a dubious quantitative exercise and bolstered by a superficial, unsystematic examination of literary sources.) Credit for the sixth, regarding the adaptability of slavery to industrial activities, belongs to a book by Robert Starobin published four years before *Time on the Cross*.[28] As for the seventh "correction," I know of no historian who argued that "slave breeding, sexual exploitation, and promiscuity destroyed the black family." None to my knowledge ever denied that slaves lived characteristically in families, though some believed that the black family played a rather truncated role in the community life of southern plantations. Indeed, numerous black and white scholars have been arguing Fogel and Engerman's case for more than a decade. The essential part of the tenth "correction," relating to southern economic growth, antedated *Time on the Cross* by fourteen years.[29] The remaining three "corrections"—numbers 5, 8, and 9—represented novel assertions of substantive content, not assaults upon straw men. Whether Fogel and Engerman have proved that slaves worked more efficiently than free laborers, that their standard of living compared favorably with free industrial workers, and that they received about 90 percent of the income they produced are major questions critically examined in the essays by the five quantitative historians noted above. In each instance they found that either the underlying reasoning or the quantitative evidence, or both, failed to justify the novel assertions set down in the Prologue to *Time on the Cross*.[30]

Contrary to Fogel and Engerman, there are in fact *two* traditional interpretations of the slave economy, one rooted in the antebellum northern abolitionist movement, the other in the antebellum southern defense of slavery. The abolitionist attack was overwhelmingly moral and religious, emphasizing the secular American commitment to freedom and equality and the Christian doctrine that all men are equal in the sight of God. Unquestionably, the moral judgments against slavery, implicit or explicit, found in the writings of twentieth-century historians stem from the abolitionist tradition; and

in this sense Fogel and Engerman were neoabolitionists themselves. Though abolitionists never argued that the physical
treatment of slaves had any decisive bearing on the issue of
the morality of slavery, their propaganda emphasized (and
doubtless exaggerated) cruelties and atrocities for the purpose
of winning converts.

Abolitionist publications devoted relatively little attention
to the economics of slavery, but their occasional comments
reveal a belief that the southern economy was backward, the
slave labor system inefficient, and capital investments in slaves
unprofitable. Fogel and Engerman correctly linked the tradition of inefficiency and unprofitability to the abolitionists, but
in explaining that tradition they made a serious error. They
wrote as follows:

> That the quality of slaves, both as ordinary workers
> and as managers, could have been so completely misrep-
> resented by the antebellum critics of slavery is testimony
> to the extent of their racist myopia. What bitter irony it
> is that the false stereotype of black labor, a stereotype
> which still plagues blacks today, was fashioned not pri-
> marily by the oppressors who strove to keep their chattel
> wrapped in the chains of bondage, but by the most
> ardent opponents of slavery, by those who worked most
> diligently to destroy the chains of bondage.[31]

That abolitionists were not free of racism is true enough—
hardly any white Americans were. However, as a group they
were decidedly less afflicted with it than the rest of their
countrymen. Moreover, many of them were self-conscious
and guilt-ridden about their surviving prejudice and struggled
to overcome it. Abolitionist societies campaigned against injustice to northern free blacks as well as to southern slaves.

Did the abolitionists, who were "the most ardent opponents
of slavery," stress the inefficiency of *black* labor?[32] Almost
never! The emphasis in their publications was on the ineffi-

ciency of *slave* labor. Abolitionists were characteristically
environmentalists who argued that in the South blacks were
what slavery had made them; in the North, what prejudice
had made them. An essay by a Garrisonian abolitionist,
Charles C. Burleigh, entitled "Slavery and the North" (1855),
was typical of countless other antislavery pamphlets:

> What if the black man is inferior to the white? It does
> not follow that he always must be. Excel him where his
> chances are equal, before you boast yourself above him.
> Give him his liberty, and as strong a motive to exertion
> as you have;—a prospect of reward as sure and ample; not
> only wages for his toil, but respect and honor and social
> standing according to his worth, and see what he can
> then become. . . . His powers have never yet been
> fairly tried, for he has always had to struggle against dif-
> ficulties and discouragements which white men do not
> meet. When free in name, he is denied a freeman's rights
> and hope and prospects, and open field of competition,
> and success to match his merit.

An argument such as this hardly suggests that abolitionists
were led to their low opinion of slave labor by "racist myopia."[33] Rather, it suggests that they were misled by one of the
naïve assumptions of classical economists—the intellectual ancestors of Fogel and Engerman—namely, that unfree labor is
necessarily inefficient and its employment unprofitable.

Time on the Cross exposed the "racist myopia" of Frederick Law Olmsted, a Northerner who traveled extensively in
the South in the 1850s and wrote three books on southern
life,[34] to illustrate the contribution of antebellum critics of
slavery to "the false stereotype of black labor." However, it
failed to inform readers that Olmsted was not an abolitionist
and that his opinions should not be confused with theirs.[35]
His writings provide evidence for almost any interpretation
of the southern economy—evidence of the efficiency and the
inefficiency of slave labor, of the profitability and the un-

profitability of investments in slaves, and of the productivity and the unproductivity of the plantations. In some passages Olmsted accepted the current stereotype of the innate inferiority of blacks; however, more commonly he attributed the deficiencies of black labor to its enslavement. The issue here is not the accuracy of his comments on slave inefficiency, but how he explained it; and the crucial point is that the great majority of his comments on the southern labor system referred not to *black* labor but to *slave* labor. Though Olmsted's racism is obvious enough, he never explicitly argued that free black labor would be inferior to free white labor. Therefore, it would be more accurate to say that he was somewhat ambiguous on the issue rather than that he was a major contributor to the "false stereotype of black labor."

Olmsted invited misunderstanding when, like so many others, he occasionally used the terms "slave labor" and "black labor" interchangeably, simply because slave labor happened to *be* black labor. The resulting ambiguity was one for which Fogel and Engerman should have shown some tolerance, for they were guilty of it themselves. For example, on page 209 of the text, they referred to the "superior quality of black labor." Surely they did not intend the inverted racism implicit in this phrase but meant to argue for the superior quality of *slave* labor. Indeed, in the next sentence, they switched phrases and referred to the "high quality of slave labor," as if both meant the same thing. Again, on page 231, they declared that "blacks were better workers than whites," but on the same page they also asserted the "superior quality of slave labor." In short, Fogel and Engerman, like Olmsted, sometimes confused their readers.

The second traditional interpretation of slavery was a product of southern proslavery writers, and this interpretation has had an interesting history. Portions of it were evident in the writings of Ulrich B. Phillips, in those of other southern and some northern historians of the early twentieth century, and now in *Time on the Cross.* Of course, the extreme defense of slavery as a positive good is dead—it was seldom heard after Appomattox. However, one part of this positive-good tradition, rather than the abolitionist tradition, bore much of the responsibility for the "false stereotype of black labor" that Fogel and Engerman so passionately condemned. The southern defense of slavery, though utilizing historical, religious, sociological, and philosophical arguments, was primarily racial; and a crucial part of the racial argument was that blacks were innately lazy and incompetent and would work only under compulsion. Slavery, the argument ran, transformed a potentially vicious and idle population into disciplined and reasonably efficient workers. In this tradition it was the *free* blacks who were inefficient, not well-managed black *slaves!*

The portion of the proslavery interpretation that lived on in the writings of the Phillips school and in *Time on the Cross* was that which stressed mild treatment, moderate discipline, wholesome and comfortable living conditions, and minimal sexual exploitation. Proslavery writers attributed the generally good treatment of slaves partly to the masters' benevolence and partly to their self-interest as practical businessmen. "When slaves are worth near a thousand dollars a head," argued George Fitzhugh, "they will be carefully and well provided for."[36] Thomas R. Dew, Professor of History, Metaphysics, and Political Law at William and Mary College, was the first Southerner to develop this line of argument in an extended and systematic essay.[37] In fact, Dew's essay, published in 1832, though borrowing heavily from earlier writers, was probably the first book-length defense of slavery ever written anywhere. If I were to locate *Time on the Cross* in the historiography of slavery, I would identify it with this second traditional interpretation; if I were looking for a label, I would be tempted to call it Neo-Dewism. Needless to say, the book was not a defense of slavery, and its argument was not racist, as was Dew's; but its highly favorable assessment of life in bondage was rooted in the traditional proslavery interpretation nonetheless.

Even the economic argument in *Time on the Cross* concerning the rationality, profitability, and viability of slavery, the efficiency of slave agriculture, and the relative wealth and prosperity of the antebellum South might be labeled, without undue exaggeration, Neo-Dewism. Proslavery writers, like the abolitionists, paid relatively little attention to the economics of slavery;[38] a few, when they did address the problem, conceded to their northern critics that free labor was cheaper and more efficient and defended their system in other ways. More often they advanced an economic defense as well. Dew argued that the productivity of slave labor was proven by the fact that slavery existed; had it not been profitable, it would have been abolished. In Virginia, he claimed, "slave labor . . . gives value to her soil . . . ; take away this, and you pull down the atlas that upholds the whole system."[39] Thornton Stringfellow presented evidence that the five Atlantic slave states during the previous two hundred years had accumulated wealth substantially greater than that of the New England states. Therefore, he asked, "Is it possible . . . to believe that slavery tends to poverty[?]" On the contrary, "slavery, as an agricultural investment, is more profitable than an investment in commerce and manufactures."[40]

Thus it is plausible to argue that Fogel and Engerman did not so much destroy a traditional interpretation of slavery as elaborate upon and reinforce one whose source runs back to southern proslavery writers. In a way, Ulrich B. Phillips was more of a maverick than they, for he built his case from a combination of the economic arguments of slavery's critics with the racial and sociological arguments of its defenders. On the other hand, the Neo-Dewists, Fogel and Engerman, rejected only the racism and positive-good doctrines of pro-slavery writers, while retaining their economic and sociological arguments almost intact.

The so-called traditional interpretation of slavery was the largest straw man of *Time on the Cross*, but the book was well populated with lesser figures made of the same stuff. Because of the rather breathless claim in the Prologue that the book was replete with "unbelievable" discoveries, readers may easily assume that as each straw man toppled the history of slavery had been rewritten in some fundamental way. For example, Fogel and Engerman reported that "the common belief that all slaves were menials is false."[41] What they meant by a menial is not clear, and among whom this belief was common they did not say. The statement was at best misleading, for no historian of slavery has ever believed this, and all of them, at the very least, have offered evidence that substantial numbers of slaves were not field hands. One finds no acknowledgment in either the text or the supplemental volume that Fogel and Engerman were not the discoverers of this well-known fact.

The passive voice sometimes enabled the authors to avoid telling their readers precisely who were the believers in the myths they appeared to be exploding. On page 24 they wrote: "It has been frequently asserted that slavery was dying in the United States from the end of the Revolution to 1810. . . ." Again, Fogel and Engerman did not name those who had asserted this, or when, or where; nor did they give citations in the supplement. Some earlier historians did argue that in the late eighteenth century slavery was a dying institution, and the myth is by no means dead. But this has not been the prevailing opinion in recent years, and in 1964 Robert McColley published a book (not cited in *Time on the Cross*) effectively disputing the notion that slavery was moribund even in post-Revolutionary Virginia.[42] Fogel and Engerman would have stated the case more accurately, though less dramatically, if they had expressed it as an old myth no longer accepted by most modern historians, thus eliminating the straw man and crediting the work of other historians.

A survey of the books on slavery and of general histories of the antebellum South written by historians in the last twenty-five years provided no evidence of many of the myths that Fogel and Engerman claim to disprove. The following are examples of these straw men, each of which was undocumented in either the text or supplement:

1. Page 41: "The notion that slaveowners relied on the lash alone to promote discipline and efficiency is a highly misleading myth." Every twentieth-century historian of slavery described the variety of positive incentives planters used to promote diligent labor.

2. Pages 53-54: Fogel and Engerman disputed "the notion that speculative purchases and sales of slaves were common among southern planters, that slaves were frequently bought and sold to take advantage of temporary aberrations of price, in much the same way as planters sought to profit from daily, weekly, or monthly gyrations in the prices of cotton or railroad bonds." Their explanation of why it would not have been practicable to speculate in slaves in this manner was rather pointless, because they were arguing with no one but the straw man of their own creation.

3. Page 55: "While historians have been well aware of slave renting, it has received insufficient attention in their writings." Having lodged this complaint, Fogel and Engerman devoted a page and a half to the subject, adding nothing to what earlier historians had said. Frederic Bancroft, in his study of slave trading, gave an entire chapter to slave hiring practices, and Robert Starobin treated the subject at length.[43] *Time on the Cross* failed to acknowledge the contribution of either historian.

4. Page 75: "The frequent contention that slaveowners preferred to work slaves to death at early ages, in order to

avoid the burden of maintenance at late ages is unfounded." This was an old staple of nineteenth-century abolitionist propaganda, but no twentieth-century historian of slavery or of the Old South made such a claim.

5. Page 78: "The thesis that the *systematic* breeding of slaves for sale in the *market* accounted for a major share of the net income or profit of slaveholders, especially in the Old South, is espoused in one degree or another by most members of the anti-Phillips school." Fogel and Engerman defined breeding for the market as "1, interference in the normal sexual habits of slaves to maximize female fertility through such devices as mating women with especially potent men, in much the same way as exists in breeding livestock; 2, the raising of slaves with sale as the main object, in much the same way as cattle or horses are raised." This was another common charge of nineteenth-century abolitionists, but no conventional historian of the past generation claimed that slaves were bred in the Old South in the manner here described. Moreover, Fogel and Engerman distorted the way in which the subject of slave-rearing had been treated recently by several quantitative historians.[44]

6. Page 79: Fogel and Engerman claimed that in spite of "many thousands of hours of research," historians "have failed to produce a single authenticated case of the 'stud' plantations alleged in abolitionist literature." They did not identify the historians who invested all that time in such an enterprise, nor did they explain what they meant by a stud plantation. There is scattered evidence that an occasional slaveholder took an unusually active interest in slave breeding; but, as historians know, evidence of slave plantations that were managed in a way analogous to stud farms is rare indeed.

7. Page 126: Fogel and Engerman questioned "the widely asserted contention that slaves were always feigning illness." No historian of slavery has made so absurd an assertion. What

many have contended is precisely what *Time on the Cross* admitted on page 119: that "planters worried about slaves who feigned illness."

8. Page 133: Fogel and Engerman challenged "the contention that a large proportion of slave children must have been fathered by white men." They did not define the vague quantitative term "large proportion," but if one were to assume that it means at least 20 percent, no historian has come anywhere near such a contention.

9. Page 133: *Time on the Cross* disputed "the widespread assumption that because the law permitted masters to ravish their slave women, they must have exercised that right." In this case it quoted, but did not identify, "one scholar" who made the following rather curious statement: "Almost every [white] mother and wife connected with the institution [of slavery] either actually or potentially shared the males in her family with slave women." There is not much to be said for this statement, except that it is indisputably true! The book did not explain among whom this assumption existed, what proportion of the masters were assumed to have ravished slave women, or what proportion of slave women were assumed to have been ravished. Since the verb "ravish" is a common synonym for rape, it is important to know that the law of *no* southern state "permitted masters to ravish slave women"—or, for that matter, to have sexual relations even with consenting slave women. In this case, *Time on the Cross* created a two-headed straw man, suggesting, first, that slaveholders had a legal right to ravish slave women, and, second, that a "widespread assumption" existed that masters exercised their right in numbers significantly larger than they actually did.

In another paragraph on the same page, Fogel and Engerman gave a variation of their statement in the passive voice: "it has been presumed that masters and overseers must have ravished black women frequently. . . ." Again, they did not say *who* had presumed this; nor did they explain how often ravishing must have occurred to justify the use of the impressionistically quantitative term "frequently."[45]

10. Page 139: "also fallacious is the contention that slave marriages, since they were arbitrarily dictated by masters, frequently produced odd age combinations—young men married to old women and vice versa." The authors of this contention were not identified; but whoever they were, they clearly were at odds with the mythmakers who advanced the thesis that slaves were bred systematically for the market.

In addition to the straw men of *Time on the Cross*, several other characteristics require attention here. Quantitative historians criticize conventional historians, quite justifiably, for failing to quantify their data and for resorting instead to needlessly vague and imprecise quantitative terms. They also criticize conventional historians for presenting exceptional data as typical and attribute this fault to their impressionistic methodology. Therefore, it was surprising to discover that *Time on the Cross* amply illustrated both of these shortcomings. The most striking example was the manner in which it treated the subject of incentives to encourage field hands to labor diligently. Neither the census returns nor other systematic data furnish information on gifts or other pecuniary rewards to slaves; all available evidence comes from literary sources such as plantation records, travelers' accounts, and southern agricultural journals. These "fragmentary" sources provided the foundation for the book's generalizations about slave incentives.

Among the incentives that Fogel and Engerman mentioned were year-end bonuses, which they claimed were "frequently quite substantial." The only example they gave was that of a Louisiana planter, Bennet H. Barrow, who "distributed gifts averaging between $15 and $20 per slave family in both 1839 and 1840." They did not report that gifts were distributed in only one of the remaining eight years of the Barrow record.[46]

Another incentive they discussed was the awarding of patches of land on which slaves grew marketable crops. They cited four cases: 1. On the Texas plantation of Julian S. Devereaux, "in a good year some of the slaves earned in excess of $100 per annum for their families." Fogel and Engerman did not reveal what proportion of the Devereaux slaves had incomes of this or any other size, or how frequently the good years occurred. 2. On "several" Texas plantations "the leading hands . . . frequently earned between $40 and $110 per year. . . ." The plantations were unidentified; the ratio of "leading hands" to the total labor force was not given; and how frequently these earnings occurred was unclear. 3. On an unnamed Alabama plantation eight hands "produced cotton that earned them an average of $71 each." Again, Fogel and Engerman did not say how many hands were employed, or in how many years these amounts were earned. 4. "On still another [unnamed] plantation the average extra earnings of the thirteen top hands was $77." The authors provided no additional information.[47]

While plantation records are fragmentary, they are abundant enough to present a much fuller picture of slave incentives—indeed Fogel and Engerman quantified smaller amounts of data on other subjects. In view of their commitment to quantification and their strictures against using atypical data as if it were typical, there was no reason why they should not have based their generalizations about incentives on the quantified records of a wide sample of those available. From such a sample they could have obtained the percentages of slaves who received "quite substantial" year-end bonuses or cash incomes from marketing their own crops. Instead, Fogel and Engerman made the errors they attributed to conventional historians: they failed to quantify the quantifiable, and they used atypical cases to bolster their argument. The sources on which they depended do not suggest that year-end bonuses were "frequently quite substantial"; rather, a sounder impressionistic statement would be that gifts as large as those distributed by Barrow in 1839 and 1840 were not only exceptional on his plantation but on all others for which records survive. These sources also indicate that cash incomes of the size given in Fogel and Engerman's four illustrations were highly exceptional among field hands, indeed, almost unheard of, and that the majority of those for whom records exist had little or no cash income. On the other hand, there was scarcely a plantation on which punishment, or the threat of it, was negligible as an incentive. Therefore it is quite correct to say that force was the "principal basis" for obtaining labor from slaves, and incorrect to say, as Fogel and Engerman did, that "pecuniary rewards were as integral a part of slavery as punishment."[48]

Another example of placing undue emphasis on atypical data appeared in a discussion of slave housing. The census returns provide no data on slave housing, and Fogel and Engerman therefore relied on plantation records and travelers' accounts. In their description they noted that there was "a considerable range in the quality of housing." "The best," they wrote, "were three- or four-room cottages . . . with up to eight hundred square feet of space on the inside, and large porches on the outside. . . . At the other pole were single-room log cabins without windows."[49] From this description one might expect to find about as many examples of the first kind of housing as of the second. But available data indicate that housing of the first kind was quite rare, while that of the second was very common.[50] Thus by giving equal emphasis to two sets of data whose relative importance is vastly different, Fogel and Engerman have achieved a considerable distortion of the facts about slave housing.

One of the more extravagant claims of *Time on the Cross* was that it was the first book to tell black Americans the truth about their years in bondage—the first to reveal the history that "has been kept from them—the record of black achievement under adversity." It portrayed the "myths" that question the diligence and efficiency of slave labor, the cohesiveness of slave families, and the work ethic of blacks who "struggled for self-improvement" within the slave system, as major forces that kept them suffering "the agony of racial discrimination" after their emancipation from bondage. Fogel and Engerman accused all previous historians of slavery of disseminating these "myths" and the racial slurs they found implicit in each of them.[51] However, if there were racial implications in these earlier interpretations—and there may have been, for racism manifests itself in many subtle ways—*Time on the Cross* by no means managed to escape them, for there were significant racial implications in some of its interpretations as well. In fact, the very shrillness of its antiracist rhetoric was transparently patronizing and thus impeded the cause it attempted to serve.

Other quantitative historians have dealt with the "myths" about slave labor and the alleged corrections in *Time on the Cross*,[52] but certain matters relevant to racism are worth considering here. To destroy the "myth" (believed by no historian of slavery) that all slaves performed menial labor, Fogel and Engerman reported "that over 25 percent of males were managers, professionals, craftsmen, and semi-skilled workers."[53] However, it is the approximately three-fourths of the slaves whom Fogel and Engerman identified as menial laborers who deserve further consideration. In the planting, cultivating, and harvesting of southern staples and food crops, field hands performed numerous tasks that ought to be classified as skilled or semiskilled—in fact merit such classification more than some tasks that *Time on the Cross* listed in these categories. The problem is how to classify workers who at different times performed skilled, semiskilled, and unskilled tasks. At one point the authors stated that agricultural workers engaged in tasks that involved the "accumulation of skills"; elsewhere they conceded that "field hands acquired a

wide variety of farm skills."[54] Yet their occupational classification listed field hands as unskilled "menial laborers"—hardly
an accurate description of workers who performed various
tasks that involved considerable skill. Contrary to Fogel and
Engerman, the overwhelming majority of black slaves de-
serves to be counted among those performing skilled or semi-
skilled tasks either full-time or part-time. In spite of their desire to destroy racist myths, they helped to perpetuate one by
accepting the descriptively inaccurate occupational categories
of the census-takers.

Fogel and Engerman placed particularly heavy responsibility for the survival of racism on those who questioned the
efficiency of slave labor. Whether the inefficiency argument
was racial or nonracial, they contended that the result was
the same: it contributed to the "false stereotype . . . which
still plagues blacks today." However, it was not altogether
clear how *Time on the Cross* provided black Americans with
a better historic image. We must remember that the abolitionist tradition denigrated *slave* labor not *black* labor. *Time on
the Cross* contributed little to the destruction of myths or
false stereotypes by replacing the racist caricatures of free
black workers with cooperative, diligent, success-oriented
slaves, "imbued like their masters" with the values of a Vic-
torian bourgeois class.

One of the astonishing oversights of *Time on the Cross* was
the existence of black resistance to bondage—a subject highly
relevant to the question of slave efficiency and productivity.
Tension always existed in the relations of masters and slaves;
discipline was never perfect and sometimes broke down altogether; runaways, malingering, and other forms of day-to-day
resistance were problems that plagued every planter. The
effects of these problems on the productivity of slave labor
are not easy to isolate and quantify; but Fogel and Engerman
considered many other nonquantifiable aspects of slavery, and
by ignoring resistance in their discussions of slave efficiency

for disputing them, but I am a little skeptical nonetheless—first, because the sources on slavery are full of ambiguities and contradictions, presenting masters and slaves in immense variety and making *any* account of slavery without ambiguity false; second, because Fogel and Engerman themselves made many crucial and questionable decisions about the choice and use of evidence; and, last, because the five quantitative historians noted above not only managed repeatedly to expose errors and systematic biases in the quantitative material presented by *Time on the Cross* but also questioned the logic of many of the inferences Fogel and Engerman drew from their "statistical findings."

Why Fogel and Engerman presented so cheerful a view of slavery as a benign institution, how they could have missed the perplexing mixture of rational and irrational behavior of white masters and black slaves, is an interesting question. No doubt the reasons were as complex as slavery itself. As a sheer guess, their view of slavery may have stemmed in part from a desire to make everything fit comfortably in a neo-classical behavioral model. The slave-plantation system was potentially profitable—Fogel and Engerman and many of their predecessors proved that beyond a doubt—and this fact may have fathered the wish to find it totally rational as well. Whatever the reason, there was no place in their schema for masters who behaved irrationally—who, for status purposes, owned more slaves than they could employ efficiently; who neglected or abused slave property; who punished in passion; who broke up slave marriages; and who "ravished" or simply made love to slave women at the risk of upsetting "the labor discipline on which economic success depended."[59]

In summary, Fogel and Engerman appeared to have been so preoccupied with the efficiency of slave agriculture that they disregarded irrationality, friction, and conflict. As a result, two cliometricians who wanted to restore to blacks their true history in slavery have written a book which deprives blacks of their voices, their initiative, and their humanity. *Time on the Cross* replaced the untidy world of reality—in which masters and slaves, with their rational and irrational perceptions and their human passions, survived as best they could—with a model of a tidy, rational world that never was.

IV

Race, Slavery, and the Republican Party of the 1850s

Among the parliamentary democracies of western Europe and the Americas, Great Britain and the United States have been remarkable for their political stability. Without exploring the various cultural, economic, and geographic characteristics of the two countries that explain this fact, it is sufficient for my purposes merely to observe that their political systems have normally functioned through two major parties rather than many and that the parties have been relatively strong and durable.

In the United States during the course of nearly two centuries, three national party systems have developed to sponsor candidates, define issues, and bid for the responsibility of administering public affairs. This means, of course, that the country has only twice experienced the shattering of an existing party system and the emergence of a new one in its place. The first party reformation occurred in the late 1820s and early 1830s, when the Whigs and Democrats replaced the Federalists and Republicans who had organized soon after the adoption of the Constitution. The second occurred in the 1850s, when the nearly defunct Whig party was succeeded by a Republican organization whose strength was centered in the North, and when a temporarily weakened Democratic party found most of its remaining political power located in the South. The fact that there has not been another political upheaval of such magnitude in the past 125 years underscores both the stability of the American party system and the unusual intensity of that mid-nineteenth-century political crisis.

The political scientist V. O. Key has observed that fluctuations in the relative strength of the two parties have seldom occurred rapidly, but that an occasional critical election has resulted in an exceptionally large and durable voter realignment. Key contended that realignments of this kind took place only when substantial numbers of voters were profoundly concerned about issues that related to cherished values and therefore aroused strong emotions.[1] The decade of the 1850s was such a time, when the characteristic minor shifts of party strength within a stable political structure were interrupted by an upheaval of massive proportions.

What were the voter anxieties—the perceived threats to eternal verities—that fomented the intense emotions of the 1850s? In the North, the recent arrival of large numbers of Irish and German Catholic immigrants evoked deep fears among native-born Protestants and generated ethnocultural political movements such as temperance reform, nativism, and anti-Catholicism—movements that first began to undermine the old party system. By 1854 and 1855, the crusade of the nativists against the whiskey-drinking Irish Catholics and beer-drinking German Catholics had become so formidable that it was unclear whether the nativists or the newly organized Republicans would supplant the Whigs as the second major party in a two-party political system. In states where they were weak the Republicans tried to attract the nativists to their party or joined them in political coalitions.[2] For example, the Chicago *Tribune* boasted that the Republican party would not cater to "the grog shops, foreign vote, and

Catholic brethren"; it accused the Democrats of pandering "to the lowest class of foreign citizens" and of combining the "forces of Jesuitism and Slavery, of the Pope and the Devil." According to the *Tribune*, the Chicago Democratic organization was the "Irish Roman Catholic and Whiskey party of the city."

After 1856, however, nativism rapidly declined as an independent political force. Though anti-Catholicism continued to be a significant determinant of political affiliations,[3] both temperance and nativism gave way to several other issues of high emotional intensity: race, slavery, slavery expansion, and, more generally, the alleged aggressions of southern slaveholders—the so-called Slave Power. How the Republican patry responded to these issues in its formative years will be the subject of this essay.

The politics of slavery in the 1850s now appears to be a more complex matter than it once did; and the Republican party has long since lost its pristine image as the political arm of the northern crusade against slavery and racial injustice. Leon F. Litwack, in his study of the antebellum northern free Negro, and George M. Fredrickson, in his analysis of nineteenth-century racism, have amply documented the prevalence of prejudice in the free states. William H. and Jane H. Pease have shown that even the abolitionists did not succeed entirely in transcending the racism of their time.[4] "Few of us are without it," confessed one antislavery crusader, who suggested that "those who have come out openly as the *colored man's friends*, should make diligent search into the state of their own hearts." Sarah Forten, a black abolitionist, regretted that "Even our professed friends have not yet rid themselves of [prejudice]—to some of them it clings like a dark mantle obscuring their many virtues and choking up the avenues to higher and nobler sentiments. I recollect the words of one of the best and least prejudiced men in the Abolition ranks. 'Ah,' said he, 'I can recall the time when in walking with a colored

brother, the darker the night, the better Abolitionist was I.' "
Most abolitionists, however, were at least aware of their prejudices and tried to overcome them; and they were, as a group,
far less prejudiced than their contemporaries. Moreover, they
confronted a difficult tactical problem: whether to risk losing
potential recruits for the antislavery cause by denouncing
race prejudice, or to admit to their ranks those with negative
feelings about blacks. Thus, Charles C. Burleigh, who wrote
one of the strongest refutations of the argument for black inferiority, could also cater to prejudice in a bid to win support
for abolitionists: "Emancipation would both keep [the
blacks] at home [in the South] and draw back many who
were driven hither by slavery but would gladly return when
they could do so and be free."

If the abolitionists failed to transcend the prevailing racism,
the Free-Soilers of the 1840s were even less successful. Indeed, their movement to keep slavery out of the western territories was, in part, an expression of northern Negrophobia.
When, in 1846, Representative David Wilmot of Pennsylvania introduced his famous Proviso to exclude slavery from
territory that might be acquired from Mexico, he assured his
colleagues that he was concerned about the rights of white
freemen, not of black slaves: "I would preserve to free white
labor a fair country, a rich inheritance, where the sons of toil,
of my own race and color, can live without the disgrace
which association with negro slavery brings upon free labor."
In support of Wilmot, Representative Jacob Brinkerhoff of
Ohio said: "I have selfishness enough greatly to prefer the
welfare of my own race to that of any other, and vindictive-
ness enough to wish to . . . keep upon the shoulders of the
South the burden of the curse which they themselves created
and courted." Expressions such as these led the historian Eugene H. Berwanger to conclude that the Free-Soil movement
was in its essence less antislavery than anti-black. White men,
he argued, opposed having blacks occupy the western terri-

tories whether they were free or slave.[5] Therefore, according to C. Vann Woodward, "One could join the free soilers not only because he opposed slavery or its expansion, but also because he feared and hated Negroes."[6]

Motives for joining the Republican party in the 1850s were seldom simple, and Negrophobia was no doubt common among Republicans as it had been among Free-Soilers. As Woodward has noted, historians have caught Republicans "mouthing the slogans of white privilege and white supremacy, appealing to [the] race prejudices of the electorate, appeasing mass phobias, and condoning compromises with discriminatory and outrageously unjust anti-Negro policies and laws."[7]

Republican leaders themselves bore witness to the prevalence of racism among their constituents. Senator Lyman Trumbull of Illinois observed that "there is a very great aversion in the West—I know it is so in my state—against having free Negroes come among us. Our people want nothing to do with the Negro." In Indiana, according to Representative George W. Julian, "our people hate the Negro with a perfect if not supreme hatred." A New York *Times* editorial of 1858 claimed that the Republicans had "uniformly and most emphatically repudiated the idea that they had anything whatever to do with negroes or negro rights . . . and declared, always and everywhere, that they aimed at the good of the *white men* of the country, and had nothing to do with negroes. . . ." The North, it concluded, "was not prepared to sacrifice or subordinate the interests of the nation to an abstract love of the negro." A letter from one Illinois Republican to his Congressman illustrated the anti-Negro basis of some opposition to slavery expansion:

> The people of the North will never consent to come in contact with the institution of slavery in the territories. To work side by side with negro slaves . . . will leave [them in a] condition little above slaves themselves. Let

[Southerners] keep their niggers if they will, but they must not bring them in contact with us. No matter whether we are opposed to the extension of slavery from our humanity and love of right and justice, or from hatred of niggers (of the latter class are many Illinois Republicans) we are terribly in earnest in our opposition to the extension of that institution.

More than a few Republican politicians took these sentiments into account when they explained their party's goals. "We, the Republican party," said Lyman Trumbull, "are the white man's party. We are for the free white man, and for making white labor acceptable and honorable, which it can never be when negro slave labor is brought into competition with it." Because Republicans believed the white race to be superior to the black, they intended, according to the Hartford *Courant*, "to preserve all of this country that they can from *the pestilential presence of the black man*." In 1858 the Springfield *Illinois State Journal* praised the Republican state platform as "the basis of the white man's party," urged the admission of Kansas as a free state, "because we are for free white men," and endorsed Abraham Lincoln for the United States Senate as "the representative of the white man, free labor, and free soil." Two years later, a Pittsburgh Republican meeting displayed a banner which proclaimed: FREE LAND FOR FREE LABOR: WITH LINCOLN NAILS AND OLD ABE'S RAILS WE'LL FENCE OUT THE NIGGER DEMOCRACY. The antislavery New York *Daily Tribune*, in a candid explanation of the reason for much of the Republican opposition to slavery expansion, regretfully confessed that it was "not a question of sympathy for the Africans or an African question at all. . . . Sympathy with the abused African is no crime—quite the reverse. It is a cause worthy of ten times the spirit and enthusiasm yet manifested in this controversy, but it is not what has thrown the Republican party across the servile track of the false Democracy. American free laboring men are to be crushed by the chattel slaves of an aristocracy; and it matters not whether they happen to be African slaves, Asiatic, or European."

Republicans who identified themselves as members of the white man's party also freely proclaimed their belief in white supremacy. Senator Trumbull, one of the most outspoken racists in the party, affirmed that God had made the distinctions between the races and that they could never be erased. "When we say that all men are created equal, we do not mean that every man in organized society has the same rights. We don't tolerate that in Illinois." In the great controversy over slavery, Trumbull denied that he had ever "contended for giving the negro equal privileges with the white man. That is a doctrine I do not advocate." Senator William H. Seward of New York also disavowed any belief in racial equality. The Negro, he said, "is a foreign and feeble element, like the Indians incapable of assimilation." According to the New York *Times*, "the great body of our Northern people prize their political privileges much too highly . . . to think of sharing them with three or four millions of emancipated blacks." Joshua R. Giddings of Ohio, an old antislavery radical, conceded that Republicans "do not say that the black man is, or shall be, the equal of the white man, or that he shall vote or hold office, however just such a position may be."

Meanwhile, numerous conservative Republicans kept alive the old idea of colonizing Negroes somewhere outside the boundaries of the United States. Among them, Lincoln advocated colonization—"a separation of the races"—as the most practical solution to the American race problem and as the one sure way to prevent "amalgamation." In explaining his support of colonization, Senator Benjamin F. Wade of Ohio declared: "I hope after that is done, to hear no more about Negro equality or anything of that kind. Sir, we shall be as glad to rid ourselves of these people, if we can do it consistently with justice, as any one else." One of Wade's political friends expressed his approval of "this new touch of Colonizing the Niggers," though he believed that "practically it is a d—n humbug." The value of the proposal, he thought, was that it explained what could be done "with the surplus Niggers" if there were to be no more slave states. "Your plan will help us out on this point. But practically I have not much faith in it."

These were the sentiments that caused historians such as Berwanger and Woodward to view the Republican crusade against slavery expansion with considerable skepticism. In stressing anti-black rather than anti-slavery attitudes among Republicans, Berwanger admitted that the extent to which race prejudice motivated opposition to slavery expansion could not be measured precisely. Yet, he argued, "if 79.5 per cent of the people of Illinois, Indiana, Oregon, and Kansas voted to exclude the free Negro [from their states] simply because of their prejudice, surely this antipathy influenced their decisions to support the nonextension of slavery." Given the prevailing racial attitudes, "Republicans were politically astute to demand the limitation of slavery and, at the same time, to refuse political equality to free Negroes." Woodward concluded that in the context of Republican racism it was possible for "some of the bitterest antiabolitionists . . . [to become] prominent antislavery politicians in the 1850s. . . . The movement that eventually democratized antislavery sentiment contrived to make it respectable at the Negro's expense. . . . The successful antislavery movement embraced anti-Negro recruits and their prejudices and triumphed over slavery in the name of white supremacy."[8]

In recent years, three other historians—Eric Foner, Richard H. Sewell, and, somewhat more cautiously, George M. Fredrickson—have offered a more favorable assessment of Republican racial attitudes. Though all admitted that the party had a plenitude of racism, they seemed to suggest that a distor-

al risks involved, Republicans proved vastly more
n Democrats wherever the question of Negro suf-
debated."

g the 1850s, Foner concluded, "a distinctive Republi-
ition on the rights of free Negroes finally became
t was not accepted by everyone in the party, but it
present what may be called the mainstream of Repub-
opinion. Fundamentally it asserted that free Negroes
human beings and citizens of the United States, entitled
e natural rights of life, liberty, and property. Given the
sm which pervaded northern society, the Republicans'
stence on the humanity of the Negro was more of a step
rward than might appear." Moreover, their stand on race
lations "went against the prevailing opinion of the 1850s,
nd proved a distinct political liability." Fredrickson identified these mainstream Republicans as "ex-Whigs of mildly
antislavery antecedents like Abraham Lincoln . . . who not
only held a middle ground on questions of antislavery policy
but also espoused a moderate racial philosophy in the tradition
of Henry Clay. Men of this persuasion offered some resistance to extreme racism while at the same time carefully
avoiding what they regarded as the dangerous racial utopian-
ism of the abolitionists."[9]

Although the two interpretations of Republican opinion
about race and slavery summarized here conflicted in significant ways, they were by no means totally different. Berwanger and Woodward recognized that genuine antislaveryism was a force in the Republican party and that some
members had liberal racial views; Foner, Sewell, and Fredrickson acknowledged the racial basis of much Republican
opposition to slavery expansion and the Negrophobia that
obsessed many party adherents. The difference between them
was one of emphasis, and the question to be considered is
which of the two emphases was a relatively more cogent
description of Republican attitudes.

tion had resulted from ov˅
identified Republicans with ˴
all of which were evident in tʰ
cratic charges that they favore
publicans denounced the prejudı
tion; some ridiculed it; some declaı
was not to support racial equality;˅˴
race issue out of politics, ignored it; ˴
their party was the white man's party,
charges. Foner claimed that many of thᵉ
to racism were merely "political replies tо
sations rather than gratuitous insults to the bᵥ
emphasized the near universality in the Westᵉ
belief in white racial superiority, and he concₗ
publicans simply recognized "that political succ
upon some measure of accommodation to thᵉ
racism."

Negrophobia, Foner believed, was strongest amoɳ
Democrats in the Republican coalition. They "took ˴
in racist appeals. They represented in the most eᵥ
degree the racism from which no portion of the Repuᵦ
party could claim total freedom." On the other hand, Fₑ
noted that many Republican leaders had "long histories
support for Negro rights, and many areas of the North whicı
gave Republicans their largest majorities had distinguished
themselves in the past by their endorsement of Negro suffrage and opposition to the Negro exclusion laws." In 1857,
in a Wisconsin referendum, though Negro suffrage was voted
down, more than 60 percent of Republican voters supported
it. In New York state, in 1860, all but five of the 89 Republicans in the Assembly voted for an equal suffrage amendment
to the state constitution. As in Wisconsin, the amendment
was defeated in a popular referendum, but the majority of
Republican voters supported it, while nearly all the Democrats opposed. Indeed, Sewell argued that, "notwithstanding

The answer to this question depends upon the perspective from which one views the matter. One way to view ante-bellum Republicans, which is both valid and useful, is from the perspective of today. From our vantage point we can hardly avoid being struck by the pervasiveness of racial prejudice in northern society—by the fact, in Woodward's words, that even "the radical, antislavery, and abolitionist Republicans . . . have been found wanting in their racial attitudes and policies."[10] To present-day liberal integrationists who fancy themselves free of prejudice, the racism of so-called "enlightened" Republicans appears to be nothing short of appalling.

Another way to view Republican racial attitudes is from the perspective of the 1850s; and most historians agree, when they are pressed, that this is the way that historical events *should* be viewed. The "supreme task of the historian," according to David M. Potter, "and the one of most superlative difficulty, is to see the past through the imperfect eyes of those who lived it and not with his own omniscient twenty-twenty vision." Potter did not suggest "that any of us can really do this, but only that it is what we must attempt."[11] When Republicans are examined from the perspective of their own time, Foner and Sewell (though perhaps too often giving them the benefit of the doubt) and Fredrickson seem to come off somewhat better than Berwanger and Wood-ward. Because, as Foner conceded, "no portion of the Republican party could claim total freedom" from racism, Wood-ward comes close to throwing all of them, even the political abolitionists, along with the Democrats, into the same racist pot.

This is what we may feel impelled to do from our present perspective. However, during the 1850s the great majority of Northerners—nearly all the Democrats and a large pro-portion of the Republicans—did *not* understand the new party system in terms of a universal and scarcely distinguishable racism. On the contrary, racial attitudes played an important role in the political realignments of that decade. As a general rule it can be said that those northern voters whose major anxiety was the "black peril"—those who were obsessed with fears of racial equality, "amalgamation," or inundation by a "black tide" flowing northward from the southern states—were heavily concentrated in the Democratic party. In the case of the Republicans, granted the racism in the party, it is nevertheless true that collectively they were somewhat more relaxed about race, somewhat less tormented by fantasies of the "black peril," and somewhat more sympathetic to the plight of blacks in America. At the very least it can be said that Republicans gave certain other anxieties they shared a higher priority.

In spite of the attempt of some racist Republicans to portray their party as *the* white man's party, their strategy was in fact a failure. Race was an issue on which the Republicans were always on the defensive, for the Democrats were quite successful in establishing themselves as preeminently the anti-Negro party. In fact, as Sewell observed, "Republican racist pronouncements palled before the brutish negrophobia of Northern Democrats." To them belonged the responsibility for first introducing racial demagoguery on a large scale into national politics—and racism continued to be the party's stock-in-trade from the 1850s to the end of Reconstruction.

Since no substantial Democratic faction embarrassed the party by advocating civil rights for blacks, the Democrats could easily outbid the Republicans for the racist vote, and they pressed their advantage to the full. They constantly branded the Republican party as the "Black Republican party," or the "nigger party," or the "amalgamation party." According to Senator Stephen A. Douglas of Illinois, the Republicans ignored "every question which has for its object the welfare and happiness of the white man—every question which does not propose to put the Negro on an equality with the white man, politically and socially." In 1858 the Democratic Chicago *Times* warned that if Lincoln were elected Senator, Illinois would become "the nigger state of the Northwest," because he was "in favor of bringing into the state the free Negro population of Kentucky and Missouri" to compete with white labor. In Massachusetts, Caleb Cushing charged that Republicans, "in their love for the black race," were "actuated by demonic hatred of the white race." During political campaigns nearly every issue of many Democratic newspapers contained racist attacks on Republicans, the viciousness of which was startling even in that age of irresponsible personal journalism. For example, during the two months before the presidential election of 1860, the Cleveland *Plain Dealer* almost daily stressed the theme that "the only distinctive creed and policy" of the Republican party was "Abolitionism and Niggerism, and the assertion of equal rights for the black man with the white man." One issue contained a cartoon of a Republican with a "cougar body, Congo head, and coon tail"; another claimed that Republicans favored "social equality . . . amalgamation, a mongrel population, and a mixed government"; two others accused them of favoring "Negro superiority" over white immigrants and white women; and, on the eve of the state election, the issue of October 3 devoted an entire page to racist caricatures of Republicans and Negroes. Indeed, the Democrats repeatedly questioned the legitimacy of the Republican organization, because it allegedly placed the interests of blacks above those of whites.

If the great majority of the most rabid Negrophobes viewed the Democrats as the anti-Negro party, nearly all of those who favored political action against slavery or slavery expansion perceived the Republicans as the antislavery party —though not as aggressively dedicated to the cause as the radicals would have liked. In fact, many moderates feared that their party was *too* closely identified with abolitionism, for this was a second issue on which the Democrats took the offensive and questioned Republican legitimacy. The Republicans, they charged, were a sectional, antislavery party, a threat to the survival of the Union, and therefore a reckless, illegitimate political organization. According to the Milwaukee *Daily News*, the Republican party was an organization of "rabid abolitionists" who plotted to "undermine and sap the foundations of the republic." In their defense, Republicans denied that they were abolitionists, or that they contemplated unconstitutional attacks on slavery in the southern states.

Nevertheless, in spite of these quite accurate Republican disavowals of radical antislavery ideas or programs, the Democrats could accuse the party of antislaveryism with greater justification than they could accuse it of preaching racial equality. In its formative years the Republican party had absorbed most of the political abolitionists, while the Democrats portrayed themselves as the party not only of white supremacy but of anti-abolitionism as well. The Republicans, one must remember, in addition to opposing slavery expansion, wrote into their national platform of 1856 a denunciation of slavery as a "relic of barbarism," thus becoming the first major party to take an official stand against it. As one abolitionist, Elizur Wright, observed, "the greatest recommendation of the Republican party is, that its enemies do not quite believe its disclaimers, while they do believe that [it is] sincerely opposed to slavery as far as it goes." A party whose leadership included veteran antislavery crusaders such as Charles Sumner, Salmon P. Chase, Joshua R. Giddings, and George W. Julian could hardly have avoided being tarred with the abolitionist brush. "The evidence strongly suggests," Foner contended, "that outside of [William Lloyd] Garrison's immediate circle [of extremists], most abolitionists voted with the Republican party despite their wish that the party adopt a more aggressive anti-slavery position. . . . The fact that so many abolitionists, not to mention radical Republicans, supported the Republican party, is an indication that anti-slavery formed no small part of the Republican ideology."[12]

This is not to dispute the assertions of some historians that many Republicans appeared to be at heart more anti-slaveholder, or anti-Slave Power, or anti-southern, or even anti-Negro than they were anti-slavery on moral grounds. Yet, in recognizing the presence of these less elevated motives of sectional self-interest and personal prejudice, several qualifications and certain mitigating circumstances need to be considered. First, many Republicans did *not* exploit the racist argument against slavery expansion—that is, the argument that the territories should be preserved for white settlers. Neither the national platform of 1856 nor that of 1860 used such language to justify its demand that slavery be confined to its existing limits. Rather, the platform of 1856 defended the Republican position on moral grounds alone; and, in 1858, as Sewell has noted, except for Indiana every state platform reaffirmed the principles formulated by the party at its first national nominating convention.[13] Throughout the 1850s Republican conventions in only a few conservative states, such as New Jersey and Illinois, resorted to racist arguments in opposing slavery expansion. Far more commonly the state party gatherings identified themselves as "a party that hates slavery" (Michigan), or one founded on "hatred of oppression" (New York), or one that regarded slavery as "a great evil and wrong" (Ohio), or one opposed to "the guilty fantasy that there can be property in man" (Vermont). Indeed, considering the prevalence of racism in the North, Republicans exploited anti-black sentiment less than one might have expected—less often than Democratic racist attacks must have invited such a response. For the party contained a substantial body of members whose moral commitment to antislavery was of long standing and who scorned racist defenses of their cause.

Second, there is evidence that some Republicans with genuine antislavery convictions resorted to racist arguments against slavery expansion simply as a matter of political tactics—as an expedient appeal to the undecided and to those who constituted the lowest common denominator in their party. As Don E. Fehrenbacher observed, "Opponents of slavery everywhere had to contend with the charge that they advocated Negro equality . . . and political survival more often than not appeared to depend upon repudiation of the epithet."[14] Horace Greeley scolded the Republican politicians who seemed to think that to prevent Democrats from raising "the cry of 'nigger' against them . . . they must be as harsh, and cruel, and tyrannical, toward the unfortunate blacks as possible, in order to prove themselves 'the white man's party.' " But a practical Republican explained that, because of northern racial attitudes, "we must make some concessions for the success of our party." Even the abolitionist Lydia Maria Child wrote Senator Trumbull that she was "well aware of the difficult position of the Republican members of Congress" and, while criticizing him for his conservatism, conceded that she could not "try your doings by *my* standard." Lincoln believed that the feelings "of the great mass of white people . . . whether well or ill founded, can not be safely disregarded." Accordingly, in order to win maximum support for an antislavery platform, Republican realists seemed ready to place their moral ends above some rather disagreeable means. With this in mind, another abolitionist, Maria Chapman, despaired of understanding the ways of God. Thinking of the racist opponents of slavery expansion, she exclaimed: "God makes use of instruments that *I* wouldn't touch."

Third, it was quite possible for Republicans of the 1850s—

and abolitionists as well—to be burdened with a considerable amount of racial prejudice and still oppose slavery on moral grounds. Republicans repeatedly declared that their anti-slavery sentiments did not inevitably lead them to a belief in the equality of the races. On several occasions Lincoln, for example, said: "I do not understand that because I do not want a negro woman for a slave I must necessarily want her for a wife." Charles S. Wilson, of the Chicago *Evening Journal*, opposed slavery as "a wrong to the down trodden and oppressed" and "resolutely opposed . . . the equalizing of the races." To him, "it no more necessarily follows that we should fellowship with negroes, because our policy strikes off their shackles, than it would to take felons to our embraces, because we might remonstrate against cruelty to them in our penitentiaries."

Fourth, it is no doubt a mistake to assume that either race prejudice or moral opposition to slavery was present in individual Republicans in some fixed and unalterable blend. More likely, a change in circumstances affected the degree to which either of these attitudes motivated the individual. A period of heightened sectional tension brought with it an intensification of anti-southern feelings and a tendency for anxiety about the Negro to give way to increased anxiety about the designs of southern slaveholders. A rise in anti-slaveholder or anti-southern sentiment probably aroused greater moral opposition to slavery and reduced, at least temporarily, hostility to blacks. The diary of George Templeton Strong, a conservative New York lawyer, illustrated this point with particular clarity. Soon after the passage of the Compromise of 1850, Strong recorded his conviction that southern slaves were "happier and better off than the niggers of the North," and that the principles of the abolitionists were "false, foolish, wicked, and unchristian." In the spring of 1854, while Congress debated the Kansas-Nebraska Act, he was "resisting awful temptations to avow myself a

Free Soiler." Two years later, after Representative Preston Brooks of South Carolina attacked Charles Sumner of Massachusetts on the Senate floor, Strong feared that "the reckless, insolent brutality of our southern aristocrats may drive me into abolitionism yet." After another month he was ready to vote the Republican ticket and join "the insurgent plebeians of the North arming against a two-penny South Carolina aristocracy." At last, in October 1856, Strong adopted the abolitionist argument that southern slavery was "the greatest crime on the largest scale known in modern history. . . . It is deliberate legislation intended to extinguish and annihilate the moral being of men for profit; systematic murder, not of the physical, but of the moral and intellectual being; blasphemy, not in word, but in systematic action against the Spirit of God. . . ." "So I feel now," he added, "perhaps it's partly the dominant election furor that colors my notions."[15]

Finally, although several historians have argued that Republicans were characteristically more anti-southern and anti-slaveholder than they were truly anti-slavery, this distinction may have been less clear in the minds of average Republicans. It would have required an exceedingly fine discrimination to enable a Republican to have negative feelings about the South, or about slaveholders, without having similar feelings about the institution that gave the South and its social elite their power and distinct identity. No doubt sectional tension, anti-southernism, and growing suspicion of the ultimate purposes of the Slave Power were the sources of much of the antislavery sentiment that ultimately pervaded the antebellum Republican party. Thus, the Massachusetts Republican state platform of 1857 began with a denunciation of "the alarming encroachments of the Slave Power" but ended with an assertion that its aggressions were "but the natural results of the inherent wickedness of chattel slavery," whose "existence and further extension" the party would oppose "by every constitutional means." Sewell concluded that "hostility toward slavery lay at the very core of Republican ideology; that nearly everywhere it overshadowed and subsumed all other issues. Nor can there be much doubt that by 1860 the vast majority of Republicans viewed bondage as a curse and sought not merely to arrest its spread but to place it on the road to ultimate extinction."[16]

For a case study of the position of mainstream Republicans on both race and slavery there is no better place to turn than to the familiar Lincoln-Douglas debates of 1858. Needless to say, one set of debates can scarcely provide sufficient evidence to settle conclusively the various questions about Republican attitudes that historians have raised; nevertheless, for several reasons, these debates were extraordinarily significant. Douglas was the acknowledged leader of the northern Democracy, while Lincoln was at least one of the most prominent western Republicans. Moreover, Lincoln was very much a Republican of the center, associated with neither the radical antislavery left wing nor the conservative Negrophobic right wing. He is, in short, an ideal party leader to examine in order to measure the thinking of average Republicans. In addition, the occasion of these debates was the only time during the 1850s when a leading Republican and a leading Democrat confronted one another publicly for many hours—twenty-one, to be exact—in order to explain the positions of their respective parties and answer the charges of the opposition. Finally, the seven debates attracted national attention. Both participants were acutely aware that they were not merely competing for a seat in the United States Senate but were representing their parties before a much wider audience.

One of the remarkable facts about the debates is that both Lincoln and Douglas, in their statements of principles and in their criticisms of each other, confined themselves almost exclusively to three topics: race, slavery, and slavery expansion. Once or twice Douglas referred briefly to his desire for

the continued geographic expansion of the United States, but
Lincoln never departed from the three central issues. All
other public problems—the tariff, banking, land policy, the
transcontinental railroad, internal improvements, immigration,
nativism, state and local issues, even the current economic
depression—were totally ignored. Students of political behavior sometimes deny that what politicians talk about is
necessarily crucial in determining party affiliations or voter
support. However, Lincoln and Douglas, as career politicians,
had a considerable stake in knowing what was on the minds
of voters, especially the undecided ones. For this reason, the
subjects on which these contestants focused are at least highly
suggestive of what was troubling the electorate. No doubt
the great majority of those who heard the debates merely had
their convictions reinforced and did not change their minds
or their parties because of them. But it was the uncommitted
minority that each candidate was courting.

The following review of the debates raises six crucial
questions and suggests the answers to each of them indicated
in the text:[17]

1. In speaking of blacks did Lincoln ever resort to cruel
caricatures or use insulting terms such as "niggers"? Except
for one instance when Lincoln resorted to the vernacular to
make a point, he refused to indulge in these crudities—and
so did Douglas. Though Douglas frequently expressed his
low opinion of blacks and referred to the "Black Republican
party" in a context that made the term clearly derogatory,
neither debater stooped to the racial slurs that were abundant
in the Democratic press and not uncommon in the Republican.

2. Did Lincoln advance the argument that the Republican
party was the white man's party? On no occasion did he
make such a claim. In fact, this is where the first significant
difference between the candidates became evident, for Douglas tried repeatedly to identify the two parties in terms of

their racial loyalties. In the first debate at Ottawa, he urged those who believed in equal political rights to "support Mr. Lincoln and the Black Republican party, who are in favor of the citizenship of the negro." At Freeport, Douglas said that "those of you who believe that the negro is your equal . . . have a right to entertain those opinions, and of course will vote for Mr. Lincoln." At Jonesboro, he charged that Chicago Republicans advocated "negro equality, putting the white man and the negro on the same basis under the law." It was Douglas, then, not Lincoln, who professed to speak for the white man's party.

3. Did Lincoln invoke a racial justification for Republican opposition to slavery expansion? In this case the answer is almost, but not quite, never. The single occasion when he adopted that line of argument was in the last debate at Alton. Here he declared that his listeners, "as white men," had an interest in keeping slavery out of the territories. Without considering the moral aspect of slavery, he added, "I am still in favor of our new Territories being in such a condition that white men may find a home. . . . I am in favor of this not merely . . . for our own people who are born amongst us, but as an outlet for *free white people everywhere*, the world over. . . ." No doubt it is significant that Lincoln used this argument in conservative southern Illinois. That it was a surrender to expediency rather than the basic reason for his opposition to slavery expansion, is indicated by the fact that he had never used this argument before.

4. Did Lincoln ever take the initiative in raising the race issue and in proclaiming his belief in white supremacy? On no occasion did he do so; and, moreover, it is likely that he would have ignored the matter altogether had Douglas not brought it up so often and so aggressively. In Springfield, on June 16, in his famous "House Divided" speech, which key-noted his whole campaign, Lincoln said nothing about race. Douglas, however, in his keynote address in Chicago, on July

9, raised the issue at once and made the first of his numerous charges that Lincoln believed in racial equality. The following day, in replying to Douglas, Lincoln denied the charge, but his comment on the race issue was brief and slightly facetious. A few days later he responded to another volley of accusations by ridiculing Douglas for having "tormented himself with horrors about my disposition to make negroes perfectly equal with white men." Though Lincoln made it clear that he had no such desire, his statement was more a defense of certain rights that Negroes could claim than a clear assertion of white supremacy.

On August 21, when the debates began at Ottawa, Douglas spoke first and again introduced the subject of race as a major issue in the campaign. His renewed charges finally elicited from Lincoln a detailed denial of support for political or social equality of the races and an assertion of belief in white supremacy. In the second debate, at Freeport, Lincoln spoke first and made no further reference to race, thus indicating again his reluctance to make it an issue. But when Douglas took his turn, he made one of his most demagogic appeals to race prejudice and repeated his charge that Republicans believed in racial equality. Lincoln, in his rejoinder, in spite of this extreme provocation, simply ignored the matter. In the third debate, at Jonesboro, he again ignored Douglas's accusations and provocative language. But in the fourth debate, at Charleston, because, Lincoln said, someone at his hotel had asked whether he really believed in perfect equality between the races, he made his most comprehensive denial that he favored political rights or social equality for Negroes.

The Charleston statement, however, did not deter Douglas from continued exploitation of the race issue to the very end of the debates. Indeed, in the last debate, at Alton, when Douglas summed up the differences between him and Lincoln, he gave race and his charge that Republicans advocated

I would most desire would be the separation of the white and black races."

Lincoln thus took his stand with Douglas in favor of white supremacy, though in language somewhat less strident. However, this was not all that Lincoln had to say on the subject of race, and it was in his further comments that the differences between the two men became evident. In the sentence immediately following the passage from his Charleston speech quoted above, Lincoln said: "I do not perceive that because the white man is to have the superior position the negro should be denied every thing." The black man still had rights, and foremost among them was "the right to put into his mouth the bread that his own hands have earned." In this respect "he is *my equal and the equal of Judge Douglas, and the equal of every living man.*"

Lincoln disagreed sharply with Douglas's contention that the Declaration of Independence did not apply to Negroes. He did not understand it "to mean that all men were created equal in all respects," but, contrary to Douglas, he insisted that the Negro was "entitled to all the natural rights enumerated in the Declaration of Independence, the right to life, liberty, and the pursuit of happiness. I hold that he is as much entitled to these as the white man." All the historical records from 1776 to the 1850s "may be searched in vain for one single affirmation, from one single man, that the negro was not included in the Declaration of Independence." Lincoln believed that "the first man who ever said it was Chief Justice [Roger B.] Taney in the Dred Scott case, and the next to him was our friend, Stephen A. Douglas. And now it has become the catch-word of the entire [Democratic] party." Lincoln opposed this new principle "as having a tendency to dehumanize the negro—to take away from him the right of ever striving to be a man." Moreover, he asked, if one man is to say that the Declaration does not mean the Negro, "why

not another say it does not mean some other man?" In his
Chicago speech, on July 10, Lincoln made a sweeping plea
which did not square with some of his later utterances, but
which may have nonetheless expressed the liberal side of his
thought on this matter. He urged his listeners to "discard all
this quibbling about this man and the other man—this race and
that race and the other race being inferior, and therefore they
must be placed in an inferior position." Douglas never permitted Lincoln to forget that plea, and he used it to support
his accusation that Lincoln spoke one way in Chicago and
another way in the southern counties of the state.

Though Lincoln opposed granting citizenship to Negroes
in Illinois, he strongly dissented from Chief Justice Taney's
argument in the Dred Scott case that a Negro could not be a
citizen in *any* state. His position was "that the different States
have the power to make a negro a citizen under the Constitution of the United States if they choose." Finally, as to colonization, one must note that Lincoln never proposed to coerce
Negroes to leave the country. If a program of colonization
were to be undertaken, he wanted it to be voluntary. Lincoln's support of colonization is best understood as an expression of his deep pessimism about the possibility of creating a
truly harmonious biracial society.[21] With all its limitations, his
position on race is somewhat less grating on modern sensibil-
ities than that of Douglas, and, in the context of the 1850s,
significantly more liberal. In fact, he was probably as liberal
as a major-party Illinois politician could be at that time, while
hoping to obtain statewide support for public office.

6. Did Lincoln's opposition to slavery expansion stem primarily from hostility to the South, or to the so-called Slave
Power, rather than from moral opposition to slavery itself?
Quite clearly, it did not. Indeed, he explicitly denied any feelings of hostility toward the South or toward white Southerners. In the first debate he quoted an earlier speech in which
he had declared: "I have no prejudice against the Southern

people. They are just what we would be in their situation.
. . . We know that some Southern men do free their slaves,
go north, and become tip-top abolitionists; while some Northern ones go south, and become most cruel slaveholders."
Lincoln often expressed sympathy for Southerners and an
appreciation of the complexity of the problem they faced. He
wished that they would adopt programs of gradual emancipation but added that "for their tardiness in this, I will not
undertake to judge our brethren of the South." However, he
insisted that the South's predicament provided "no more excuse for permitting slavery to go into our free territory, than
it would for reviving the African slave trade by law."

Lincoln, then, addressed himself not to the evil in the hearts
of white Southerners but to the evil he believed to be inherent
in slavery. "I have always hated slavery," he said, "I think as
much as any abolitionist." In the final debate at Alton he described what he believed was "the real issue" of the national
political crisis: It was "the sentiment on the part of one class
that looks upon the institution of slavery *as a wrong*, and of
another class that does *not* look upon it as wrong. The sentiment that contemplates the institution of slavery in this country as a wrong is the sentiment of the Republican party. It
is the sentiment around which all their actions—all their
arguments circle—from which all their propositions radiate.
They look upon it as being a moral, social and political
wrong. . . ." Though Republicans had a due regard for the
difficulty of abolishing slavery, as well as for the constitutional protections surrounding it, they nevertheless insisted
"that it should as far as may be, *be treated* as a wrong, and
one of the methods of treating it as a wrong is to *make provision that it shall grow no larger*. They also desire a policy
that looks to a peaceful end of slavery at sometime, as being
a wrong."

In his "House Divided" speech, Lincoln asserted even more
forcefully that "this government cannot endure permanently

half slave and half free," that there would be no political peace until slavery was placed "where the public mind shall rest in the belief that it is in the course of ultimate extinction." In every debate Douglas attacked him for this statement and accused him of seeking to provoke disunion and civil war. The people of the South, Douglas retorted, "are accountable to God and their posterity and not to us. It is for them to decide, therefore, the moral and religious right of the slavery question for themselves within their own limits." Contrary to Lincoln, Douglas asserted that the country could "endure forever, divided into free and slave States as our fathers made it,—each State having the right to prohibit, abolish or sustain slavery, just as it pleases." But Lincoln stood firm and frequently restated the position he had taken in his acceptance speech. How is the slavery agitation to end? he asked at Charleston. "I say . . . there is no way of putting an end to [it] . . . but to put it back upon the basis where our fathers placed it, no way but to keep it out of our new Territories. . . . Then the public mind will rest in the belief that it is in the course of ultimate extinction." After preventing its expansion, Lincoln did not expect the complete abolition of slavery to come in the immediate future—it might even take a century—"but that it will occur in the best way for both races, in God's own time, I have no doubt."

There was nothing for which Lincoln attacked Douglas more persistently than Douglas's apparent lack of moral feeling about slavery. Douglas, he charged, had never expressed disapproval of it.[22] "He has the high distinction, so far as I know, of never having said slavery is right or wrong." Douglas could profess not to care whether slavery was voted up or down only if he saw nothing wrong with it; but, said Lincoln, "he cannot say so logically if he admits that slavery is wrong. He cannot say that he would as soon see a wrong voted up as voted down." According to Lincoln, Douglas's trouble was that he thought of slavery "as an exceedingly little thing—this matter of keeping one-sixth of the population of the whole nation in a state of oppression and tyranny unequalled in the world. He looks upon it . . . as something having no moral question in it." This was a position that Lincoln could not accept, and in the final debate at Alton he related the slavery issue to the history of all mankind:

> It is the eternal struggle between these two principles—right and wrong—throughout the world. They are the two principles that have stood face to face from the beginning of time; and will ever continue to struggle. The one is the common right of humanity and the other the divine right of kings. . . . It is the same spirit that says, "You work and toil and earn bread, and I'll eat it." No matter in what shape it comes, whether from the mouth of a king who seeks to bestride the people of his own nation and live by the fruit of their labor, or from one race of men as an apology for enslaving another race, it is the same tyrannical principle.

In summary, Lincoln, in his debates with Douglas, was highly successful in occupying what is called, in modern political jargon, the middle of the road. Speaking for mainstream Republicans, he outlined a program that he took pains to portray as responsible moderation between two extremes. On one side, according to his view, were the national Democrats (including Douglas) dominated by the proslavery interest—forced to betray a long-standing sectional agreement by the repeal of the Missouri Compromise, to accept the Dred Scott decision, and to follow a course that could only end in the nationalizing of slavery. On the other side were the radical abolitionists urging an unrealistic program of immediate emancipation, threatening the states where slavery existed, going to extremes on the subject of racial equality.

In the middle were the Republicans for whom Lincoln spoke: opposing the further expansion of slavery; demanding the admission of Kansas as a free state; hoping to put slavery on the road to ultimate extinction; respecting meanwhile the constitutional guarantees protecting slavery in the southern states; accepting the principle that blacks were entitled to some minimum rights. To be sure, there were right-wing Republicans who used racist arguments against slavery expansion and called their party the white man's party; and left-wing Republicans who were more aggressively antislavery and more sympathetic to the black man, even supporting Negro suffrage in the northern states.[23] But the center of gravity in the party was located around the moderate position defined by Lincoln in his debates with Douglas.

The positions of the two men on slavery and race were sufficiently different to give Illinois voters—and, two years later, all northern voters—a clear choice. Those who were seriously troubled by fear of a black threat to the white race in America—troubled to the point where their fear became a major determinant of political action—would most likely have turned to the Democrats in this period of party realignment. Those who had any substantial moral feelings about slavery— which, one must always remember, was not incompatible with a certain amount of race prejudice—would almost surely have joined the Republicans. Sewell's conclusion was a fair statement of the case: "That the antebellum Republicans . . . were often indifferent and sometimes hostile to black Americans, need come as no surprise. The remarkable fact is that the Republicans . . . showed a willingness to recognize the Negro's humanity and to protect his most basic freedoms which went well beyond the narrow racism of most other contemporary Americans, North and South."[24] A year after Lincoln's debates with Douglas, when he was actively seeking a presidential nomination, he again attacked the new Democratic doctrine that the Declaration of Independence did not apply to Negroes. The tendency of that principle, Lincoln said, "is to bring the public mind to the conclusion that when men are spoken of, the negro is not meant; and when negroes

even would have doubted the wisdom and propriety of such a political phenomenon as a national nominating convention.

American political practices had undergone some basic changes since 1800, when the Jeffersonians named their presidential candidate in a private congressional caucus and appealed to a somewhat restricted electorate—and then only indirectly, for presidential electors were still chosen by state legislatures. In subsequent years, western farmers, eastern workingmen, and middle-class reformers had struggled successfully to broaden the base of democracy. In political terms, this "rise of the common man" had involved reforms such as the direct election of presidential electors, the abolition of property qualifications for voting and officeholding, and the substitution of the national nominating convention for the congressional caucus. Advocates of the nominating convention claimed that it would give rank-and-file party members a greater voice in choosing candidates and writing platforms. Thus, by 1860, the "common man" supposedly had gained increased opportunities to make his influence felt in government.

How wisely, how effectively, the "common man" would use his political power would depend upon his level of literacy, his comprehension of the problems of his society, his willingness to defend such essentials of democracy as freedom of speech and assembly, and his sense of individual responsibility for the effective working of the political process. To the extent that voters were deficient in these matters, they were likely to become in the same degree the pawns and not the masters of political machines. It was all too easy for the delegates to national conventions to be controlled by powerful party leaders, who were the dispensers of patronage; for candidates and platforms to be the products of secret bargains arranged by wire-pullers and special interests; for politicians to appeal to the emotions and not the intellects of men; and for campaigns to become circuses with parades, barbecues, extravagant stump oratory, and other forms of public entertainment. The temptation to travestize political democracy was strong and ever present.

The vulnerability to such tactics of much of the American electorate had been amply demonstrated in the famous "log-cabin, hard-cider" campaign of 1840. Whig and Democratic leaders, whose followers included men of all classes, regions, and sections, had repeatedly found it necessary not only to compromise internal differences but to evade issues and confuse voters in order to hold their motley organizations together. It had become almost a tradition of the second American party system for presidential candidates to be noncontroversial mediocrities. Small wonder that elderly conservatives shook their heads in dismay as the deferential politics controlled by gentlemen of the eighteenth century gave way to the mass politics of the nineteenth.[2]

However, in the middle of the nineteenth century the course of American politics threatened to take a different turn. A cluster of social problems, including nativism, but most notably the problem of slavery and slavery expansion which divided North and South, gradually caused the two old national parties to disintegrate. In 1848, the Democrats lost some of their northern followers to the Free-Soilers; more broke away in 1854 in protest against Stephen A. Douglas's Kansas-Nebraska bill. By 1860 the two wings of the party were no longer able to agree on a platform or unite behind a single presidential candidate. And by then only a fragment of the Whig party survived to support the candidacy of John Bell of Tennessee.

The new Republican party, formed in the majority of northern states by 1855, was the most significant political product of sectionalism. At the time of its birth it was, in part, a popular mass movement relatively free from the control of political machines. Drawing its support from free-state Whigs, political abolitionists, Free-Soilers, "Anti-Nebraska" Democrats, temperance reformers, and anti-Catholic "Know-

Nothings," it appealed to the fears, aspirations, and ideals of most Protestant, middle-class Northerners. The party made an impressive showing in the election of 1856, when it carried all but five of the free states for its first presidential candidate, John C. Frémont.

The next four years had given Republicans ample time to improve their organization, to broaden their appeal, and to become increasingly realistic in their electioneering techniques. Now, on May 16, 1860, party delegates were again gathering in convention to prepare for another struggle for national political supremacy. This time the Republican campaign would end in victory—a victory that would lead to disunion, to four years of civil war, and to many years of Republican rule, during which American institutions and public policy would undergo profound change.

Since the first Republican victory produced such momentous results, the nature and proceedings of the convention that planned it have considerable historical significance. It is important to determine whether the delegates performed their duties in a manner consonant with the seriousness of their task, whether they fairly represented the will of the party rank-and-file—in short, whether the body as a whole proved to be an effective agency of political democracy. One approach to the problem—the one that will be taken here—is to investigate the matter of communication. For example, how decisive was open discussion on the convention floor in determining the action taken? How decisive were the private conferences, the secret bargains, and the outside pressures? To what extent did the delegates honestly try to explain, through their formal speeches, their party's position on various public questions? To what extent did they deliberately make their appeal vague or deceptive? These were matters of considerable consequence, for the speakers were heard not only by potential supporters in the North but by angry and often frightened critics in the South. The convention provided one of the last great public airings of national issues before peaceful discussion gave way to violence.

Chicago Republicans provided spacious accommodations for this gathering of their political friends. They had just finished constructing, for the convention's special use, a huge wooden "Wigwam"—a two-story structure, 100 feet wide and 180 feet long, capable, they claimed, of holding more people than any other building in the country. In addition to the 466 delegates and numerous newspaper reporters, it could accommodate approximately 10,000 spectators. The various state delegations sat together on a stage which ran the width of the edifice. About 1200 ladies and their escorts sat in a gallery, while the rest of the audience stood on a series of platforms which descended to the stage. These platforms were always filled to capacity, and usually a large crowd milled about in the streets outside.

The interior of the Wigwam was crude and unfinished, but the Republican ladies of Chicago had decorated it gaudily with wreaths, festoons, coats of arms of the several states, multicolored streamers, flags, and artificial flowers. Whatever its aesthetic limitations, the building served its basic purpose well. Spectators doubtless found it a painful ordeal to stand long hours on the densely packed platforms, but all were able to see and hear the proceedings on the stage. The acoustics were excellent; many witnesses testified that an ordinary voice could be heard in every part of the hall.[3]

The delegates who attended the Chicago convention were a heterogeneous lot. Most of them were obscure local politicians who played passive roles and cast their votes in conformance with instructions from state conventions or from party leaders to whom they were attached. Only occasionally was their action the product of a spontaneous impulse or a reasoned decision arrived at in the course of free debates on the convention floor. The proceedings of this body indicated that the Republican party was now better organized and disciplined and less a spontaneous mass movement than it had been in 1856, and that it was more inclined to act expediently in order to win the victory that was within its grasp. With success so likely, the practical politicians had taken control and, though by no means abandoning the basic principles of the party, charted a moderate course that would attract the more cautious opponents of slavery expansion and the Slave Power.

To many of these political realists the open discussions in the Wigwam were primarily for public consumption and rarely relevant to the business they came to transact. Their function was to applaud at the proper times and to carry out the agreements made in private conference rooms. These often anonymous figures were present in every state delegation; they were significant in groups, seldom as individuals. For example, most of the delegates from New York were the disciplined followers of Thurlow Weed, "Lucifer of the Lobby," boss of the state Republican machine, whose henchmen in the last legislature had been deeply involved in corruption related to the awarding of street railway franchises in New York City. This corruption, many thought, was the source of the huge funds New Yorkers boasted they would use to nominate and elect their favorite, Senator William H. Seward. Among Weed's followers were politicians "of the lower sort" who were, according to one reporter, able to "drink as much whiskey, swear as loud and long, sing as bad songs, and 'get up and howl' as ferociously as any crowd of Democrats. . . . They are opposed, as they say, 'to being too d—d virtuous.' " Accompanying the official delegates from New York were several thousand professional applauders and marchers under the supervision of one Tom Hyer, a celebrated prizefighter.[4]

The other delegations were only a little less colorful. The Illinois group was thoroughly controlled by Abraham Lincoln's campaign managers—David Davis, Norman B. Judd,

Leonard Swett, and Joseph Medill—who were decided political realists. They, too, were accompanied by thousands of leather-lunged Lincoln shouters. The Pennsylvania friends of Senator Simon Cameron soon demonstrated that their mentor had trained them well in the art of practical politics. Also present were men from the border slave states who had become delegates in devious ways and represented phantom constituencies. There was even a Texas delegation— recruited in Michigan among the friends of Seward.[5]

Many of the delegates who had come to Chicago merely to vote and shout and not to think seemed to treat the whole affair as a glorious excursion which temporarily freed them from the restraints of home and fireside. Murat Halstead, the brilliant reporter for the Cincinnati *Commercial,* described scenes which have long since become familiar to convention-goers. Halstead traveled to Chicago on a train loaded with delegates and their friends. He found some Republicans pained by the disposition of other members of this "supposed to be virtuous party" to use ardent spirits. The revelers, who sang "song not found in hymn-books," threw the pious "into prayers and perspiration."[6]

On the night before the convention opened, the men who shared Halstead's hotel room were in "magnificent condition." In the morning he was aroused by a "vehement debate among them, and . . . discovered that they were sitting up in bed playing cards to see who should pay for gin-cocktails all around, the cocktails being an indispensable preliminary to breakfast." On the second night the New Yorkers were "raising h——l generally," with champagne flowing "freely as water" at their headquarters. At two o'clock in the morning the Missouri delegates were "singing songs in their parlor," and "the glasses were still clinking in the bar rooms—and far down the street a brass band was making the night musical."[7]

On the last day, as the convention was about to adjourn,

the presiding officer commended the delegates for their "solemn purpose," their "sober judgments . . . [and] calm deliberations, after a . . . discussion, free, frank, brotherly and patriotic."[8] None knew better than the chairman himself how grotesquely his description had distorted much of the business of the convention. For many of those who sat on the stage of the Wigwam showed little appreciation of the seriousness of their task or of the magnitude of the growing national crisis. Each of the sessions produced a distressing amount of disorder, horseplay, bickering on small points of procedure, and hollow oratory. On the opening day much time was consumed by a discussion of whether the delegates should temporarily abandon their duties and accept an invitation from the Chicago Board of Trade to enjoy an excursion on Lake Michigan. Finally, after a prolonged turbulent debate, the excursion was put off until evening.[9] The official proceedings record other unseemly episodes, such as the controversy over the number of votes to be required to nominate a presidential candidate:

> *Mr. Goodrich, of Minnesota,* I move that the representatives . . . of Pennsylvania be excused from voting upon their own proposition. [Hisses and confusion.] . . .
>
> *Mr. Reeder [of Pennsylvania]* . . . Did I understand a gentleman just now to intimate that Pennsylvania was not entitled to a vote upon this floor? If he did, I should be glad to know who he is, and where he comes from. [Immense applause and cries of "Goodrich."]
>
> *Mr. Goodrich,* I rise, Mr. President—[Cries of "Sit down," and hisses.] I will.
>
> *The President*—Gentlemen do not forget yourselves. You must keep order.
>
> *Mr. Goodrich,* Mr. President—[Cries of "Sit down," and hisses.] I will not sit down. [Confusion.]

The President— . . . Let us act, gentlemen, in a
friendly spirit, and if men make remarks that are not
exactly correct, let them be forgotten on the moment.[10]

After listening to the debate upon the report of the committee on credentials, a reporter concluded: "There has not been
in any previous Republican Convention sharp-shooting so
keen, and sarcasm so bitter and incisive. The Convention is
very like the old Democratic article. . . . The truth is the
Republican party is rapidly becoming Democratized in its
style of operations."[11]

On some occasions long-suffering delegates deserved a
measure of sympathy when they grew restless or openly re-
belled against the turgid eloquence of their colleagues. They
would cry out impatiently, "No speech," "Time," "Sit
down," or "Dry up." Once the secretary recorded that the
members became so "vociferous in their calls to proceed to
business [that] the speaker could proceed no further." When
one delegate complained about being treated so rudely by his
political friends, an anonymous voice retorted: "If you are
our friend let us adjourn."[12]

However, the record of this convention was not entirely
one of roistering, disorder, empty oratory, and irresponsible
action by boss-ruled puppets. Nor were all the delegates obscure ward heelers oblivious of their national responsibilities,
indifferent to party principles, devoid of motives higher than
the spoils of office, and lacking reasonable political ethics. A
powerful element in the party still reflected the idealism of
the crusade against slavery and was committed to a general
program of nineteenth-century liberal reform. Even some of
the more practical delegates were models of respectability,
and many of them were distinguished party leaders.

Among the Republicans who participated in the Chicago
convention was David Wilmot of Pennsylvania, whose historic Proviso had precipitated the controversy over slavery

Mexican War. George Ashmun of Mas-
permanent president and presided with
ccording to Halstead, his "clear, full
reshing to hear amid the clamors of a
ominent delegates included such im-
as Joshua R. Giddings of Ohio and
of Massachusetts; Carl Schurz, the distin-
German-American orator from Wisconsin; Eli
Thayer of Massachusetts, promoter of the New England
Emigrant Aid Society, now serving as a delegate from Oregon; and Horace Greeley of the New York *Tribune*, also
representing Oregon. Even the New York delegation was
sprinkled with well-known businessmen, jurists, orators, writers, and statesmen, such as William M. Evarts, John A. King,
John L. Schoolcraft, George William Curtis, William Curtis
Noyes, and James W. Nye.

The convention's personnel, then, was a mixture of opportunists and idealists, of practical conservatives and moderates
and antislavery radicals, of unsavory tools of political bosses
and principled statesmen. Though crusading reformers were
not in the majority, they were far from a negligible force.
The Republican organization of 1860 was prepared to do a
certain amount of trimming to capture the "battle-ground"
states (New Jersey, Pennsylvania, Indiana, and Illinois) that
it had lost in 1856, but it could not survive if it gave up its
basic identity as an antislavery party. It was still dedicated to
the cause of free labor, and it still reflected the ideals of
northern "free society."[14]

How did Republican delegates define national issues and
interpret party policy in their discussions on the convention
floor? As in most gatherings of this size, more than four-fifths
of them had nothing to say at all. Of the 466 delegates, only
eighty-three were formally recognized by the chair on one
or more occasions during the three days that the convention
met. Most of those who were recognized merely made par-

liamentary motions or spoke briefly on matters r
procedure. This left the elaboration of broader quest
public policy to a handful of speakers.

Only a few speakers extended their remarks to unreas
able lengths. Despite instances of impatience and disord
when delegates spoke at inopportune moments and thus delayed proceedings, or when their discourses contained more
bombast than substance, the able orators were listened to with
interest and enthusiasm. Political oratory was still a favorite
popular diversion, and the audience in the Wigwam would
have been disappointed if this form of entertainment had not
been provided by some of the celebrated Republican spell-
binders. Even the overflow crowd outside begged the chairman "to send out some effective speakers to entertain twenty
thousand Republicans and their wives."[15] Hence, such men as
Andrew, Giddings, Schurz, and Curtis had no fear of imposing upon their friends when they rose to speak. They addressed a sympathetic and receptive audience, and they were
repeatedly rewarded with loud applause.

In the formal speeches of the delegates certain ideas and
concepts were common to nearly all of them. To be sure,
much of what they said was typical of convention oratory
from their day to ours. But they also explained the issues of
1860 as they understood them and outlined the positions they
hoped their party would take. They indicated the manner in
which Republicans would bid for popular support, and they
demonstrated how well they understood both the prejudices
and the aspirations of the northern people. Their contribution
to the education of the electorate may be fairly judged by
what they said on the stage of the Wigwam.

Almost every speaker assured the voters that Republicans
were fully aware of the solemnity of the occasion and the
gravity of the national crisis. "The favorite word in the Convention is 'solemn,'" wrote one reporter. "Everything is solemn. . . . Here there is something every ten minutes found

to be solemn."[16] On the first day Edwin D. Morgan, chairman of the Republican National Committee, pointed to the "momentous results" that hinged upon its proceedings. "No body of men of equal number was ever clothed with greater responsibility than those now within the hearing of my voice." In his "keynote" address, David Wilmot, the temporary chairman, stressed the "importance of the occasion," the "high duties" which devolved upon the delegates.[17] No political convention has ever belittled the urgency of its task, but the Republican party was the very creature of crisis; and at this time it was hardly possible to exaggerate the critical nature of its role. George Ashmun reminded the delegates of this fact when he assumed his duties as permanent president:

> . . . Gentlemen, we have come here today at the call of our country from widely separated homes, to fulfill a great and important duty. No ordinary call has brought us together. Nothing but a momentous question could have called this vast multitude here today. Nothing but a deep sense of the danger into which our government is fast running could have rallied the people thus. . . . The sacrifice which most of us have made in the extended journey, and in the time devoted to it, could only have been made upon some solemn call; and the stern look which I see, the solemn look which I see on every face, and the earnest behavior which has been manifested in all the preliminary discussion, shows full well that we all have a true, deep sense of the solemn obligation which is resting upon us.[18]

Another common theme in convention oratory is political harmony. Whatever the facts may be, it is vitally important to convince the electorate that complete agreement and unity of purpose exists within the party. The Republican speakers of 1860 were no exception. Harmony, said Ashmun, was the "striking feature" of the convention. He praised the delegates for their spirit of "brotherly kindness . . . which marked

every conversation and every discussion, showing a desire for
nothing else but their country's good." He had heard not
"one unkind word uttered by one man towards another." A
facetious reporter, seeking an explanation for Ashmun's unrealistic appraisal, suggested that he "must have kept very
close," or that his hearing was "deplorably impaired."[19] But
the convention's president had conveyed an impression essential to victory.

Convention speakers, especially those representing the party
out of power, never fail to exploit the blunders of their opponents, or to equate political victory with national salvation.
This the Republicans did with enthusiasm. Even the call for
the convention had invited the support of all who opposed
"federal corruption and usurpation." Morgan of New York
referred to the "stupendous wrongs, absolutely shocking to
the moral sentiment of the country, . . . fastened upon the
people by the party in power." The mission of the Republicans, said another delegate, was to rescue the government
"from the deep degradation" into which it had fallen. He
impeached the Buchanan administration "of the highest crimes
which can be committed against a Constitutional government,
against a free people, and against humanity. [Prolonged
cheers.] The catalogue of its crimes . . . is written upon
every page of [its] history."[20] It was certainly time for a
change!

That the Republican party was the party of the people, the
defender of democratic institutions, was a major text of most
of the speeches. Ashmun called his colleagues "delegates of
the people." They were performing "the great work which
the American people [had] given into [their] hands to do,"
work which would be done "with the help of the people."
Norman B. Judd of Illinois, as a token of this support, presented the chairman with a gavel carved by "one of the working mechanic Republicans of Chicago," who thus showed his
"warmth and zeal in the Republican Cause."[21]

This "People's party" (the name then used by Pennsylvania Republicans) was mobilized against the "sham Democracy," which had fallen under the control of arrogant southern slaveholders. These aristocrats had established a merciless tyranny in their own section. Delegates from border slave states frequently described the dangers they had endured for professing Republican principles in the South, and they received generous praise from their colleagues in the North.[22] Chauncey F. Cleveland of Connecticut insisted that many southern voters sympathized with the Republicans but dared not avow their sentiments. The duty of his party was to get these Southerners "out from under the heel of the slave oligarchy."[23]

Even more urgent, Republican speakers contended, was the need to prevent slaveholders from spreading their despotic rule over the whole nation. Their ultimate purpose was to destroy the liberties of all the people. A great "aristocratic party" had "for years dominated with a high hand over the political affairs of this country." It would impose "a despotism more dreadful, and grasping and audacious than that of Naples, Austria or Russia"; it was guilty of "lawless violence, of tyranny such as the world never saw in a civilized and Christianized land."[24] Giddings offered a resolution expressing sympathy for those who had been driven from their homes in the South "on account of their opinions," and accusing the Democrats of failing to defend the civil rights of American citizens. Hence, said Orville H. Browning of Illinois, the preservation of "free institutions" was at stake in the approaching political contest.[25]

Yet, though Republicans painted terrifying pictures of aggressive slaveholders, frontal attacks upon slavery itself and demands for its abolition were less common in their convention oratory. One reporter observed: "We only occasionally hear the sentimental twang, the puritanical intonation that indicates the ancient and savory article of anti-slaveryism."[26] Few speakers would risk offending conservative Northerners with utterances that would give substance to the persistent charges of Democrats that the "Black Republicans" were a party of abolitionists. Their assaults were usually aimed not directly at slavery in the southern states but at the Slave Power and slavery expansion. It was in defiance of "the whole slave power and the whole vassalage of hell" that men such as Carl Schurz spoke.[27]

Again, in contrast to the convention of 1856, the generally more discreet speakers of 1860 placed less emphasis on the need for congressional action to exclude slavery from the territories. Instead, they harped upon the threat to freedom from the new doctrine, proclaimed by the Supreme Court in the Dred Scott decision, that the Constitution of itself opened all the territories to slavery. This decision was part of the plot of the "filibustering, Slavery-extending, sham Democracy" to "guarantee to slavery perpetual existence and unlimited empire," to reopen the African slave trade, to adopt a national slave code, and to plant Negro servitude "wherever the banner of this Union floats."[28] The Democratic party, said Andrew of Massachusetts, "exists only today in two sections, one of which is absolutely devoted to slavery, and the other of which is opposed to liberty. [Loud cheers and laughter.]"[29]

It followed, therefore, that the Democracy, devoted to the interests of southern slaveholders, was the real sectional party. Republicans shrewdly exploited this theme in order to absolve themselves from charges of sectionalism, a matter about which they felt especially vulnerable. The Republican program, they said, was truly national, for it encompassed the needs of the whole country. Its aim was "to resist . . . [the] policy of a sectional interest," to defeat "the leaders of a sectional party."[30] Andrew declared: "The Republican party is today, gentlemen, the only united national party in America. . . . [It] is the only party in the nation which stands by the Union and holds no secessionists in its ranks. Now, since the result . . . is known of the Convention at Charleston, the Democratic party is the only secession party in existence."[31]

Various speakers warmly commended the presence of delegates from the border slave states, for this helped to validate their disavowals of sectionalism. Some even predicted a rapid growth of their party throughout the South, while others gave assurances that no attack upon southern institutions was contemplated. Chauncey F. Cleveland told Southerners that their rights would be respected: "I say, sir, and I wish it to be understood everywhere, I am not here for the purpose of making war on the slave states, nor do I believe that there is a man in this house who is. We have been charged with that. It is false and they know it. We are here for the purpose of satisfying the American people that we are willing to give the slave states their entire rights."[32]

Another means of establishing the conservatism and respectability of the Republican party was to identify it with the sanctified doctrines of the Founding Fathers. The convention call announced the party's determination to restore "the federal administration to a system of rigid economy and to the principles of Washington and Jefferson." Browning claimed that Republicans cherished "the same principles which embalmed the hearts and nerved the arms of our patriot sires of the Revolution . . . the same principles which were vindicated upon every battlefield of American freedom."[33] "Fortunately," said Morgan of New York, "you are not required to enunciate new and untried principles of government. This has been well and wisely done by the statesmen of the Revolution. [Applause.] Stand where they stood, avowing and maintaining the like objects and doctrines; then will the end sought be accomplished; the Constitution and the Union be preserved, and the government be administered by patriots and statesmen."[34] Wilmot proclaimed: "It is our purpose to restore the Constitution to its original meaning; to

give to it its true interpretation; to read that instrument as our
fathers read it." The country would return to "those broad
constitutional doctrines that were recognized for the first
sixty years of the existence of our government."[35]
In many ways, then, convention speakers attempted to
make their appeal broad enough to attract every shade and
variety of opposition to the "proslavery Democracy," and to
assure voters that the Republican party was basically sound
and conservative. This purpose was also clearly evident in the
party platform. Horace Greeley, who served on the platform
committee, was convinced that Republicans could not win
"on a square slavery issue."[36] Consequently, the document
made a bid for the support of several "free-labor" groups on
grounds other than opposition to slavery expansion. To the
manufacturing interests of the East, particularly of New Jersey and Pennsylvania, it promised an adjustment of the tariff
to give increased protection; to western farmers it promised
legislation providing for free homesteads on the public do-
main—a measure many thought to be strongly antislavery in
its consequences; and to all involved in the national market
economy it promised to facilitate trade by subsidizing internal
improvements, including a Pacific railroad. The convention
secretary recorded that the reading of the platform "was interrupted by tremendous outbursts of applause—the most en-
thusiastic and long continued being given to the tariff and
homestead clauses."[37]
The increased power of pragmatic and conservative Republicans was evident in those portions of the platform which
related to slavery. In 1856, in a platform notable for its brev-
ity and forthrightness, the party had affirmed that Congress,
in exercising its "sovereign power" over the territories, had
"the right and the imperative duty . . . to prohibit . . .
those twin relics of barbarism—Polygamy and Slavery." In
1860 this clause was dropped. The new platform promised to

respect "the right of each state to order and control its own domestic institutions according to its own judgment exclusively." It stated less directly that slavery ought to be excluded from the territories and that this could be accomplished by congressional action if necessary. The platform denounced as a "dangerous political heresy" the new dogma "that the Constitution, of its own force, carries slavery into any or all of the territories of the United States." It affirmed that the "normal condition" of the territories was "that of freedom," and it denied "the authority of Congress, of a territorial legislature, or of any individuals, to give legal existence to slavery in any territory. . . ." The commitment to oppose the spread of slavery was still there, but it seemed to take more words to acknowledge the commitment somewhat less militantly.

The original report of the platform committee made another significant concession to expediency. In contrast to the document adopted in 1856, this committee failed to incorporate the bold statement from the Declaration of Independence: "That all men are created equal; that they are endowed by their Creator with certain unalienable rights; that among these are life, liberty and the pursuit of happiness. . . ." But this retreat was more than veterans of the antislavery crusade such as Giddings could bear. As soon as the platform was read, Giddings was on his feet demanding recognition amid calls for the previous question. In an impassioned speech he demanded the restoration of those words from Jefferson's immortal document. "I propose," he said, "to maintain the fundamental and primal issues upon which the government was founded. . . . I offer this because our party was formed upon it. It has existed upon it—and when you leave out this truth you leave out the party." Giddings won the audience over to his side, but the delegates voted his amendment down.[38] It was a tense and dramatic moment. "The old man quickly rose, and made his way slowly toward the door. A dozen delegates begged him not to go. But he considered everything lost, even honor."[39]

Everything was not yet lost. A few minutes later, George William Curtis of New York overcame all points of order and introduced the Giddings amendment again. His eloquent speech provided one of the rare instances when oratory on the floor had a decisive impact upon the convention's proceedings. His appeal was one that the delegates could not ignore:

> . . . I have to ask this Convention whether they are prepared to go upon the record and before the country as voting down the words of the Declaration of Independence? [Cries of "No, no," and applause.] . . . Bear in mind that in Philadelphia in 1856, the Convention of this same great party were not afraid to announce those principles by which alone the Republican party lives, and upon which alone the future of this country in the hands of the Republicans is passing. [Tremendous cheering.]
>
> Now, sir, I ask gentlemen gravely to consider that in the amendment which I have proposed, I have done nothing that the soundest and safest man in all the land might not do; and I rise simply . . . to ask gentlemen to think well before, upon the free prairies of the West, in the summer of 1860, they dare to wince and quail before the men who in Philadelphia in 1776—in Philadelphia, in the Arch-Keystone State . . .—before they are to shrink from repeating the words that these great men enunciated. [Terrific applause.][40]

Curtis's "captivating burst of oratory" apparently "took the convention by storm." The Giddings amendment was then adopted, and the Declaration of Independence again became part of the Republican platform.[41] With honor thus saved, Giddings returned to his seat. There were limits beyond which the old antislavery radicals could not be pushed.

However, on the third day, when the presidential candidate was nominated, the pragmatic, middle-of-the-road moderates again had things their own way. Though Abraham Lincoln was an antislavery man and firm in his opposition to slavery expansion, his selection was in no sense a triumph for the antislavery radicals in the party. Nor was it the result of a mass movement among rank-and-file party members. Rather, it was achieved through adroit political maneuvering and through the understandings and bargaining that are usually needed to win the prize for a presidential aspirant. Lincoln won the nomination in 1860 because of the skill of his political managers, because he was a former Whig from a doubtful state, because his position on all the issues seemed to be precisely what the Republicans needed at that particular time, because he proved to be less offensive to more people than any other candidate, and because so many delegates turned to him as a second choice. As Lincoln himself explained, "I suppose I am not the *first* choice of a very great many. Our policy, then, is to give no offence to others—leave them in a mood to come to us, if they shall be compelled to give up their first love." In short, his nomination was the "triumph of availability."[42]

The debates and discussions, the planning and bargaining that preceded the balloting were not, of course, conducted in the open. Ordinary Republicans had little direct influence upon the nomination, and they knew practically nothing of what went on behind the scenes. Only occasionally did the war of the factions spread to the convention floor, and then only the "insiders" knew what was at stake. For example, the opponents of Seward tried to force the adoption of what, in effect, was a two-thirds rule governing a presidential nomination, which they believed would weaken the New Yorker's position. In this they were defeated. They also demanded a reduction in the number of votes given to slave-state delegations, most of which were assumed to be in Seward's pocket.

On this point the anti-Seward forces won a partial victory.[43] But for the most part, the maneuvering was carried on in private caucuses and secret conferences behind the closed doors of hotel rooms.

As late as the morning of the balloting, Seward remained the leading candidate, and most observers regarded his nomination as almost inevitable. He came closer than any other candidate to being the popular favorite among Republicans throughout the country. He had the solid support of the delegations from New York, Michigan, Wisconsin, and Minnesota, and much strength in many others. Thurlow Weed, his close friend and political manager, handled the preparations before and during the convention with great skill. Weed dispensed champagne and cigars freely at his Chicago headquarters; he was generous in his promises of political rewards; and he boasted that he had ample funds to wage successful campaigns in various key states, especially Pennsylvania. Accordingly, Seward's partisans looked to the outcome of the balloting with confidence.[44]

But Seward also had some weaknesses. Many feared that the notorious corruption of the last New York legislature, and the suspicion that some of Weed's funds came from that source, might compromise Republicans during the campaign.[45] Also dangerous to Seward was the fact that, in spite of his control of the New York delegation, a group of party leaders from his own state was opposed to him. This faction was headed by Greeley, an influential figure among the delegates at Chicago, who sought to punish Weed and Seward for failing to gratify his political ambitions in earlier years.[46] Moreover, Seward had antagonized the Know-Nothing element when he served as governor of New York. Finally, and most crucial, this expounder of the "higher law" and "irrepressible conflict" doctrines was regarded, quite unjustly, as the very symbol of Republican radicalism. The need to gain the support of conservative northern Whigs in order to win Pennsylvania and at least one other "doubtful" state (New Jersey, Indiana, or Illinois) seriously damaged Seward's chances. He did not have a majority of the delegates pledged to him, and that could be fatal *if* the opposition could unite behind a single candidate.

Accordingly, Lincoln's managers set out to attract anti-Seward delegates by convincing them that there was no other way to block Seward's nomination. In the kind of work that had to be done to achieve this result, David Davis and Norman B. Judd, who commanded the Lincoln forces, proved to be just as adept as Weed. They, too, made careful preparations before the convention met, and they brought up an Illinois delegation unanimously pledged to Lincoln. Months before, they had begun the job of winning friends in other states, and Lincoln quietly assisted them, offering in one case to pay the expenses of a prospective delegate from the territory of Kansas.[47]

The appeal formulated by Lincoln's managers stressed the "unavailability," in one way or another, of each of Lincoln's rivals. Salmon P. Chase of Ohio, like Seward, was too radical and could not carry Pennsylvania. Edward Bates of Missouri, on the other hand, was far too conservative ever to be acceptable to antislavery Republicans; and, as a former Know-Nothing, he would lose the support of the powerful German element in the Northwest. Lincoln, though a moderate ex-Whig, was less conservative than Bates—at least his "House Divided" speech of 1858 would reassure the radicals. He had never joined the Know-Nothings and therefore was not offensive to the Germans. Simon Cameron of Pennsylvania, Lincoln's only other serious rival, had an unsavory political reputation; nothing commended him to the Republicans except that he controlled the delegation from the most crucial doubtful state. But Lincoln was sound on the tariff, the economic issue which most interested Pennsylvanians.[48] Arguments such as these eventually began to increase Lincoln's strength.

Lincoln's managers also did effective work in the various caucuses, especially in those of the doubtful states. "They are suing us and wooing us," reported an Indiana delegate. At these meetings the supporters of Lincoln repeatedly outmaneuvered the partisans of both Bates and Seward. Gustave Koerner of Illinois brandished threats of a German bolt in the event that Bates should be nominated. Orville H. Browning argued persuasively that only Lincoln could command the confidence of all anti-Democratic factions.[49] As a result, by the evening of the second day Lincoln had clearly become Seward's most dangerous rival.

However, after the convention adjourned that night, much still remained to be done. What happened then was best described by Murat Halstead: "There were hundreds of Pennsylvanians, Indianians, and Illinoisans, who never closed their eyes that night." Halstead saw Henry S. Lane, Republican candidate for governor in Indiana, at one o'clock in the morning, "pale and haggard, with cane under his arm, walking as if for a wager, from one caucus room to another, at the Tremont House." The objective of Lane and his friends was "to bring the delegates . . . to consider success rather than Seward," and it was this appeal that finally caused the "fatal break" in Seward's ranks. "It was reported, and with a well-understood purpose, that the Republican candidates for Governor in Indiana, Illinois and Pennsylvania would resign, if Seward were nominated. . . . Henry S. Lane . . . asserted hundreds of times that the nomination of Seward would be death to him, and that he might in that case just as well give up the canvass."[50] Lincoln's managers completed their private bargaining with some specific pledges. Caleb B. Smith and Simon Cameron were promised cabinet posts for the delivery of the votes of Indiana and Pennsylvania. Lincoln was alleged to

and of large experience in national affairs."[56] But no one knew better than Weed that such considerations were quite irrelevant and that it would be fatal to rest Seward's case upon them. Hence, he put far more emphasis upon the funds he had with which to wage campaigns in the doubtful states.

Seward's prominence and long participation in politics, if anything, lessened his availability as a presidential candidate. His positions on national issues were too well known, and he had had time enough to make numerous political enemies. And so, as one disappointed New Yorker complained, "Seward, like Calhoun, like Clay, and like Webster, was slaughtered in the home of his friends, and . . . expediency had done for him what it always has done for the great men of this confederacy."[57] It is doubtful that Seward would in fact have been a better President than Lincoln. But such a judgment can only be credited to hindsight, not to the foresight of the delegates at Chicago.

Some Republican newspapers did not even know the first name of their candidate; the New York *Times* announced the nomination of "Abram" Lincoln of Illinois.[58] Nevertheless, in the closing hours of the convention, Republican orators quickly discovered elements of greatness in Lincoln, as well as one source of the popular appeal he would make. They found in him the embodiment of the American success story, the vindication of American institutions, the fulfillment of the promise that Northerners believed was open to free labor. "Thirty years ago on the Southern frontier of Indiana," said Caleb Smith, there was "a humble, ragged boy, bare footed, driving his oxen through the hills, and he has elevated himself to the pinnacle which has now presented him as the candidate of this convention. It is an illustration of that spirit of enterprise which characterizes the West. . . ." Lane called the Illinois railsplitter the "most beautiful illustration of the power of free institutions and the doctrine of free labor in the United States."[59]

The business of the convention was finished. After "the usual stump speeches . . . complimentary resolutions . . . and the 'three times three' for the candidate," the delegates went home.[60] Their public discussions on the floor of the Wigwam, vague though they were on many points, had faithfully expressed the concerns and aspirations of a large segment of the northern people. Their private caucuses, with all their concessions to expediency, were no doubt essential to the efficient transaction of the convention's business; they exemplified the normal behavior of professional politicians in a party that was fast becoming institutionalized. In short, the Chicago convention provided a fair illustration of political democracy at work in mid-nineteenth-century America. The lust for office, the practical interests of various economic groups, the crusade against slavery, and, more broadly, the ideals of northern middle-class society all played a part in shaping its deliberations. The forces that were driving the country to disunion and war were, after all, beyond the control of this single small body of men.

VI

Lincoln and the Secession Crisis

"Lincoln never poured out his soul to any mortal creature at any time. . . . He was the most secretive—reticent—shut-mouthed man that ever existed."[1] This, the studied opinion of his former law partner, William H. Herndon, defined the perplexing quality in the character of Abraham Lincoln that caused both contemporaries and historians to view him as something of an enigma. This is why his acts frequently permit antithetical explanations; perhaps, too, why forthright motives sometimes appear devious. Because we tend to assume that "shut-mouthed" men are necessarily complex, his reticence always seemed to belie his self-professed simplicity.

As President-elect during the months of the secession crisis, Lincoln kept his own counsel even more rigidly than usual. The confessions of close associates such as Herndon and Judge David Davis that they knew nothing of his plans verified the remark of a newspaper correspondent that "Mr. Lincoln keeps all people, his friends included, in the dark. . . . Mr. Lincoln promises nothing, but only listens."[2] This may help to explain why the available evidence has led some historians to conclude that Lincoln deliberately provoked hostilities at Fort Sumter, while others contended that the Sumter episode was precisely what he had hoped to avoid. The debate over Lincoln's intentions began during the war itself, but Charles W. Ramsdell introduced it to modern scholarship in 1937 with an article that accused Lincoln of cynically maneuvering the Confederates into firing on Fort Sumter. His action, according to Ramsdell, resulted from a belief that a war was necessary to save not only the Union but his administration and the Republican party.[3] Three years later, James G. Randall replied to Ramsdell in an article claiming that Lincoln's policy was at all times peaceful and that his Sumter strategy was designed to minimize the danger of war.[4] David M. Potter, in a book-length study of the Republican party during the secession crisis, amplified Randall's thesis. Lincoln's policy, Potter argued, was based on a common northern belief that Unionism was still strong in the South and that a pro-Union reaction was bound to come. His aim, therefore, was to avoid further irritation of the South and thus to provide both time and the best possible conditions for southern Unionists to regain control. Potter, like Randall, believed that Lincoln was still trying to maintain the peace at the time of the crisis at Fort Sumter, that he considered evacuation under certain circumstances, and that ultimately he tried to relieve the fort in the manner least likely to provoke a hostile Confederate response. Therefore, Potter concluded, the Confederate attack on Sumter was a defeat, not a victory for Lincoln's policy.[5] However, the same scanty evidence suggests still another possible interpretation.

Fortunately, the President-elect left the record unmistakably clear on two points. First, there can be no doubt that he was an intense nationalist and that he regarded the Union as indestructible. Lincoln was an old Whig, an admirer of Webster and Clay, and he repeatedly expressed pride in his political origins and scoffed at the dogmas of the state-rights school. In his first inaugural address, he took pains to prove that "the Union of these States is perpetual." While he added little to the classical nationalist argument, he showed that the thought of acquiescing in disunion never entered his mind:

> It follows from these views that no State, upon its own mere motion, can lawfully get out of the Union,—that *resolves* and *ordinances* to that effect are legally void; and that acts of violence, within any State or States, against the authority of the United States, are insurrectionary or revolutionary, according to circumstances.
> I therefore consider that, in view of the Constitution and the laws, the Union is unbroken. . . .[6]

Second, through private and confidential letters to political friends in Congress, Lincoln expressed firm opposition to any compromise on the issue of slavery expansion. His past speeches, he contended, provided sufficient evidence that he assumed no right to interfere with slavery in the states where it already existed, that he had no desire to menace the rights of the South, and that he would enforce the fugitive slave law. He would tolerate slavery in the District of Columbia and the interstate slave trade—"whatever springs of necessity from the fact that the institution is among us"—and he might even agree to the admission of New Mexico as a slave state. But he was "inflexible" on the territorial question, and he cautioned his friends to "hold firm as with a chain of steel."[7]

Any explanation of Lincoln's opposition to compromise must be speculative, for his words are sometimes ambiguous and subject to varying interpretations. He objected to the restoration of the Missouri Compromise line on the grounds that it would settle nothing, that it would simply stimulate "filibustering for all South of us, and making slave states of it. . . ."[8] He also expressed a distaste for the personal humiliation involved in proposals to "buy or beg a peaceful inauguration" through concessions, thus indicating that considerations of prestige and "face-saving" were involved.[9] He seemed to be no less concerned about the prestige of the federal government itself: "I should regard any concession in the face of menace the destruction of the government . . . and a consent on all hands that our system shall be brought down to a level with the disorganized state of affairs in Mexico."[10] In addition, Lincoln apparently had decided that this was an appropriate time for a final settlement of the questions of secession and slavery expansion. If concessions were made, he warned, Southerners "will repeat the experiment upon us *ad libitum*. A year will not pass, till we shall have to take Cuba, as a condition upon which they will stay in the Union." Hence, he advised, "Stand firm. The tug has to come, and better now, than any time hereafter."[11] Many Republican politicians and editors shared his determination to resolve the sectional crisis this time, whatever the cost. "If we must have civil war," wrote the conservative Edward Bates, "perhaps it is better now than at a future date." A western Republican paper asserted that "we are heartily tired of having this [secession] threat stare us in the face evermore. . . . We never have been better prepared for such a crisis than now. We most ardently desire that it may come."[12] Throughout the secession crisis it is remarkable how often Lincoln shared, or merely reflected, popular Republican views.

In his private advice against compromise the President-elect made some rather vague remarks to the effect that as soon as a compromise was adopted "they have us under again; all our labor is lost, and sooner or later must be done over." Compromise "would lose us everything we gained by the election," he wrote, adding that it would be "the end of us."[13] These apprehensions might indicate deep concern for the well-being of the Republican party and a fear that compromise would spell its ruin. Most of Lincoln's political friends and advisers were acutely aware that concessions to the South would threaten their organization and that the radical wing might bolt the new administration. They remembered the fate of the Whig party, which, one Republican insisted, had "died of compromises." Thurlow Weed, on a visit to Washington, found the Republicans overwhelmed by this fear. Open the territories to slavery, warned one of the faithful, and "Republicanism is a 'dead dog.' "[14]

Yet there was little in Lincoln's remarks on compromise to invalidate the possibility that, in opposing it, he was thinking less of party than of what he regarded as the best interests of the North, perhaps of the whole nation. More than likely the two concerns were fused in his mind. Politicians have a happy facility for identifying personal and party interests with broad national interests, and Lincoln may have believed sincerely that what was good for the Republican party was good for everyone.

Having flatly rejected both compromise and acquiescence in disunion, Lincoln could have hoped to deal with the secession crisis in only two other ways. Either he could encourage loyal Southerners to overthrow the secessionists, voluntarily renew their allegiance to the federal government, and thus achieve a peaceful reconstruction of the Union, or he could resort to whatever force might be necessary to collect federal revenues and to recover or maintain possession of federal property. To that extent, in other words, he could have coerced the secessionists, defining coercion broadly as any attempt to enforce federal laws against the wishes of state authorities or large bodies of disaffected citizens.

In all probability Lincoln regarded neither the device of peaceful reconstruction nor coercion as a basic policy. These were merely tactical alternatives to be used according to circumstances. From the traditional viewpoint of practical statesmanship the preservation of peace and the launching of war are never the supreme objects of policy. They are potential means to some desirable end; the more fundamental goal is to preserve, defend, or advance primary national interests. These interests are guarded by peaceful means when possible, but the use of force is never ruled out as a last resort. "National interest" is a loose concept easily abused, but it has ever been a prime concern of governments.

When Lincoln's problem is placed in this context, his words and acts during the secession crisis appear to be rational, realistic, and remarkably consistent. Because he opposed compromise and peaceful secession it does not follow that his basic purpose was to resort to force any more than it was to risk everything on a policy of peace. Rather, his chief concern was the maintenance of the Union, a national interest which he regarded as vital enough to take precedence over all other considerations. And the integrity of the Union continued to be his paramount objective throughout the ensuing conflict—even his Emancipation Proclamation was conceived and justified with that goal in mind. There is no reason to doubt that Lincoln would have accepted peaceful and voluntary reconstruction as a satisfactory solution within the time limits fixed by political realities, especially northern public opinion. But there is abundant evidence that the possible necessity of coercion entered his calculations as soon as he understood the seriousness of the crisis.[15] Lincoln was not a pacifist, and as both a practical statesman and a mystical believer in an American mission to the world, he looked upon disunion as a sufficient threat to justify resistance by military force if necessary.

"The most distinctive element of Mr. Lincoln's moral composition," wrote Henry Villard, the shrewd and observant correspondent of the New York *Herald*, "is his keen sense and comprehensive consciousness of duty. Upon taking his oath of office he will not be guided so much by his party predilections as by the federal constitution and laws. . . . That he will endeavor to fulfill the obligations thus imposed upon him faithfully and fearlessly may be expected with the utmost certainty."[16] Making due allowances for spells of irresolution, Villard was essentially correct in his surmise that Lincoln was strongly impressed with his obligation to "enforce the laws" under all circumstances and whatever the consequences. "I see the duty devolving upon me," he told a friend in early January, adding bitterly that he was "in the garden of Gesthemane now."[17] Lincoln was perhaps as frank and blunt on this point before he assumed the presidency as he could have been under the circumstances. Certainly he had no desire to provoke a conflict before the fourth of March; the peaceful inauguration of his administration was essential before decisive action could be taken.

Nevertheless, it requires no unwarranted inferences or tortured meanings to read coercion implications into Lincoln's public and private utterances before his inauguration. As early as December 3, 1859, in a speech at Leavenworth, Kansas, he warned Southerners that if the Republicans elected a President, "and therefore you undertake to destroy the Union, it will be our duty to deal with you as old John Brown has been dealt with. We shall try to do our duty."[18] A month after the election, John G. Nicolay, one of Lincoln's private secretaries, recorded Lincoln's current views on the matter: "The very existence of a general and national government implies the legal power, right, and duty of maintaining its own integrity. . . . It is the duty of the President to execute the laws and maintain the existing government."[19]

One of the earliest acts of the President-elect was to establish contact with General Winfield Scott, whom he urged "to be as well prepared as he can to either *hold*, or *retake*, the forts, as the case may require, at, and after the inauguration." On several occasions he assured friends that if the southern forts were occupied by secessionists, "my judgment is that they are to be retaken." The most revealing of these letters was one, dated December 29, to James Watson Webb, editor of the New York *Courier and Enquirer*, in which he anticipated much of what he would say in his inaugural address. Webb had written to ask Lincoln's view on how to deal with secession, to which Lincoln replied: "I think we should hold the forts, or retake them, as the case may be, and collect the revenue. *We* shall have to forego the use of the federal courts, and *they* that of the mails, for a while. We can not fight them in to holding courts, or receiving the mails. This is an outline of my view; and perhaps suggests sufficiently, the whole of it." His response to the request of Pennsylvania's governor-elect, Andrew G. Curtin, for advice regarding Curtin's inaugural address was equally clear:

> I think of nothing proper for me to suggest except a word about this secession and disunion movement. On that subject, I think you would do well to express, without passion, threat, or appearance of boasting, but nevertheless, with firmness, the purpose of yourself, and your state to maintain the Union at all hazards. Also, if you can, procure the Legislature to pass resolutions to that effect.

It was no doubt significant that in none of these letters was there a hint that Lincoln had confidence in voluntary reunion as a likely solution to the crisis.[20]

More than once during his journey to Washington in February, Lincoln gave additional evidence that the possible need for a coercive policy was very much on his mind. His carefully prepared remarks to an Indianapolis audience on February 11 were aptly described as his "keynote." By the simple process of putting suggestive questions to his audience, he indicated his intention to hold or retake federal property in the southern states and to collect the duties on foreign imports.[21] From these remarks the Washington correspondent of the New York *Tribune* concluded that Lincoln believed "that he has a right to use force against the seceding States to the extent of recovering United States property, collecting the revenues and enforcing the laws generally." To the New

York *Herald* the speech was "the signal for massacre and bloodshed by the incoming administration."[22] Thereafter, perhaps alarmed by the sensational response, Lincoln spoke with greater caution. Yet, he told the New Jersey General Assembly, on February 21, that "it may be necessary to put the foot down firmly. . . . And if I do my duty, and do right, you will sustain me, will you not?"[23]

Meanwhile, the President-elect had been revising and polishing his inaugural address. In its original form the document had contained a blunt threat to the seceded states: "All the power at my disposal will be used to reclaim the public property and places which have fallen." While rejecting William H. Seward's proposal to substitute a meaningless vagary, Lincoln accepted the advice of Orville H. Browning and omitted the phrase. But this deletion did not necessarily mean that he had abandoned his intention of recovering lost federal property, for Browning had defended his suggestion purely on the ground of expediency. "The fallen places ought to be reclaimed," he wrote. "But cannot that be accomplished as well, or even better without announcing the purpose in your inaugural?" Even after this change, the address still indicated that the new President might feel constrained under certain conditions to use force. Besides referring to contingencies which could produce civil war, Lincoln announced his intention to see "that the laws of the Union be faithfully executed in all the States," to "hold, occupy, and possess the property and places belonging to the government, and to collect the duties and imposts."[24] To one northern Democratic paper the inaugural was "a tiger's claw concealed under the fur of Sewardism."[25] Secessionists agreed almost unanimously that it threatened war. The Republican Boston *Daily Advertiser* penetrated its meaning with remarkable acumen. The President, it believed, had indicated that he would be discreet and conciliatory, but that he recognized "the natural limits of that discretion."

The address itself [it concluded] contemplates the possibility of an interruption of the peace. We understand the President to disclaim the intention of doing many things which he thinks himself authorized to do, but which he can forbear doing without detriment to the claims of the government. . . . But there is obviously a limit to this forbearance, and a limit to the concessions which the government should make for the preservation of peace. . . . Such powers are as confided to him . . . the President will use, with a due regard to practical policy, but with no thought of foregoing the exercise of a right essential to the existence of the government, because resistance is threatened.[26]

The fact that Lincoln intimated the possible use of force does not necessarily imply that he visualized, as an inevitable consequence, a long civil war, or the need for any war at all. Like many others, he may have thought that "a little show of force," entailing a minimum of bloodshed, would suffice to crush the southern rebellion. Better still, a sufficient demonstration of federal power might result in the immediate collapse of the Confederacy without so much as a skirmish. However, the consequence of coercive measures was really out of the President's hands. It would depend upon the secessionists. And from this critical fact Lincoln formulated his basic strategy.

From the outset the new President, in dealing with the disunion crisis, had three clear advantages. First, the northern people, with few exceptions, agreed with him that the states did not have a constitutional right to secede. However many may have favored compromise and hoped to avoid the use of military force, the masses of Republicans and Democrats alike shared the belief that the Union was perpetual. It was not difficult, or even necessary, to convince them that the preservation of the Union was both a moral obligation and a vital national interest. Second, the burden of direct action rested upon the seceding states, which, after all, were seeking to disturb the political *status quo*. In order to make their independence a reality, they thought it essential to seize government forts and other property, and to destroy the symbols of federal authority. As a result, the Union government could easily claim that it would avoid aggressive action and merely assume a defensive posture. In other words, the exigencies of the situation would almost certainly suggest to a wise and practical political leader a strategy of defense—of throwing the initiative to the South.

This is where Lincoln's third important advantage made itself evident. Given the general northern belief that, in spite of southern ordinances of secession, the Union was not and could not be dissolved, the government was entitled to make a number of "defensive" moves. These presumably nonaggressive acts might include such things as collecting the revenues, holding federal property, perhaps even reinforcing the forts or recovering those that had been seized. Action of this kind, most Northerners believed, would be far different from marching a hostile army into the South to overawe and coerce it. "There is no form in which coercion . . . can be applied," wrote a northern editor. "The general government can do no more than see that its laws are carried out."[27] Of course, secessionists, who regarded the dissolution of the Union as an accomplished fact, brushed aside these fine distinctions and branded any federal intervention in the South as coercion. Perhaps abstract logic was on their side, but to Lincoln that was irrelevant. Always holding the preservation of the Union above peace, he exploited his three strategic advantages in order to cast coercion in the mold of defense and to shift responsibility for any resulting violence to his "dissatisfied fellow-countrymen."

This defensive concept was in no sense an original idea of Lincoln's. Soon after the election of 1860 the Republican press began to propose the strategy with remarkable spontaneity. "The Republican policy," predicted the Springfield (Massachusetts) *Republican*, "will be to make no war upon the seceding states, to reject all propositions for secession, to hold them to the discharge of their constitutional duties, to collect the revenues as usual in southern ports, and calmly await the results. There can be no war unless the seceders make war upon the general government."[28] The New York *Evening Post* suggested that if South Carolina should make it impossible to collect duties at Charleston, Congress could simply close it as a port of entry. "Here then we have a peaceful antidote for that 'peaceful remedy' which is called secession. It is no act of war, nor hostility, to revoke the permission given to any town to be opened as a port of entry; but when that permission is revoked it would be an act of hostility . . . to disregard the injunction."[29] A northern clergyman summed up the strategy precisely in advising the South: "Secede on paper as much as you please. We will not make war upon you for that. But we will maintain the supremacy of the constitution and laws. If you make war on the Union, we will defend it at all costs, and the guilt of blood be on your heads."[30] Thus the strategy, occasionally defined as one of "masterly inactivity," had been outlined in advance; Lincoln had only to read the newspapers to discover its value.

From the time the President-elect left Springfield in February until the firing on Fort Sumter, the central theme of his public utterances was the further development and clarification of a strategy of defense. Holding inflexibly to the conviction that his fundamental purpose must be the preservation of the Union, he chose his words carefully and shrewdly to protect himself from any charge of aggression. Appreciating the possibility that hostilities might ensue, Lincoln seemed preoccupied with an intense desire to leave the record clear, to make it evident to the northern people that war, if it came, would be started by the South. His words were not those of a man confused about the true situation, about what his policy should be, or about possible consequences. The coercive intimations were nearly always of a sort that would be perceived as such only by southern secessionists, seldom by northern Unionists.

During his first stop, at Indianapolis, Lincoln began at once to expound his defensive strategy. In a speech from the balcony of the Bates House he denied any intention to invade the South with a hostile army and made it clear that the government would only defend itself and its property. On February 21, he assured the New Jersey General Assembly that he would do everything possible to secure a peaceful settlement. "The man does not live who is more devoted to peace than I am." The next day, before the Pennsylvania legislature, he expressed regret "that a necessity may arise in this country for the use of the military arm. . . . I promise that, (in so far as I may have wisdom to direct,) if so painful a result shall in any wise be brought about, it shall be through no fault of mine." On the same day, in Philadelphia, Lincoln spoke with unusual clarity: "Now, in my view of the present aspect of affairs, there is no need of bloodshed and war. There is no necessity for it. I am not in favor of such a course, and I may say in advance, there will be no blood shed unless it is forced upon the Government. The Government will not use force unless force is used against it."[31]

Lincoln rounded out his strategy with additional assurances to the South that its rights would be respected, thus denying the need for it to secede in self-defense. Hence, he could insist that "there is really no crisis except an *artificial one*," that "there is nothing that really hurts anybody."[32] Always embarrassed by the popular election returns, Lincoln also sought to convey the impression that a major issue was the right of the majority to rule. Finally, he placed the question of the Union squarely in the hands of the American people. He was but their servant, elected to do their wishes. Without their support he was helpless; with it the Union must triumph. Summing up, he said:

> In all the trying positions in which I shall be placed . . . my reliance will be placed upon . . . the people of the United States—and I wish you to remember now and forever, that it is your business, and not mine; that if the union of these States, and the liberties of this people, shall be lost, it is but little to any one man of fifty-two years of age, but a great deal to the thirty millions of people who inhabit these United States, and to their posterity in all coming time. It is your business to rise up and preserve the Union and liberty, for yourselves, and not for me. . . . I appeal to you again to constantly bear in mind that with you, and not with politicians, not with Presidents, not with office-seekers, but with you, is the question, "Shall the Union and shall the liberties of this country be preserved to the latest generation."[33]

Having already outlined his defensive strategy on several occasions, Lincoln's inaugural address contained no surprises on that score—only a final clear exposition of his nonaggressive intentions. Once more he insisted that in upholding the authority of the government "there needs be no bloodshed or violence; and there shall be none, unless it be forced upon the national authority." He would refrain from doing many things which he had a right to do, but which could be forgone without injury to the prestige of the government. However, though he desired a peaceful solution, the matter was beyond his control: "In *your* hands, my dissatisfied fellow-countrymen, and not in *mine*, is the momentous issue of civil war. The government will not assail *you*. You can have no conflict, without being yourselves the aggressors. *You* have no oath registered in Heaven to destroy the government, while *I* shall have the most solemn one to 'preserve, protect and defend it.' "[34]

Thus, by the time of his inauguration, Lincoln had firmly established his intention to preserve the Union by measures that Unionists would accept as purely defensive. With consummate skill he had at once hamstrung the South, satisfied the great majority of Northerners that he contemplated no aggression, and yet conveyed his determination to defend the authority of the federal government. The Republican press glowed with appreciation. "No party can be formed against the administration on the issue presented by the inaugural," observed one friendly editor. Another noted that "the fiat of peace or war is in the hands of Mr. Davis rather than of Mr. Lincoln." Samuel Bowles of the Springfield *Republican* believed that the inaugural had put "the secession conspirators manifestly in the wrong, and hedges them in so that they cannot take a single step without making treasonable war upon the government, which will only defend itself."[35] By the fourth of March, Lincoln had already cornered the disunionists.

It should be evident, then, that Lincoln's reaction to the problem of supplying Fort Sumter, which confronted him immediately after his inauguration, was in perfect harmony with the strategy he had already conceived. His decision to sustain the Sumter garrison involved no change of plans—no reluctant abandonment of a policy of voluntary reunion, no sudden determination to provoke a war.[36] It was a logical consequence of the President's fixed determination to defend the Union even at the risk of hostilities. Had the Sumter crisis not arisen, or had Lincoln been convinced ultimately that military necessity dictated evacuation,[37] his strategy almost certainly would have led to a similar violent confrontation somewhere else. In fact, while he was exploring the possibility of sending supplies to Major Robert Anderson, he was also searching for other means of developing his defensive policy. For example, he instructed General Scott "to exercise all possible vigilance for the maintenance of all the places within the military department of the United States, and to promptly call upon all the departments of the government for the means necessary to that end."[38] In addition, he offered the deposed Unionist governor of Texas, Sam Houston, military and naval support if Houston would put himself at the head of a Union party; and he considered the collection of duties from naval vessels off southern ports, or even a blockade of the Confederacy.

However, Lincoln's most important action, aside from his decision to supply Sumter, related to Fort Pickens, on Santa Rosa Island near Pensacola, one of the few southern forts remaining in federal hands. In January, President Buchanan had sent reinforcements on the U. S. S. *Brooklyn* to Pensacola harbor, but, because he agreed to a truce with certain secessionist leaders, they were not landed. On March 11, Lincoln ordered Scott to instruct the commander to land these troops at once. But, on April 6, a special messenger arrived from Fort Pickens with the news that the reinforcements had not disembarked, for Captain H. A. Adams of the *Brooklyn* denied that Scott's orders could supersede those of the former Secretary of the Navy. The President dispatched new instructions immediately, and the troops landed on April 12 while Anderson was still in possession of Sumter.

Yet, in his message to the special session of Congress which convened on July 4, Lincoln claimed that he had intended to order the evacuation of Fort Sumter if Fort Pickens had been reinforced before Anderson had exhausted his supplies. Evacuation under those circumstances would not have damaged the national cause, Lincoln said, because he would have demonstrated that he was yielding only to military necessity. Apparently still seeking to impress the nation, especially his northern critics, with his peaceful intentions, he declared that not until April 6, when he received news of the failure to reinforce Pickens, did he make the final decision to send the relief expedition to Sumter. His decision was motivated, he added, by the desire to prevent "our national destruction" and to give "bread to the few brave and hungry men of the garrison."[39]

In stating that the voluntary surrender of Sumter hinged upon the successful reinforcement of Pickens, Lincoln gave evidence of a rather faulty memory, for it is impossible to harmonize his interpretation with the known facts. No member of the Cabinet, at any time, indicated that he had heard the President discuss such a possibility. Indeed, on April 1, when Secretary of State William H. Seward himself proposed the reinforcement of Pickens and the evacuation of Sumter, Lincoln categorically rejected the idea. He reminded Seward of the pledge in his inaugural address to "hold, occupy and possess" government property, and he declared, without qualification, that he did "not propose to abandon Fort Sumpter [sic]."[40] Moreover, the debate on supplying Sumter went on in the Cabinet and in Lincoln's own mind *after* he had given the order to reinforce Pickens, an order that he had no reason to believe would not be executed forthwith. Most damaging to Lincoln's claim is the fact that Captain Gustavus Vasa Fox, who commanded the Sumter relief expedition, received his final instructions to go forward on April 4, the same day that Lincoln wrote and mailed a letter to Anderson notifying him that supplies were being sent. Thus Lincoln's decisive action on the Sumter question occurred two days *before* the news arrived that reinforcements had not landed at Fort Pickens.[41] Finally, since reinforcements actually entered Pickens on April 12, he *did* in fact achieve that objective before Anderson's capitulation. Clearly, Lincoln had approached Sumter and Pickens as separate problems, although his action in each case was part of a unified program.

Not only Lincoln's Sumter plan, but all of his activities during March and early April illustrate the rapid development of his defensive strategy. Step by step he was quietly moving to assert and vindicate federal authority in the South. Before each advance Confederate leaders would have had to retreat, until they found themselves discredited before their own people and, for all practical purposes, back in the Union. Their only alternative was resistance, but always the burden of aggression would be upon them. Lincoln's record would remain clear in the eyes of the northern people.

If Lincoln ever seriously believed that the secession crisis could be solved by voluntary reconstruction—and there is nothing to indicate that he had completely ruled it out in the weeks immediately after the election—he seemed to have lost whatever hope he may have had for it long before the guns of Charleston began to speak. The transparent hostility of the leading secessionists to reasonable compromise proposals, the seizure of federal property, the rapid organization of a Confederate government, and the military preparations in the South hardly encouraged confidence in this passive and patient approach. Besides, the Republican press had confidently predicted that Lincoln would pursue a "vigorous policy." Amid the denunciations of Buchanan for his "weakness" and "submission to treason" came assertions that the new President would soon demonstrate that "we still have a government." The following comment was typical:

> Mr. Buchanan may strive to get rid of his obligations to the Constitution and the Union, imposed by his oath of office and 'the Supreme law of the land;' but Mr. Lincoln . . . is not the man to shrink from the performance of any duty. Like Jackson he may regret the necessity of shedding blood in the faithful discharge of his duties; but having accepted the Presidency, and solemnly sworn to sustain the Constitution, preserve the Union, and execute the laws, he will not be wanting in the hour of trial.[42]

These early prognostications, together with the secrecy which covered the development of Lincoln's policy, threatened to discredit his administration unless there was immediate and visible action. The widespread rumors in March, for which Seward was in large part responsible, that Sumter was to be evacuated gave the anti-Republican press an opportunity to taunt the new President. "This administration," gloated one Democratic editor, "after all its bluster about 'enforcing the laws in all the states,' not only surrenders Sumter but South Carolina and the whole South."[43] Indeed, critics insisted, Lincoln was merely continuing Buchanan's "weak" policy.

Even before Lincoln's inauguration there were abundant signs that the general uncertainty was becoming intolerable. More and more it appeared that time was not on the side of the Union, that the secession movement was actually gaining in strength. After March 4, Republican leaders bombarded Lincoln with advice favoring decisive action, and with warnings that the people would not tolerate the abandonment of Sumter. Meanwhile, the differences between Union and Confederate tariff schedules frightened many conservative merchants into a mood for drastic remedies.[44] By the end of March numerous businessmen had reached the point where they felt that anything—even war—was better than the existing indecision which was so fatal to trade. "It is a singular fact," wrote one observer, "that merchants who, two months ago, were fiercely shouting 'no coercion,' now ask for anything rather than *inaction*."[45] Even anti-Republican and anti-coercion papers could bear the suspense no longer and urged that something be done. Lincoln might well have hoped for a little more time to organize his administration before dealing with the secessionists; but the general unrest in the North, as well as the Sumter crisis, forced his hand at once. The time for delay had passed.

Such was the atmosphere in which Lincoln dispatched a relief expedition to Fort Sumter. Every circumstance combined to make this a satisfactory culmination of his defensive strategy. Popular attention had long been focused on the small federal garrison in Charleston harbor. A southern attack was almost certain to consolidate northern opinion behind the new administration, while permitting the garrison to receive supplies would seriously damage Confederate prestige. Having authorized Seward to promise the Confederate Commissioners in Washington that relief would not be sent without due notice, the President could be doubly sure that this step, one way or another, would be decisive. Equally important, the fact that he could force the issue merely by sending supplies served to underscore the defensive nature of his move. He instructed his messenger, Robert S. Chew, to notify Governor Francis W. Pickens of South Carolina that "an attempt will be made to supply Fort-Sumpter [sic] with provisions only; and that, if such attempt be not resisted, no effort to throw in men, arms, or ammunition, will be made, without further notice, or in case of an attack upon the Fort."[46] After that, whether the Confederates attacked or submitted, Lincoln would triumph.

The President himself pointed to the Sumter expedition as the fulfillment of the policy he had outlined in the past. He did so first in his reply to Seward's memorandum of April 1, in which the Secretary of State proposed, for all practical purposes, Lincoln's own strategy, except that he favored the evacuation of Sumter. Professing surprise at this, Lincoln reminded Seward that his inaugural embraced "the exact domestic policy you now urge," except that he would not give up Fort Sumter.[47] Even more emphatic was his response, on April 13, to a delegation sent by the Virginia convention to inquire about his policy. "Not having, as yet, seen occasion to change," he said, "it is now my purpose to pursue the course marked out in the inaugural address." He would hold federal property in the South. However, if it proved true that "an unprovoked assault" had been made upon Sumter, he would feel free "to re-possess . . . like places which have been seized before the Government was devolved upon me." It was at this point, more clearly than ever before, that Lincoln expressed his unqualified decision in favor of coercion. Yet, he still insisted that his policy was altogether defensive, for he added that he would simply "repel force by force."[48] The Confederate attack upon Fort Sumter was, in effect, a striking victory for Lincoln's defensive strategy. Just as Republican editors had first suggested the formula, their appreciation of its success was immediate and spontaneous. In one great chorus they denounced the Confederates as the aggressors. "It was," wrote one, "an audacious and insulting aggression upon the authority of the Republic, without provocation or excuse." A Boston editor piously described the event as one furnishing "precisely the stimulus which . . . a good Providence sends to arouse the latent patriotism of the people." "*Let it be remembered*," cried the Providence *Journal*, "*that the Southern government has put itself wholly in the wrong, and is the aggressor.* On its head must be the responsibility for the consequences."[49] These were accurate expressions of the feelings of an indignant northern people.

Only a few cynical editors survived in those exciting days. Early in April, the Albany *Argus* hinted "that the administration of Mr. Lincoln is disposed to secretly provoke a fight; and that it looks to some collision at the South, commenced on that side, to arouse Northern feelings." Another critic believed that the Sumter expedition was designed "*to provoke and draw the first fire from the Montgomery government.*" "By this cunningly contrived plan," added a Democratic editor, "it is hoped the responsibility of commencing hostilities will be thrown upon the South." The reason: "Nothing but a war can keep together the Republican party."[50] Within a few days after the fall of Sumter, however, the doubters were either converted or silent.

That Lincoln understood the probability of Confederate resistance at Charleston is beyond a reasonable doubt, for the messengers he sent there in March informed him of the state of opinion in South Carolina. During the period of preparation the President strove to organize the defenses of Washington and urged Governor Curtin of Pennsylvania to prepare for an emergency. Lincoln's secretaries, John G. Nicolay and John Hay, believed that it was "reasonably certain" that he expected hostilities to ensue, and they observed that when the news arrived of the attack upon Sumter he was neither surprised nor excited.[51] Indeed, if he had believed that Sumter could be supplied peacefully, there was no reason why he should ever have considered evacuation as a possible military necessity. During the weeks when members of the Cabinet and military officers discussed the Sumter crisis, they simply took for granted that a federal relief expedition would result in a Confederate attack.

There is no evidence that Lincoln regarded the result of his strategy with anything but satisfaction. Having derived his policy from his determination to preserve the Union at all costs, he had reason to congratulate himself, for with a united North behind him he was likely to succeed. "You and I both anticipated," he wrote Captain Fox, "that the cause of the country would be advanced by making the attempt to provision Fort-Sumpter [sic], even if it should fail; and it is no small consolation now to feel that our anticipation is justified by the result."[52] A few months later, after Lincoln had gained greater perspective, he told Senator Orville H. Browning of Illinois that he had "conceived the idea" of sending supplies without reinforcements and of notifying the governor of South Carolina in advance. According to Browning, Lincoln added: "The plan succeeded. They attacked Sumter—it fell, and thus did more service than it otherwise could."[53]

Nicolay and Hay believed that Lincoln regarded the success or failure of the Sumter expedition as "a question of minor importance." More significant was his determination that the Confederates "would not be able to convince the world that he had begun civil war." According to Nicolay, Lincoln's "carefully matured purpose" was "to force rebellion to put itself flagrantly and fatally in the wrong by attacking Fort Sumter."[54] Showing the greatest admiration for Lincoln's political skill, his secretaries reached an accurate conclusion:

> When he finally gave the order that the fleet should sail he was master of the situation; master of his Cabinet; master of the moral attitude and issues of the struggle; master of the public opinion which must arise out of the impending conflict; master if the rebels hesitate or repent, because they would thereby forfeit their prestige with the South; master if they persisted, for he would then command a united North.[55]

Professor Potter, in analyzing the Sumter crisis, asked whether Lincoln, given his determination to save the Union, could "have followed any more peaceable course than he did." After all, he gave the governor of South Carolina advance notice that the relief expedition was coming, and he assured the governor that his aim was to supply the fort with provisions only. Historians who attribute to him a coercive policy must "name a less provocative course that he might have followed," or they are guilty "of arguing that a man may pursue a course which offers the maximum possibility of peace and may at the same time be open to the accusation of scheming to bring about war."[56]

However, the crucial point about the Sumter crisis was that, except for the important consideration of northern public opinion, it mattered little whether Lincoln attempted to supply Sumter in the least provocative or the most provocative way, because, as he had reason to know, *any* attempt was bound to open hostilities. Moreover, it is possible to argue that Lincoln's Sumter policy was not in fact the least provocative course he might have followed. For example, he might have done what he subsequently claimed that he had hoped to do— that is, evacuate Fort Sumter and reinforce Fort Pickens, as Seward suggested. The reinforcement of Pickens was accomplished with ease, and the federal position there was so strong that the fort was never lost to the Confederates. As to Sumter, before sending a relief expedition, Lincoln might have directed Major Anderson to try to obtain the needed supplies in Charleston. South Carolina authorities might well have refused such a request (though they permitted Anderson to purchase fresh meats and vegetables in the Charleston market), but the request was never made. Finally, although Lincoln assured the governor of South Carolina that the relief expedition would land provisions only, he also hinted that an attempt (with notice) to land "men, arms, or ammunition" might be made at some future time. A Sumter policy designed to minimize provocation would hardly have suggested such a possibility at that crucial juncture. Yet, it is not to accuse Lincoln of deliberately starting a war to conclude that the Confederate attack on Sumter was a triumph, not a defeat, for his policy.

With the fall of Sumter Lincoln's defensive policy had served its purpose, and instantly he changed his ground. In his proclamation of April 15, calling for 75,000 volunteers, he did not propose merely to "hold" or "possess" federal property and to collect the revenues. Instead, he summoned the militia to suppress an insurrection, "to re-possess the forts, places, and property which have been seized," "to cause the laws to be duly executed," to preserve the Union, and "to redress wrongs already long enough endured."[57] A few days later, when addressing the Frontier Guard in Washington, Lincoln gave additional evidence that he had always preferred coercion to disunion. While professing peaceful intentions, he predicted that "if the alternative is presented, whether the Union is to be broken in fragments . . . or blood be shed, you will probably make the choice, with which I shall not be dissatisfied."[58]

Although Lincoln accepted the possibility of war, which, in retrospect, was the almost certain consequence of his defensive strategy, the indictment—if such it be—can be softened considerably by surrounding circumstances. It was a burden that he shared with many others, for his standards of statesmanship and his concept of the national interest were those common to his age—and, for that matter, to ours as well. The Union was a thing worth fighting for! If Lincoln was no pacifist, neither were his contemporaries. The growing impatience in the North and the widespread demand for action no doubt helped to shape his final decision. And it is still a moot question whether politicians in a democracy are morally bound to yield to popular pressures or to resist them. Moreover, without quibbling over who was guilty of the first act of aggression, the case would be distorted if one overlooked the fact that southern leaders shared with Lincoln the responsibility for a resort to force. Richard N. Current argued persuasively that "the Ramsdell thesis, turned inside out, could be applied to [Jefferson] Davis with as much justice as it has been applied to Lincoln," for Davis had as strong political reasons for authorizing the attack upon Fort Sumter as Lincoln had for attempting its relief. In any case, Current concluded, "Lincoln did not order the guns to fire. Davis did."[59] Thus, the Confederates, too, preferred war to submission.

One final mitigating circumstance was the quite justifiable uncertainty as to whether acquiescence in disunion was, in the long run, necessarily a peace formula. Many Northerners were convinced that the clash of interests and the bitter feelings resulting from a divided Union would lead, sooner or later, to armed conflict. Lincoln contended "that far less evil and bloodshed would result from an effort to maintain the Union and the Constitution, than from disruption and the formation of two confederacies."[60] That this was more than a Republican rationalization was attested by the fact that some conservative Democrats held the same opinion. For example, the pro-Breckinridge Boston *Post* declared: "We have no faith, if the States separate, that there can be a peaceable issue of the vast interests, and the public property at stake."[61] To understand Lincoln's decision to risk hostilities through the Sumter expedition, it is of the utmost importance to see the probable consequences from his perspective. He had no way of knowing that he was helping to pave the way to four years of bloody war and the loss of more than half a million lives. He doubtless shared the common belief that the contest would be short. As one editor described it, "There will be no prolonged and doubtful struggle. The country is coming down like an avalanche upon the conspiracy, and it will be annihilated at one fell swoop."[62]

It may well have been true, as Ramsdell claimed, that the outbreak of war saved the Republican party from disintegration and that a practical politician such as Lincoln could not have ignored the political consequences of his action. But the Machiavellian implication of that hypothesis is based on sheer speculation. We cannot read Lincoln's mind; and the available evidence makes equally valid the counter-hypothesis that he considered only the country's best interests. Or, again, he may have had a comprehensive understanding of what both the country and political expediency demanded. Perhaps it was simply Lincoln's good fortune that personal, party, and national interests could be served with such favorable coincidence as they were by his strategy of defense.

Civil War Causes and Consequences

system, from which emerged a ruling class with a world view
and a cluster of "prebourgeois" values markedly different
from those of the middle-class North. Rejecting "the crass,
vulgar, inhuman elements of capitalist society," Southerners
found it increasingly difficult to coexist with a "hostile, powerful, and aggressive Northern capitalism." By the mid-nine-
teenth century the South had developed "a special civilization
built on the relationship of master to slave," and, according to
Genovese, this was "the root of its conflict with the North."
The slaveholders' decision to secede was both a recognition of
the threat of the bourgeois world and their ultimate protest
against it.[7] Eric Foner, focusing on the North, stressed the
free-labor ideology of the Republicans, "their devotion to the
mores and values of northern society, and . . . their conviction of the superiority of the North's civilization to that of
the South." The final crisis grew out of the Republicans' confidence "that in the sectional struggle, which one newspaper
summarized as a contest between 'Northern Progress and
Southern Decadence,' southern civilization must give way
before the onslaught of the modern world."[8] Thus Genovese
and Foner together portrayed two sections with goals and
cultural values so antagonistic as to make conflict a logical if
not inevitable result.

Early in the twentieth century some historians, while
equally certain that the sectional conflict was irrepressible, denied the importance of the slavery issue and emphasized instead
the differences between the northern and southern economies
and the clash, not of cultures and ideologies, but of material
interests. "To say that the Republican party was organized, or
the Civil War waged to abolish chattel slavery," argued the
Marxist Algie M. Simons, "is but to repeat a tale invented . . .
as a means of glorifying the party of plutocracy. . . ." Rather,
the crisis took shape with the emergence of a northern capitalist class, which, by 1850, was "destined soon to seize the
reins of political power." When at last this political revolution

occurred, the southern slaveholders had no alternative but to secede. "The Civil War therefore was simply a contest to secure possession of the 'big stick' of the national government"; it was fought "that the capitalist class might rule."[9]

However, economic determinism as a frame of reference for the irrepressible conflict made its impact on American historiography less through the writings of Marxists than through those of the Progressive Charles A. Beard. Noting the tendency of historians to stress slavery as the source of sectional tension, Beard observed that slavery was "no simple, isolated phenomenon." It was a labor system, "the foundation of the southern aristocracy." This aristocracy, in alliance with western farmers, opposed public policies that were favorable to capitalism and thus frustrated the efforts of northern merchants and manufacturers to obtain federal protection and support. Hence, Beard contended, "It took more than a finite eye to discern where slavery as an ethical question left off and economics—the struggle over the distribution of wealth—began." He found the southern claim that state rights was the basic issue equally superficial. At the root of every congressional debate over state rights and federal power was some concrete economic issue, not a mere constitutional abstraction. Thus, again, "It took more than a finite eye to discern where . . . [southern] opposition to the economic system of Hamilton left off and . . . their affection for the rights of the states began." Beard thought it significant that in the North abolitionists were always a small minority, that no major party ever wrote a platform demanding the abolition of slavery, and that Southerners were far from consistent supporters of state rights.[10]

Turning to the productive systems of the North and South, Beard explained the sectional crisis as a consequence of their "inherent antagonisms" intensified during a period of rapid economic growth. "The periphery of the industrial vortex of the Northeast was daily enlarging, . . . and the area of virgin soil open to exploitation by planters was diminishing with rhythmic regularity—shifting with mechanical precision the weights which statesmen had to adjust in their efforts to maintain the equilibrium of peace." Spokesmen for the planters charged that their northern economic rivals had organized politically to plunder the agricultural interest, while northern entrepreneurs viewed the planters as "a huge, compact, and self-conscious economic association bent upon . . . the possession of the government" for the aggrandizement of their class. Given the irrepressible conflict between these antagonistic interests, Beard was convinced that a violent resolution—"a transfer of the issues from the forum to the field"—was bound to come. "Each side obdurately bent upon its designs and convinced of its rectitude, by the fulfillment of its wishes precipitated events and effected distributions of power that culminated finally in the tragedy foretold by Seward."[11]

Beard's concept of the irrepressible conflict was a logical extension of his earlier portrayal of the federal Constitution as an economic document and of its framers as motivated primarily by economic self-interest. It was the background for his interpretation of the Civil War era as a "Second American Revolution" marking the triumph of the masters of capital over the tillers of the soil. His economic determinism, with its unsentimental assumption that practical economic concerns, not vague ideologies, were at the core of reality, won numerous converts among historians of his day, especially among graduate students during the depression years of the 1930s. As late as 1951, C. Vann Woodward, in his study of the sectional Compromise of 1877, paid tribute to Beard "as the originator of the concept of the Civil War and Reconstruction as . . . the Second American Revolution" and acknowledged that his own book was "built upon that conception."[12]

Ultimately, Beard's economic determinism as applied to the sectional conflict failed to supersede the slavery-cultural interpretation—indeed, in recent years, the number of its advocates has diminished, primarily because a convincing case for it has not been made. Although Nevins's *Ordeal of the Union* was essentially a synthesis of modern scholarship, it nevertheless rejected Beard's schema, declaring that "of all the monistic explanations for the drift to war, that posited upon supposed economic causes is the flimsiest."[13]

Most historians of the sectional conflict, whatever differences they may have on other matters, now see no compelling reason why the divergent economies of the North and South should have led to disunion and civil war; rather, they find stronger practical reasons why the sections, whose economies neatly complemented one another, should have found it advantageous to remain united. Beard oversimplified the controversies relating to federal economic policy, for neither section unanimously supported or opposed measures such as the protective tariff, appropriations for internal improvements, or the creation of a national banking system. Except for the nullification crisis of 1832-33, economic issues, though sometimes present, were not crucial in the various sectional confrontations. During the 1850s, federal economic policy gave no substantial cause for southern disaffection, for policy was largely determined by prosouthern Congresses and administrations. Finally, the characteristic posture of the conservative northeastern business community was far from antisouthern. Most merchants, bankers, and manufacturers were outspoken in their hostility to antislavery agitation and eager for sectional compromise in order to maintain their profitable business connections with the South.

The conclusion seems inescapable that if economic differences, real though they were, had been all that troubled relations between North and South, there would be no substantial basis for the idea of an irrepressible conflict. In the historiography of sectionalism the slavery-cultural concept easily survived the challenge of Beardian economic determinism and remains the dominant interpretation.

In the long run, the more interesting and persistent challenge to the slavery-cultural concept came from historians
who thought the sectional conflict was, in Seward's words,
"accidental, unnecessary, the work of interested or fanatical
agitators, and therefore ephemeral." This alternative hypothesis has always had its ardent champions in the course of a
long and sometimes tempestuous life, and, though in recent
years rather on the wane, it is by no means dead. Avery
Craven, a distinguished exponent of the idea of an unnecessary, or repressible, conflict, once labeled it "revisionism," and
that, unfortunately, is the name by which it has been known
ever since.[14] It originated among certain of Seward's contemporaries who believed that no sectional difference was too
serious to be disposed of by compromise, if only irresponsible
agitators would hold their tongues. These precursors of revisionism, who went by many names, were numerous among
northern Democrats, southern Whigs, border-state people of
all parties, and northern businessmen. During the 1850s, Senator Stephen A. Douglas of Illinois was the most influential
spokesman for this point of view; in a sense, he was the original revisionist, for most of the ideas associated with that interpretation can be found in his speeches and writings.

Revisionist historians were not all alike. Some advanced
certain parts of the case for a repressible conflict but ignored
or rejected others. One, Avery Craven, tried to combine revisionism with a measure of Beard's economic determinism;
another, James G. Randall, considered the idea of economic
causation to be as superficial as all other supposedly rational
causes propounded in support of the concept of an irrepressible conflict. In portions of *Ordeal of the Union* Nevins appeared to be attempting to reconcile the case for revisionism
with that for a slavery-cultural interpretation, but he did not
succeed and merely introduced an element of ambiguity in his
work. In spite of the differences among revisionists, it has
been the custom to treat them as a fairly coherent group and

to associate them with a historiographical trend during a
rather short period of time. But revisionism is in fact best
understood as a body of ideas about the sectional conflict first
advanced by certain politicians of the 1850s, and then by
various historians in a variety of ways from the late nineteenth century to the present day.[15]

The case for a repressible conflict rested on a foundation of
beliefs about slavery as a moral question, of attitudes toward
antislavery agitators, and of conclusions about slavery expansion as a political issue. In their earliest form revisionist ideas
and attitudes often betrayed, either implicitly or explicitly, a
kind of racist resentment that Negroes should have been the
source of so much political turmoil in antebellum years.
Stephen A. Douglas, though no defender of slavery, resorted
to much racial demagoguery in denouncing those who joined
the antislavery crusade. Slavery, he repeatedly said, was a
matter that concerned the South alone, and he was willing to
let white Southerners deal with it as they saw fit. If the people
of a western territory wanted slavery, "let them have it," and
that would be "entirely satisfactory" to him. This attitude of
moral indifference—the feeling that slavery was hardly a matter over which sane men and women would create a crisis—is
evident in much revisionist writing. Ulrich B. Phillips's influential study of southern slavery was in this respect a decidedly revisionist work, for it portrayed the institution as, in
the main, benevolent and a civilizing force which did much
good for the blacks at little cost to them. As Phillips understood them, the slaves were, "by racial quality," "submissive,"
"light-hearted," "amiable," "ingratiating," and "imitative,"
and their progress "was restricted by the fact of their being
negroes."[16] The slave-plantation system aroused in him not
ethical concerns but nostalgia.

Without the explicit racism of Phillips, the theme that slavery was nothing to get excited about and a matter which historians of the irrepressible conflict emphasized too much, was

fundamental to revisionism. Frank L. Owsley, whose writings
wavered uncertainly between Beardian economic determinism and the concept of a repressible conflict, asserted that
"slavery as a moral issue has too long been the red herring
dragged across the trail," for it "was no essential part of the
agrarian civilization of the South."[17] Randall was perplexed
by the moral fervor of antebellum abolitionists, for, like Phillips, he found little justification for their passionate attacks.
According to Randall, black slaves "adapted . . . to bondage
with a minimum of resistance, doing cheerfully the manual
work of the South. . . ." As for abuses, "there was truth in
the common declaration that Southern abuse of the slave was
often a matter of mistreatment through leniency"; thus, "in a
real sense the whites were more enslaved by the institution
than the blacks." Randall's admiration for the statesmanship
of Douglas was based in part on Douglas's effort "to subordinate the slavery factor to larger issues."[18] Craven's estimate of
the significance of slavery was evident in his assertion that
the differences between North and South "were not much greater
than those existing between East and West." Abolitionist agitation made it "very difficult to understand the more modest
place . . . [slavery] occupied in the actual life of the section
and of the Negro." According to Craven, what slavery
"added to the usual relationship between employer and em-
ployee . . . is difficult to say," but in most ways the lives of
slaves were "much like those of other American workers."
During all the controversy over slavery, "The patient Negro
. . . went on with his tasks generally unconscious of the
merits or the lack of them in the system under which he
toiled." Craven concluded: "Perhaps the idea [of slavery]
was always worse than the fact itself."[19]

David Potter, whose thoughtful writings about the antebellum period revealed his many revisionist attitudes, believed
that a compromise permitting slavery to survive and even ex-
pand had the merit at least "of being better than war." He

conceded that the Civil War had the "immense value" of emancipating four million slaves, but he found it appalling that it cost the life of one soldier for every six slaves who were freed. "A person is entitled to wonder," he wrote, whether "the slaves could not have been freed at a smaller per-capita cost."[20] While Potter suggested no alternative solution—instead, endorsed the Crittenden Compromise, which would have guaranteed slavery perpetually in the southern states and protected it in the territories south of the Missouri Compromise line—he probably had in mind a fundamental assumption of nearly all revisionist historians: by the 1850s, slavery had reached the "natural limits" of its potential expansion and would soon have died of natural causes.

That the westward expansion of slavery was controlled by geographical conditions was a common idea among contemporary advocates of compromise. Douglas, taking a deterministic position, held that slavery would spread only into areas where soil and climate were hospitable to the cultivation of staple crops, and that none of the remaining territories, including Kansas, was suitable for that purpose. Revisionists defended Douglas's statesmanship in part because they believed that his principle of popular sovereignty—permitting the people living in a territory to decide the question of slavery for themselves—would have prevented slavery expansion as surely as federal intervention. Among them, Charles W. Ramsdell developed the natural-limits hypothesis most fully and effectively. Insisting that the growth of slavery was tied to the expansion of the Cotton Kingdom, Ramsdell concluded that by the eve of the Civil War "the western limits of the cotton growing region were already approximated." From this it followed that "the institution of slavery had virtually reached its natural frontiers"—there was "no further place for it to go."[21] Echoing Ramsdell, another revisionist, Henry H. Simms, affirmed that the territorial question "was a mere abstraction. . . . Congress might legislate and courts might adjudicate, but the inexorable laws of nature had decreed that slavery had no place in the western territories."[22] Since slavery lacked room for expansion, revisionists concluded that it could not have survived much longer.

However, their belief in slavery's imminent decline did not rest on the natural-limits idea alone, for they found other forces at work which, if left undisturbed, would have helped to bring the institution to a peaceful and orderly end. After the Civil War southern partisans frequently recalled the anti-slavery attitudes of their ancestors in Washington's and Jefferson's day, and they claimed that a promising manumission movement had been destroyed by attacks from the outside. In due course this claim became an integral part of the revisionist case. Had it not been for northern meddling, Phillips contended, "it is fairly probable that . . . slavery would have been disestablished in some peaceable way in response to the demand of public opinion in the South."[23] Owsley asserted that slavery "must have soon begun to decline and would probably have ceased to exist before the end of the nineteenth century,"[24] while Randall was convinced that it "was crumbling in the presence of nineteenth century tendencies."[25] Craven stressed the substantial southern opposition to slavery in the early years of the republic and concluded: "The impartial observer might have prophesied a peaceful solution of the problem because of . . . the presence of a vague undercurrent of belief in the ultimate extinction of the evil."[26]

According to some revisionists, even after the collapse of the southern antislavery movement certain impersonal and irreversible conditions made the peaceful demise of slavery inevitable. Ramsdell believed that after 1860 the development of labor-saving machinery, as well as overproduction and low cotton prices, would have made slaves a burden to their owners and thus changed southern attitudes. Therefore, he concluded that "within a comparatively short time [slavery] would have begun to decline and eventually have been abol-

ished by the Southerners themselves."[27] Since revisionists
viewed slavery as an institution whose evils were much exaggerated, which in any case had passed its prime, and which
was destined soon to disappear, one can understand the dis-
gust Ramsdell expressed for antebellum politicians. Those
who wanted slavery abolished, he wrote, "had only to wait a
little while—perhaps a generation, probably less. . . . One is
tempted at this point to reflections on what has passed for
statesmanship on both sides of that long dead issue. But I have
not the heart to indulge them."[28]

Ramsdell's bitter comment drove to the heart of the problem as revisionists understood it—what it was that *really*
caused the sectional conflict and, ultimately, the Civil War.
Douglas offered a partial answer as early as 1858 when he
asked, "Why should this slavery agitation be kept up? . . .
Who does it benefit except the Republican politicians, who
use it as their hobby to ride into office?" Former President
James Buchanan, in his recollection of the crisis, placed the
blame on the "misguided fanatics" who wasted the time of
Congress "in violent debates on the subject of slavery" and
provoked Southerners to form a party "as fanatical in advocating slavery as were the abolitionists of the North in denouncing it."[29] This, in brief, is what eventually became the
revisionist explanation: political opportunists and irresponsible agitators exaggerated sectional differences that could
easily have been resolved peacefully, fomented an artificial
crisis, and thus brought on a needless war.

Historians of the repressible conflict, in their individual
ways, wrote variations on this theme. Mary Scrugham, minimizing the differences between the sections and emphasizing
the element of irrationality, suggested that "there need have
been no appeal from the ballot to the bullet in 1861, had the
American people of that day possessed sufficient political
sagacity to distinguish between appearance and reality."[30]
Ramsdell, describing what he considered the pointless con-

worked. . . . The conflict was the work of politicians and pious cranks!"[35]

In his later writings, beginning with an essay in 1947, Craven shifted his position in some respects and presented what can best be described as a recasting of the revisionist case. He became somewhat ambiguous about whether the sectional conflict was repressible; and, while emphasizing the "psychological causes which ultimately permitted emotions to take the place of reason," he explicitly recognized that the Civil War had "economic causes, constitutional causes, social causes, moral causes, [and] political causes." He agreed that slavery, "a great evil," provoked "a sharp moral reaction against it which had a major part in producing the Civil War." The error of the South was its failure to recognize that its institutions "were not safe anywhere in the nineteenth century and the emerging modern world." Craven's heightened emphasis on industrialization and the northern free-labor ideology made him sound somewhat more Beardian and indicated a partial acceptance of the slavery-cultural interpretation.

However, the result of Craven's revised revisionism was not so much a coherent new synthesis as a lumpy mixture of contradictions, in which the flavor of the old revisionism was still most pronounced. His portrait of the abolitionists remained highly unflattering; he claimed that Lincoln and Seward "brought the moral issue [of slavery] into politics and used it to advance their political fortunes"; and he described a South under "relentless attack," being forced to "yield its ways and values," facing an adversary wearing an air of "moral superiority and self-righteousness." Moreover, having conceded that the Civil War did have rational causes, Craven insisted that "the important question is not *what* the North and South were quarreling about half as much as *how* their differences got into such shape that they could not be handled by the process of rational discussion, compromise, or the tolerant acceptance of majority decision." Thus he turned away from the causes and, as in his earlier writings, stressed the exaggerations and distortions, the oversimplification of concrete issues into abstract questions of right and wrong. In short, it was still not the issues themselves but the "blundering which made the war inevitable."[36] Even so, Craven's later writings are perhaps the most interesting in the historiography of revisionism, because they define a problem that is relevant to all interpretations of the sectional conflict: how the crisis of the 1850s ended in war and thus came to represent the greatest failure of the democratic process in American political history.

In 1960, David Donald propounded a modified and subtle version of one crucial revisionist theme. Rejecting the view that antebellum politicians were exceptionally incompetent or malignant, Donald argued that they were logical products of contemporary American society—a society in which "all the recognized values of orderly civilization were gradually being eroded," in which precedents were being rejected and authority repudiated. The adoption of white manhood suffrage made it increasingly difficult to cope with problems "requiring subtle understanding and delicate handling." Suffering from an "excess of liberty," Americans were "unable to arrive at reasoned, independent judgments upon the problems which faced their society. . . . Fads, fashions, and crazes swept the country," along with "hysterical fears and paranoid suspicions," and the electorate was ripe for the "propagandist, the agitator, the extremist." Donald described the political crises of the 1850s as "not in themselves calamitous experiences. Revisionist historians have correctly pointed out how little was actually at stake." After accepting the argument that slavery would not have spread into the territories, he concluded: "When compared to crises which other nations have resolved without great discomfort, the true proportions of these exaggerated disturbances appear."[37] Thus, after shifting responsibility from irresponsible individuals to a more general condition of society, Donald joined the revisionists in minimizing

new issue," tried to "exploit the revived sectional conflict."
Thus, he asserted, "The Kansas-Nebraska Act had been
shaped largely by the divergent intentions of politicians who
had specifically partisan and not sectional goals in mind." He
agreed with a Kentucky editor who charged that politicians
"constructed a new arena for party gladiators at the expense
of the repose and temper of the nation." One of Holt's major
generalizations restated the concept of a "whipped-up" crisis:

> The sectionalization of American politics was emphati-
> cally *not* simply a reflection or product of basic popular
> disagreements over black slavery. . . . [It] is a mistake
> to think of sectional antagonism as a spontaneous and
> self-perpetuating force that imposed itself on the political
> arena against the will of politicians. . . . Some one has
> to politicize events. . . . Politicians who pursued very
> traditional partisan strategies were largely responsible for
> the ultimate breakdown of the political process. Much of
> the story of the coming of the Civil War is the story of
> the successful efforts of Democratic politicians in the
> South and Republican politicians in the North to keep
> the sectional conflict at the center of political debate.
> . . . Republican politicians quite consciously seized on
> the slavery and sectional issue in order to build a new
> party.[41]

Clearly, the thesis that political agitators were the source of
the sectional conflict has not altogether lost its appeal.

The origin of revisionism, with its concept of a repressible
conflict and needless war, has been explained in various ways.
Craven himself simply dismissed the "orthodox" point of
view as a biased "northern explanation of events" and claimed
that it had been upset by the findings of scholars who went
back to the sources "as scientists and not as partisans."
Equating revisionism with a new objectivity, he denied that
he had been "interested in defending or attacking any sec-

tion." Rather, he had tried "to come as nearly to the truth as possible regardless of personal or sectional interests."[42] Several revisionists, including Scrugham, Randall, and Craven, linked their interpretations to the insights of modern psychology. Thus, Craven, in his assessment of the abolitionists, observed:

> The modern psychologist . . . talks of youthful experiences, maladjustments, inferiority complexes, and repressed desires. He is not sure about the sources of the reform impulse or the unselfish character of the reformer. The student of social affairs is likewise less inclined to grant unstinted praise to the fanatic and is not certain about the value of the contribution. . . . He sees the triumph of emotion over reason in the extremist's course and sometimes wonders if the developments of history might not have been more sound without him.[43]

Similarly, Randall suggested that, "When nations stumble into war, . . . there is at some point a psychopathic case. Omit the element of abnormality . . . and diagnosis fails." Given "the artificiality of war-making agitation," the theory that "fundamental motives make war" is one of "the most colossal misconceptions." Accordingly, Randall concluded: "to suppose that the Union could not have been continued or slavery outmoded without war . . . is hardly an enlightened assumption."[44] These explanations of the psychological foundations of revisionism were obviously premised on a belief that rationality is the norm in human behavior and that the irrational element in the sectional conflict was a tragic exception.

One critic, Arthur Schlesinger, Jr., described Randall's interpretation as "optimistic sentimentalism" which "evades the essential moral problems in the name of a superficial objectivity and asserts their unimportance in the name of an invincible progress." Accepting Reinhold Niebuhr's tragic view of the human predicament, Schlesinger found in revisionism "a touching afterglow of the admirable nineteenth-century faith in the full rationality and perfectibility of man; the faith that the errors of the world would all in time be 'outmoded' . . . by progress." According to Thomas J. Pressly, revisionists thought that "war was always useless, that war never settled any issue in a desirable manner, and that war was always the worst possible alternative in human relations." Contrary to this alleged revisionist view, Schlesinger insisted that historians must face the "unhappy fact . . . that man occasionally works himself into a log-jam; and that the log-jam must be burst by violence."[45] Written during the Cold War following World War II, the Schlesinger and Pressly critiques seemed to represent tough realism; a quarter-century later the realists in this historiographical dispute might be somewhat more difficult to discern.

Harry V. Jaffa, in a study of the Lincoln-Douglas debates, developed an equally unflattering but less presentist explanation of the revisionists. He, too, found implicit in their writings a naïve belief in the inevitability of progress, but he considered this belief the only possible moral justification of Douglas's policy, "as of revisionist historiography." However, Jaffa reasoned that if, as the revisionists think, Douglas could have kept slavery out of the territories, and if Lincoln kept the issue alive solely for political reasons, Lincoln is given "a character that, in the profundity of its immorality, is beyond treason." Jaffa rejected the premise and concluded that the needless-war doctrine was "an apology for the South."[46] Don E. Fehrenbacher found the sources of revisionism in the horrors of four years of Civil War and in the traditional negative view of Reconstruction disseminated by William A. Dunning and his students. "Thus an intense dissatisfaction with the consequences of the war encouraged revolt against the deterministic view of its coming" and tempted some sensitive scholars "to confront Americans with the impatient question, 'Was it worth the price?' "[47]

By far the most common explanation of the needless-war doctrine was that it reflected the disillusionment of the 1930s with the involvement of the United States in the First World War. Bernard DeVoto attributed it to the "climate of the time"—to the fact that "an intellectual fashion was developing the (erroneous) thesis that the United States could and should have stayed out of the First World War and the (false) theorem that we were betrayed into it by propaganda." Howard K. Beale thought it significant that revisionism reached its peak "at a time when men were feeling the futility of one world war and facing the possibility of another."[48] Thomas N. Bonner speculated more cautiously that there may have been a connection between revisionism and "the feeling of disillusionment and futility regarding war which overtook Americans in the 1920's, followed by the economic collapse, wars, and threats of war in the 1930's and 1940's."[49] Pressly noted the widespread belief in the 1930s "that the entrance of the United States into war in 1917 came not because of any justifiable concern over important issues but because certain 'devils' had employed 'propaganda' to stir up emotions and thereby induce people to fight." These were the attitudes that "furnished the general framework" for the revisionist interpretation.[50] In short, a clear relationship existed between attitudes toward involvement in the First World War and attitudes toward the Civil War and wars in general. The exposure of the prowar propagandists of 1914-17 presumably stimulated a more critical view of the agitators of the 1850s.

Beale, without really believing it, advanced one small caveat: "This timing may be accidental."[51] He was right—and therein lies a caution to historians who are necessarily involved with problems of human motivation and ever tempted to advance "obvious" but simplistic explanations. In actual fact, although several prominent revisionists did much of their writing during the 1930s, there is no evidence of a significant connection between what they said about the causes of the

Civil War and what some other historians were then saying about the causes of America's declaration of war in 1917. The needless-war argument, of course, antedated the First World War, and it was still evident in much historical writing after the Second. Yet it was not a dominant trend in Civil War historiography even between the First and Second World Wars, for in the 1930s Beard's economic determinism made a considerably stronger appeal. Most important, no historiographical study has demonstrated convincingly that a single revisionist projected disillusionment with American involvement in the First World War back to the sectional crisis prior to the Civil War. Indeed, Scrugham, who is sometimes mistakenly identified as the first revisionist, appears to have based her interpretation of the Civil War in part on her *satisfaction* with the results of the First World War. Writing shortly after the formation of the League of Nations and the World Court, she affirmed optimistically that public opinion was turning against war as a means of settling international disputes and concluded: "Because of this new trend . . . the civilized world may yet reverse its present decision on the Civil War."[52] Scrugham's faith in progress—her naïve belief that the recent war marked a fortuitous turning point in human affairs—not postwar disillusionment, informed her Civil War revisionism.

Randall was the only revisionist who made frequent allusions to twentieth-century international crises and wrote more generally about the problem of war causation, but he provided no basis for the belief that his view of the Civil War originated in disillusionment with the results of the First World War. Quite the reverse, in an essay entitled "Lincoln's Peace and Wilson's," Randall strongly defended Wilson's foreign policy, American participation in the war, and the League of Nations, and he held American isolationists and those who appeased the Nazis responsible for the outbreak of another World War. "One [cannot] . . . base successful international policy on isolation," he wrote. "Realities cannot be ignored. Human interdependence cannot be violated with impunity."[53]

Since those comments appeared in 1943, they might be seen simply as evidence of a changed Randall made wiser by Pearl Harbor. However, his writings thereafter continued to support an unmodified revisionist interpretation of the sectional conflict; moreover, the tone of his earlier and best-known revisionist essay, "A Blundering Generation," was quite consistent with that of the essay comparing Lincoln and Wilson. In its original form the earlier essay concluded with a rather misleading analogy between revisionist writing about the Civil War and revisionist writing about the First World War: "Just as Americans beginning about 1935 executed something like an about-face in their interpretation of the World War, including American participation in it and attitudes preceding it, so the retelling of the Civil War is a matter of changed and changing viewpoints." In a later version, published in 1947, this analogy was deleted, perhaps because it sounded rather dated after the Second World War.[54] Whatever the reason, both versions of the essay make it clear that Randall does not agree with revisionist writings about the First World War and that they were not the inspiration for his interpretation of the Civil War.

In his blundering-generation essay Randall drew his illustrations of the irrationality of war-making in the twentieth century exclusively from the examples of German, Italian, and Japanese nationalism and expansionism. In the case of the Germans, he doubted that "war arose from valid fundamental motives of culture or economics." He discounted all rational explanations for the aggressions of the Axis powers, and, applying his blundering-generation analysis to them, he concluded: "War-making is too much dignified if it is told in terms of broad national urges, of great German motives, or of compelling Italian ambitions."[55] The "abnormality," the "bogus leadership," the "psychopathic cases" about which he wrote involved only the leaders of those countries, not the Wilson or Franklin D. Roosevelt administrations, or the governments of the European allies. Randall made no unfavorable reference to American involvement in the First World War, and in no respect did he betray disillusionment with its results. In short, as an internationalist and firm supporter of the League of Nations, he drew his analogy between the irresponsible politicians and antislavery agitators of the Civil War generation and the war-making adversaries of the United States in two World Wars. Revisionist historians of the First World War received no support from him.

Several critiques of Civil War historiography alluded briefly to another possible explanation of revisionism. Jaffa, as noted above, asserted that it was "an apology for the South," and Fehrenbacher suggested that the "emotional basis of 'revisionism' was . . . to some extent an affection for the South."[56] Bonner stated with more certainty that historians of the repressible conflict belong "to a 'southern school' of interpretation," and he demonstrated it by locating their geographic origins in the former Confederate states. Noting the "natural aversion of Southerners for a moral interpretation of the Civil War," Bonner concluded that southern historians had always favored one "which is least unflattering to the motives of the defeated South, yet consistent with good scholarship and academic respectability."[57] Pressly, though finding it understandable that revisionists could be accused of "pro-Southernism," was not satisfied with that explanation and preferred to make a distinction between them and three southern historians (Phillips, Ramsdell, and Owsley) whose writings he labeled "The New Vindication of the South."[58] The distinction is a tenuous one, for all three contributed to the development of, and subscribed to, major tenets of the revisionist case. Though it is true that by no means all southern historians of the sectional conflict have been revisionists, it is also true that nearly all revisionists have been Southerners, the one notable exception being Randall.[59]

The dominant interpretation of the sectional conflict, in both its late nineteenth-century moralistic form and its less judgmental twentieth-century slavery-cultural form, was always easier for Northerners than for Southerners to accept. Craven understood this when he called it the "Northern interpretation" and when he complained that the antebellum South was "hidden by the lingering clouds of abolitionist propaganda." His intention was to be objective, but in his major revisionist work he explained that he would approach the sectional conflict "from the angle of the South" in order to distinguish "realities" from "distortions."[60] One must take care not to substitute one facile explanation of the revisionists as victims of postwar disillusionment for an equally facile explanation of them as mere southern apologists. Yet, Southerners they were, and as a group they did show considerable affection for the Old South.

In revisionist writings the sectional conflict developed not because of the survival and expansion of slavery but because of the northern attack upon it. Though southern fire-eaters bore a share of the responsibility for precipitating a needless war, northern troublemakers were almost always the aggressors, and hence primary responsibility belonged to them. "The abolitionists made certain false charges against the Southern system," wrote Phillips. "In repelling these calumnies the Southern leaders thought it advisable . . . to praise the institution . . . and to advocate its permanent maintenance instead of its gradual disestablishment. This change in the Southern attitude was to a large extent involuntary."[61] Simms found that radical groups in both sections resorted to "exaggeration and violent abuse" but that "the bitter verbal assault" began "with the abolitionists."[62] Chauncey S. Boucher denied the charge of aggression hurled at the antebellum South—a charge that persisted because most historical works "have been based on sources which, in the final analysis, are really of abolitionist origin." According to Boucher, the South was "on the defensive throughout almost the entire antebellum period," though individual Southerners sometimes did take "a stand which may perhaps best be termed 'aggressively defensive.' "[63]

Craven had no doubt who the aggressors were. To him, writing a narrative of the sectional conflict was a matter of tracing "the steps by which the South was pounded into self-consciousness and moved to ultimate secession. . . ." Southern unity "was primarily the result of a drive launched first against her labor system and then broadened into an attack against the character of her people and their entire way of life." Craven held abolitionists responsible for the fact that the South's "intellectual life was almost frozen, not so much to justify a questionable labor system as to repel a fanatical attack!"[64] Owsley's explanation of the sectional conflict was much like Craven's, except that his resort to hyperbole made it a good deal more colorful. The crisis, he claimed, occurred because Northerners failed to respect the dignity of Southerners and assaulted them with "crude, discourteous, and insulting language." Indeed, even the Nazi propagandist Dr. Goebbels did not "plumb the depths of vulgarity and obscenity reached and maintained by . . . abolitionists of note." Eventually, Owsley concluded, a "slow and consuming fury" took hold of the southern people; but even then the response of the fire-eaters "was not usually coarse or obscene in comparison with the abolitionists. . . ."[65]

As the revisionists took up the various episodes of the sectional conflict, almost invariably they put the onus for each crisis on northern politicians and agitators. Thus, the Gag Rule of the 1830s, which prevented either house of Congress from hearing or discussing antislavery petitions, resulted from "the action of overzealous [northern] fanatics."[66] The Wilmot Proviso, a proposal to exclude slavery from territories ceded by Mexico, was motivated by the pure opportunism of certain northern politicians. During the 1850s, though Southerners showed considerable indifference to affairs in Kansas, a crisis in that territory was brought on by northern agitators. The disastrous Dred Scott decision resulted from the personal ambition of two northern Associate Justices, who forced the majority to consider the subject of congressional power over slavery in the territories. Crazy John Brown's attack on Harpers Ferry did not alarm the South as much as the fact that prominent Northerners made him a hero and a martyr. Finally, when secession came in 1860-61, war resulted not from the action of Southerners but from the refusal of northern Republicans to support a reasonable settlement, such as the Crittenden Compromise. In short, revisionism is something like Rhodes's history of the sectional crisis stood on its head.

Perhaps no military conflict in history has produced more anguished writing about whether it was evitable or inevitable than the American Civil War. The problem, of course, is one that can never be solved conclusively even by the most exhaustive research, because it involves metaphysical questions about free will and psychological questions about the limits of human choice. Yet historians do sometimes indulge in "counterfactual history"—informed speculation about how things would have been if certain other things had or had not happened—and that essentially is the kind of history that revisionists have written. They were interested not only in explaining why the Civil War occurred but in showing how, by a different course of action, it could have been avoided and how much better off the country would have been if its history had been one of continued peace.

The Civil War settled the issues of the sectional conflict at a cost of more than half a million lives. The revisionists' alternative to the war was compromise, delay, patience, and the avoidance of recrimination and confrontation in order to maintain a milieu of political tranquillity in which sectional differences could have been rationally resolved. Their conviction that evolutionary forces would soon have ended slavery peacefully was a basic premise of their case. In his account of the crisis, James Buchanan contended that, "If left to the wise ordinances of a superintending Providence, which never acts rashly, [slavery] would have been gradually extinguished in our country . . . without bloodshed. . . ."[67] Ramsdell, though relying on economic and geographic forces rather than Providence, made this the moral of his argument that slavery had extended to its natural limits. "[Can] we say with conviction," he asked, "that this war accomplished anything of lasting good that could not and would not have been won by the peaceful processes of social evolution? Is there not ground for the tragic conclusion that it accomplished little which was not otherwise attainable?"[68] E. Merton Coulter made the point concisely: "The Civil War was not worth the cost. . . . What good the war produced would have come with time in an orderly way; the bad would not have come at all."[69]

Precisely when slavery's peaceful end would have come no revisionist could say, but most of them guessed that it could have lasted no longer than another generation, or no later than the end of the nineteenth century. In any event, when emancipation came, it would not have cost the life of one soldier for every six slaves freed—a per capita cost that Potter quite understandably found rather staggering. On the other hand, the postponement of emancipation for a generation, while saving the lives of soldiers, would have exacted its own price. It would have meant that the four million slaves of 1860, as well as their descendants, would have remained in bondage until the forces anticipated by the revisionists moved white masters in their own good time to grant freedom to their black laborers. How to balance the lives of half a million soldiers against the prolonged bondage of four million slaves is

a question with profound moral implications; how one re-
solves it will doubtless depend in part on one's judgment of
slavery itself. Clearly, the revisionists believed that the survival of black bondage for another generation would not have
been too high a price for avoiding the bloodshed of the Civil
War. Given their characteristic view of southern slavery,
their resolution of this moral dilemma was logical enough.

In considering the plausibility of the case for a repressible
conflict, one must note that the writings of historians who
advanced it were not always models of measured and temperate discourse.[70] Some revisionists wrote with a passion that
approached the intensity of those antebellum orators whose
verbal excesses they so roundly condemned. More important
than style, however, was a logical inconsistency that lay at
the heart of their argument. Revisionists advanced a highly
deterministic explanation of how slavery would have been
abolished if the Civil War had not occurred. Unalterable conditions and uncontrollable trends—the realities of western soil
and climate, the impact of the laws of supply and demand on
cotton and slave prices, "the processes of social evolution,"
and the resulting realization of rational Southerners that slavery was a burden—would have led inevitably to the ultimate
adaptation of southern agriculture to a free-labor system. Yet,
revisionists rejected the deterministic concept of an irrepressible conflict as an explanation of the Civil War itself. They
discerned no logical, fundamental forces operating to bring
on this great and tragic event, only the unnecessary, irrational
behavior of a blundering generation of politicians and agitators. But if one generation of Northerners could produce a
needless war over issues irrationally perceived, might not another generation of Southerners have defied all the presumably sound reasons for abandoning slavery and preserved it
for irrational—say, for example, racist—reasons? Revisionists,
though apparently assuming that history normally follows a
rational course, by their analysis of the sectional crisis, them-

both beneficiaries and victims of the rapid social changes oc-
curring during their lives.

The necessity to assume the existence of an antebellum
abolitionist movement that would attract quite normal people
arises from the existence then of powerful secular intellectual
trends associated with the eighteenth-century Enlightenment
and nineteenth-century Romanticism, and religious trends
associated with evangelical Protestantism, trends that explain
the crusade against slavery not as a historical aberration but
as a logical and predictable development of Western, including American, culture.[73] In a society notable for its doctri-
naire belief in individual liberty, its plethora of reform movements, and its religious revivals in a millennial context, the
failure of an abolitionist crusade to materialize would have
been a difficult fact for historians to explain. To presuppose
abolitionism in this manner still leaves room for speculation
about why it was stronger in some northern regions than in
others, why it made more of an impact on some Protestant
churches than on others, and why it appealed to some individuals and repelled others.

Abolitionism, of course, was always a movement of a minority, for even in an era of reform most men and women
were absorbed in the problems of their own daily lives and
were either indifferent to reformers or regarded them as disturbing nuisances. Nationalists disliked abolitionists for disre-
garding constitutional restraints and endangering the Union;
practical men of business viewed them as a threat to their rich
southern trade; and conservative clergymen feared them as a
disruptive force in the churches. Above all, the racism that
was nearly universal in nineteenth-century America, by fos-
tering anxieties about the consequences of liberating millions
of black slaves, severely limited the abolitionist appeal. Indeed, as historians have amply demonstrated, the abolitionists
themselves, though far in advance of their contemporaries,

were by no means free of race prejudice.[74] To appreciate the importance of racism as a deterrent to abolitionism one needs merely to consider how much stronger the movement would have been if the South's slave population had been white rather than black.

Revisionists disparaged the abolitionists by observing that their purpose was to disrupt the southern economy and promote radical social change at no cost to themselves or risk to their own society. The point was a telling one, especially when revisionists noted in addition that most abolitionists were indifferent to the problems of northern factory workers. Unfortunately, their criticism described a general characteristic of nearly all reform movements. As British abolitionists crusaded for emancipation at the expense of planters in the distant West Indies, so northern abolitionists crusaded for emancipation at the expense of planters in the South. Reform movements seem always to attract mostly those whose own interests and security are not too deeply involved, not only because they will not bear the cost and the risks but because their judgment and sense of justice are not clouded by self-interest, as those of white Southerners were. Being an abolitionist did in fact entail certain risks, for more than a few activists were victims of violent attack by northern mobs. In any case, abolitionism, with all its defects and limitations, was a normal product and inextricable part of antebellum northern society.

Not only must antislavery be accepted as a given, its characteristic rhetoric, tactics, and goals must also be recognized as quite normal for that age. As Martin Duberman has argued, "the evangelical rhetoric of the movement, with its thunderous emphasis on sin and retribution . . . [was] in its day common enough to abolitionists and nonabolitionists alike."[75] The highly moralistic tone of abolitionist lectures and literature was as characteristic of the British crusade as of the American—in fact, the two movements were very much alike.

Both contemporaries and historians criticized abolitionists more often for their commitment to "immediatism" than for any other alleged shortcoming. Only impractical, irresponsible fools, they charged, would ignore all the social problems of emancipation, the need for a period of gradual transition, and call for slavery's immediate end. But this criticism was an oversimplification of the abolitionist goal and took it out of the context of the times. Immediatism, as abolitionists usually understood the term, was not a naïve program to abolish slavery in a day; rather, it meant that the process of abolishing slavery, a sin, should commence at once, though its completion would probably take some time. It also meant a rejection of the gradualism that would postpone even the commencement of emancipation until some future date.

To this antebellum generation of reformers, familiar with religious revivalism, with the spectacle of mass responses to the sermons of preachers such as Charles G. Finney, and with the miraculous experience of conversion and the instant renunciation of sin, the goal of immediatism did not seem unrealistic. In the early years of their crusade, abolitionists dared hope that their tactic of "moral suasion"—trying to convince slaveholders that slavery was sinful and imperiled their salvation—might, like a great revival, bring masses of slaveholders to an immediate decision to emancipate their slaves. In any case, moral suasion was the only tactic open to them, for the federal government had no power to interfere with slavery in the southern states, and the abolitionists, committed as they were to peaceful methods, did not countenance a slave insurrection. They never addressed their appeals to the slaves themselves, only to white masters, and the danger of slave rebellions if emancipation were not adopted was a persistent theme in their literature.

Thus, it is possible to argue that historians who developed the concept of a repressible conflict and needless war have looked in the wrong place for the abnormality which they believed would explain the antebellum period. The abnormal irritant that created sectional tensions and placed so great a burden on the American political structure was the persistence of southern slavery far into the nineteenth century. The revisionists were also mistaken in holding abolitionists responsible for the failure of Southerners to develop their own program of emancipation. In the states of the Deep South an organized antislavery movement never existed, and individual public expressions of antislavery sentiment were rare even during the Revolutionary generation and almost unheard of thereafter. In the Upper South, in the late eighteenth and early nineteenth century, private emancipations increased and some public men acknowledged the evils of slavery and hoped for its abolition at some future and more propitious time. But even then the number of voluntary emancipations never approached the natural increase of the slave population, and the great majority of Virginia slaveholders defended slavery and resented discussions of the subject in the state legislature.[76]

Though as late as the 1820s a scattering of manumission societies existed in the Upper South, early in the next decade organized antislavery activity virtually ceased, not as a reaction to northern abolitionism but as a result of conditions in the South itself. The manumission movement collapsed because of the growing profitability of slavery, the expanding market for surplus slaves in the new areas of the Southwest, the general belief that whites and free blacks could not live together in peace, the harsh state laws designed to suppress antislavery agitation, and mob violence. The critics never posed a serious threat to slavery in any southern state, and in the end they were unable to point to a single success. In January 1832, after the Nat Turner insurrection, Virginia's emancipationists waged their last battle in the state legislature and went down to overwhelming defeat. At the Tennessee constitutional convention of 1834 the antislavery forces could muster only ten votes. In 1849, Kentucky emancipationists failed to elect a single delegate to a state constitutional convention, and the proslavery forces underscored their victory by inserting a clause protecting slave property in the new constitution's bill of rights.

Northern reformers thus saw all the optimistic predictions of Revolutionary liberals that slavery would soon succumb to the progressive tendencies of an enlightened age end in disappointment, the efforts of southern manumissionists a total failure. Meanwhile, except for Cuba and Brazil, slavery was abolished in the West Indies and Latin America, but in the Model Republic to the north it was spreading through the Southwest and across the Mississippi River into Missouri, Arkansas, and Texas. It could no longer be viewed as a decrepit institution about to die; rather it showed enormous vitality, remarkable flexibility as a labor system, and every prospect of a long life.

One event of the 1820s brought home with special force how deeply embedded slavery had become in the social and economic life of the South. In 1824, the Ohio legislature adopted resolutions proposing a plan of gradual emancipation, colonization of the freed blacks outside the boundaries of the United States, and federal compensation to slaveholders "upon the principle that the evil of slavery is a national one, and that the people and the states of this Union ought mutually to participate in the duties and burthens of removing it." Eight northern states endorsed Ohio's conservative proposals, and Senator Rufus King of New York urged that the proceeds from the sale of public lands be used to defray the cost of the plan. The response of the Upper South was negative, that of the Deep South hostile and threatening. The South Carolina Senate vowed that it would not permit slave property "to be meddled with or tampered with" by outsiders, and Governor George M. Troup of Georgia denounced the "combination of fanatics" who sought to destroy "everything valuable in the Southern country." He urged the legislature "to step forth, and having exhausted the argument, to stand by your arms."

A decade before the northern abolitionist movement began, a citizens' meeting in Charleston had petitioned the legislature to expel all free blacks "that we may extinguish at once every gleam of hope which the slaves may indulge of ever being free." Finally, in 1836, the Mississippi legislature gave its answer to the appeal of the northern moral suasionists. It resolved that the people of the state regarded slavery "not as a curse, but a blessing . . . and that they hope to transmit this institution to their posterity, as the best part of their inheritance. . . . We hold discussion upon this subject as . . . impertinent . . . and we will allow no present change, or hope of future alteration in this matter." Northern abolitionism, then, did not destroy the southern antislavery movement; rather, the failure of that movement and the vitality of slavery, together with the temper of the age, ultimately produced abolitionism. The northern movement would never have developed to wage a campaign against a declining institution which Southerners themselves seemed ready to abandon.

If abolitionism of a moralistic, immediatist type is accepted as a logical and quite inescapable product of antebellum society, and slavery as an exotic aberration, the task of historians who would make a case for a repressible conflict is not to wish away the abolitionists but to explain how an atmosphere favorable to political tranquillity, compromise, and patient delay might have been maintained in spite of the irritant of an antislavery crusade. This would require a rather radical reformulation of the problem as revisionists customarily perceived it, for much of the responsibility for avoiding sectional confrontation would be transferred from the North to the South. In effect, antebellum Southerners asked for the tolerant acceptance of an institution which, however vital it may have been economically, was a moral anachronism in their age, until they found a convenient and safe way to give it up.

They asked a great deal of their generation, and their best hope of avoiding a national crisis—of keeping the conflict repressible—was to defuse the antislavery movement by minimizing its appeal to the northern public, and thus to soften the impact of some quite compelling ideological forces. To consider how this might have been possible involves another exercise in counterfactual history, one premised on the existence of *both* southern slavery and northern antislavery.

The first requirement was that Southerners avoid aggressively proslavery postures which would diminish the traditional expectation that through a natural progression slavery would give way to a free-labor system. The fact that many post-Revolutionary Southerners conceded the evils of slavery and assumed at least a vague antislavery stance encouraged northern reformers to be temperate and patient. However, the gradual change to a less apologetic tone—a change that antedated abolitionism—eventually altered perceptions of the possibility for emancipation without intervention from the outside.

During the eighteenth century some Southerners had defended slavery occasionally on racial and religious grounds; during the Missouri controversy they justified it more vigorously; and during the following decade their defense accelerated until, in 1832, Thomas R. Dew of Virginia published the first book-length treatise upholding slavery as a positive good. As the defense became increasingly sweeping, invoking biblical authority, historical experience, scientific evidence, and racist concepts, southern intellectuals romanticized slavery into an ideal paternal relationship beneficial to both master and slave. Reacting to these changed circumstances, a northern reformer expressed dismay at "the sentiments openly expressed . . . that slavery is not an evil . . . [and] that it is criminal toward the South . . . to indulge even a hope that the chains of the captive may some day or other, no matter how remote the time, be broken." The positive-good hypothesis, an aggressive vindication of slavery about which many Southerners themselves had uneasy feelings, by shocking northern reformers into organized activity, played a major role in undermining sectional peace. It was, in the terminology of revisionism, an irresponsible blunder that needlessly heightened tensions between North and South.

A second basic condition for the preservation of political tranquillity was a southern program to reform the institution of slavery in those aspects where it was most exposed to sensational abolitionist attacks. To this end, and at the cost of compromising somewhat the property rights of slaveholders, southern legislatures should have given legal protection to slave marriages, prohibited the breakup of slave families when estates were sold for debt or divided among heirs, reduced the brutal aspects of the slave trade, given slaves greater protection from violent assault, defined the rape of a slave woman as a crime, given slaves a stronger position in courts of law, regulated more strictly their labor and living conditions, and repealed the laws against teaching them to read and write, thus shifting the emphasis in the legal codes from slaves as property to slaves as persons. Reforms such as these would not have made bondage acceptable to abolitionists, but they would have blunted their attack by depriving them of some of their most effective propaganda weapons. The vulnerable slave woman, exposed to her master's lust, faced with the dissolution of her family at her master's will, required to engage in heavy field labor; the slave coffles driven to the plantations of the Southwest by unfeeling traders; the physical punishment inflicted by some callous masters—these were the materials from which abolitionists constructed their accounts of slavery. By improving the condition of the slave the southern states would not only have reduced the abolitionist appeal but checked the growing sense that without external pressure nothing would ever change.

The most significant reforms in the post-Revolutionary South were the laws defining the deliberate killing of a slave as murder in the same degree as if it were committed on a white person. All the codes recognized the humanity of the slaves and provided some limited regulation of labor and living standards, but the conditions which the abolitionists exploited most frequently remained unchanged. Indeed, the codes became more rigorous in some respects, especially in the control of slave movement and assemblages, and private emancipations were made more difficult by various restrictive acts. In 1860, it was still possible for Senator Charles Sumner, in a typical abolitionist attack, to stress all the old themes in portraying "The Barbarism of Slavery":

> Slavery paints itself . . . in its complete *abrogation of marriage*, recognized as a sacrament by the Church, and as a contract by the civil power wherever civilization prevails. Under the Law of Slavery no such sacrament is respected, and no such contract can exist. The ties formed between slaves are all subject to the selfish interest or more selfish lust of the master, whose license knows no check. Natural affections which have come together are rudely torn asunder: nor is that all. Stripped of every defense, the chastity of a whole race is exposed to violence, while the result is recorded in telltale faces of children, glowing with master's blood, but doomed for their mother's skin to Slavery through descending generations. . . . Surely, Sir, is not Slavery barbarous?

Sumner's description of slavery was hardly fair to the average slaveholder, but he and other abolitionists were able to say with perfect truth that this was what the laws of the southern states tolerated. That southern churches failed to call for state action to meliorate the conditions of bondage, especially to demand legal protection for slave families, is one of the most distressing chapters in the history of American Christianity.

By their timidity the churches, too, shared responsibility for arming the abolitionists and for another major blunder of the antebellum South.

A third essential requirement for avoiding an irrepressible conflict was acceptance of a federal policy of confining slavery to the fifteen states that recognized it at the time of the Mexican War. Nothing alarmed Northerners more than the aggressive demand of southern politicians that the western territories be opened to slavery; nothing lent more credence to the abolitionist charge that a Slave Power conspired to make slavery a national institution. The fact that much of the northern opposition to slavery expansion was less an expression of moral feelings than of race prejudice does not in the least diminish its importance as a political force.[77] Traditionally, historians of the repressible conflict placed the onus on the North for agitating what they thought was an issue without substance; but Daniel E. Somes, a congressman from Maine, shifted the responsibility to those who probably most deserved to bear it. "You say it is a mere abstraction for which we are contending," he told Southerners. "And yet you regard this abstraction of so much importance to you that you say you are willing to dissolve the Union . . . to secure it. If it is an abstraction with us, of course it must be an abstraction with you." For this alleged abstraction, this issue without substance, southern politicians waged a bitter fight against the adoption of the Wilmot Proviso. In 1854 they secured the repeal of the Missouri Compromise before they would permit the passage of legislation to organize the territories of Kansas and Nebraska, thus provoking an unprecedented uprising of the northern people, encouraging the formation of the purely sectional Republican party, and doing severe damage to the conservative national Democratic party.

By the 1850s many southern politicians and editors supported Calhoun's doctrine that the Constitution protected

slavery in all the territories; and in 1857 they rallied behind
the Supreme Court's decision in the Dred Scott case, which
denied that slavery could be barred by either Congress or a
territorial legislature. Subsequently, when Douglas claimed
that, in spite of the Court's decision, the people of a territory
could exclude slavery simply by refusing to protect it, southern politicians proposed a remedy so extravagant as to suggest
not merely irresponsibility but a flight from reality. They demanded that Congress adopt a code protecting slavery in all
the territories and, in 1860, that the Democratic party incorporate their demand in its national platform. The reckless
southern agitation of the slavery expansion issue was a blunder whose consequences included the fragmentation of national political organizations and the destruction beyond re-
pair of the conditions essential to continued sectional peace.

A fourth requirement was that Southerners set an example
of temperate response to antislavery criticism and of open-
mindedness to moderate proposals for eventual manumission.
Instead, southern defenders of slavery sought to prevent discussion altogether; they seemed prepared, if necessary, to
violate the federal Bill of Rights and thus to threaten the
liberties not only of black slaves but of white freemen as well.
Southern laws designed to protect the white community from
slave insurrections were interpreted so broadly as to prevent
all discussion of slavery in the schools and colleges, in the
press, or in public meetings. "The expression of Black Republican opinions in our midst is incompatible with our honor
and safety as a people," wrote a North Carolina editor during
the presidential campaign of 1856. "Let our schools and semi-
naries of learning be scrutinized, and if Black Republicans be
found in them, let them be driven out. That man is neither
a fit nor a safe instructor of our young men, who even in-
clines to . . . Black Republicanism." By constructing an "intellectual blockade," as Clement Eaton called it, proslavery

Southerners gave northern reformers additional reason to despair that slavery would ever be abolished by internal forces alone.[78]

One of the most serious tactical blunders southern politicians ever made was supporting the passage of a Gag Rule to prevent congressional discussion of petitions and memorials relating to slavery. Between 1836 and 1844, while the rule was in effect, the right of petition was seriously compromised, and abolitionists could argue plausibly that the Slave Power would even subvert the Constitution to preserve their evil institution. Rather than reducing agitation, the Gag Rule increased the flood of petitions and enabled abolitionists to present their cause to the country in a manner most favorable to them. Meanwhile, angry southern congressmen made wild threats and uttered indiscreet remarks that provided more grist for the abolitionists' mill.

In addition to encroaching on freedom of speech and the press and the right of petition, Southerners violated the United States mails in order to prevent the circulation of abolitionist literature. In 1835, the American Anti-Slavery Society, as part of its campaign of moral suasion, began to mail abolitionist pamphlets to slaveholders. The pamphlets were never addressed to slaves or designed to incite an insurrection, only to persuade white masters that slavery was a sin. Nevertheless, in July 1835, a mob broke into the Charleston post office, seized packages of the pamphlets, and burned them in the streets. Similar seizures occurred in other southern communities. Mob violence of this kind was hardly calculated to advance the cause of sectional harmony, nor was the response of a southern Postmaster General, Amos Kendall, and a southern President, Andrew Jackson. Though admitting that he had no authority to exclude antislavery literature from the mails, Kendall did not condemn the action taken in Charleston. "We owe an obligation to the laws," he wrote, "but a higher one to the communities in which we live." A postmaster who refused to distribute "inflammatory papers" would "stand justified before country and all mankind." President Jackson, in his annual message to Congress in 1835, erroneously described the antislavery pamphlets as "inflammatory appeals addressed to the passions of the slaves." He placed full responsibility on the "misguided" abolitionists and urged Congress (unsuccessfully) to adopt legislation prohibiting, "under severe penalties, the circulation in the Southern States, through the mail, of incendiary publications intended to instigate the slaves to insurrection."[79]

Matching all the other blunders relating to civil liberties was the southern demand, as a fundamental provision of the Compromise of 1850, for a new fugitive-slave law to replace the old law of 1793. As adopted the law was a tissue of injustices and a standing provocation to the North. It provided for the appointment of federal commissioners in each county to hear cases involving blacks alleged to be fugitives, and it empowered federal marshals to require citizens to assist in their capture. In all hearings the alleged fugitive was denied trial by jury and the right to testify in his own behalf; the commissioner received a fee of $10 if he found the black to be a slave, and $5 if the black was released. During the 1850s, though several sensational slave rescues occurred, the law was effectively and vigorously enforced, not only against recently escaped fugitives but against some who had escaped many years earlier. Northern conservatives promised to respect the law, but it was a disrupting irritant; even those who hated abolitionists and were strongly infected with racism were sometimes moved by accounts of fugitives captured and carried back to slavery. If, in the 1850s, the North experienced a steady growth of hostility to the South and slaveholders, the fugitive-slave law was a significant force in building these negative attitudes.

Having flouted every requirement for the preservation of an atmosphere conducive to compromise and political tranquillity, politicians of the Deep South committed the ultimate blunder of attempting secession after the election of the first Republican President, Abraham Lincoln. Their action was swift and impetuous—all seven states had seceded within less than three months after the election—and they gave Congress no opportunity to consider a compromise plan. As early as December 13, 1860, thirty southern congressmen signed a letter to the southern people declaring, "The argument is exhausted. All hope of relief in the Union . . . is extinguished. . . . We are satisfied the honor, safety and independence of the Southern people require the organization of a Southern Confederacy." Before the end of January nearly all the congressmen from the Deep South had resigned, and northern and border-state moderates had no one with whom to discuss a compromise and the restoration of peace and political tranquillity.

Since only one of the seceding states submitted its ordinance of secession to popular ratification, the debate among historians whether the secession conventions represented the will of the people will doubtless go on indefinitely. Yet, granted that the people might have changed their minds six months or a year later, there is little reason to doubt that secession was the will of a substantial majority at the time the decision was made. The majority for secession was overwhelming in every secession convention, the closest vote being 61-39 in Alabama. Texas was the only state to provide for a popular referendum, and there secession was approved by a plurality of approximately three to one.

Northern and southern conservatives argued in vain that secession was a reckless act, that, so far from giving the South greater security, secession would heighten the dangers it faced and threaten the supreme disaster of defeat in war. They reminded secessionists that Lincoln was not an abolitionist, that he acknowledged slavery to be a local institution over which the federal government had no jurisdiction, and that he recognized his duty to enforce the fugitive-slave law. Secession, they warned, would prevent slaveholders from recovering fugitives, for the federal government would no longer be obligated to assist them; it would strengthen the abolitionists, for love of the Union would cease to be an inhibiting force; and it would deprive the seceding states of all the territories, for none would be open to them. The conservatives insisted that Lincoln's election was not a threat to the South, for as a minority President with less than 40 percent of the popular vote his position would be weak. The new Congress would have an anti-Republican majority; hence the Republican legislative program would be effectively blocked, and Lincoln's appointments would require the approval of a hostile Senate. Finally, the conservatives described the Republicans as internally divided, a loose coalition of discordant elements which might fall apart before the next presidential campaign. How, then, could secession be viewed as anything but the last and greatest blunder of an irrational and irresponsible generation of southern politicians?

Since traditional revisionism and the alternative interpretation suggested here are both attempts at counterfactual history, it is tempting to speculate further about what might have happened to the Republican party during the four years after Lincoln's election if secession and the Civil War had not occurred. Given the embarrassingly weak position in which the election of 1860 had placed it, the party's record of positive achievement could hardly have been impressive. Moreover, it is difficult to imagine what damage Lincoln could have done to the southern slaveholding interest, especially if one accepts the revisionist belief that slavery expansion was an issue without substance. Thus, had the South remained in the Union, Lincoln's presidency could still have afforded it additional time to make a peaceful transition from slavery to a system of free labor. But that was not to be. In the end, Southerners themselves, by their decision to disrupt the

Union, took the decisive step that ended all hope for the compromises, delays, and rational decisions that eventually might have brought the issues of the sectional conflict to a peaceful resolution. Accordingly, the burden of responsibility for the failure of the democratic process falls rather heavily on the politicians of the South.

The alternative case for a repressible conflict presented here has the merit of taking into account some of the fundamental conditions of northern antebellum society that traditional revisionists chose to ignore. But in a different way it, too, is flawed. While accepting northern antislavery tendencies as an inescapable force in sectional relations, it is premised on an assumption that Southerners were exposed to no comparable social pressures—that they were free to choose between the acts they committed, which brought on a profound crisis and Civil War, and a more rational, controlled, and peaceable course. In short, like the old revisionist interpretation, it is one-sided, for it fails to recognize the predicament of the South.

In a slave society, especially one in which racial and cultural differences separated masters and slaves, certain intrinsic stresses existed that added another factor to the antebellum political equation and made southern behavior as understandable and predictable as the rise of abolitionism in the North. These southern stresses, together with the circumstances that produced northern antislavery, make untenable either the revisionist concept or the alternative concept of a repressible conflict. They bring us back to Seward's "irrepressible conflict between opposing and enduring forces," but not to the clash of economic interests seen by Beard, or even to the clash of cultures variously described by, among others, Channing, Nevins, and Genovese. Slavery produced in the South not a unique culture in any primordial sense, but a special set of problems.[80]

population had to be forever on guard—to maintain special patrols, to restrict the movements of slaves, to prohibit them from gathering in large numbers unless whites were present, to give whites despotic power over slaves, and almost never to question a white man for his treatment of a slave. The antebellum South was a land troubled by a nagging dread of slave insurrections; indeed, it is impossible to understand the psychology of white Southerners, or the events of the sectional conflict, without taking this fact into account.

If the fear of slave violence was a constant, at certain times, when a conspiracy was discovered, or more commonly, when rumors of a conspiracy were afloat, the fear bordered on the pathological, if it did not explode into pure hysteria. John Randolph once told his fellow congressmen: "I speak from facts when I say, that the night bell never tolls for fire in Richmond, that the mother does not hug the infant more closely to her bosom. I have been witness to some of the alarms in the capital of Virginia." In 1822, a group of Charlestonians sent a memorial to the state legislature asserting that there was "only [one] principle that can maintain slavery, the 'principle of fear.' . . . We should always act as if we had an enemy in the very bosom of the state, prepared to rise upon and surprise the whites, whenever an opportunity afforded."

These candid statements of the anxieties that were endemic in the antebellum South tell a great deal about the sources of the American sectional conflict. In the name of white supremacy and to protect the South from the horrors of Santo Domingo, as well as to secure the slaveholders' economic interests, the agitation of abolitionists *had* to be suppressed, the Gag Rule enforced, the mails censored, the "intellectual blockade" maintained. These were the inescapable imperatives of southern life as surely as abolitionism was an unavoidable product of intellectual currents in the nineteenth-century North. Without these imperatives John Brown's raid on

Harpers Ferry might have been dismissed as a ridiculous event, at most a minor irritant, and would not have induced the acute slave-conspiracy hysteria that swept the South during the crucial presidential election of 1860.

A significant number of Southerners seemed not to have found the proslavery argument a fully convincing defense of their peculiar institution, and consequently the pressure on them in this tension-ridden society was all the more severe. Many, perhaps most, slaveholders accepted the system because the slaves were black, but great numbers of them were tormented by the accusation that they were parties to a betrayal of the principles embodied in the Declaration of Independence.[83] Those who were troubled by moral uncertainties seldom resolved their problem by surrendering their investments and abandoning a profitable labor system, and certainly their private doubts made them love their abolitionist critics none the more. Rather, they united with those who firmly believed in the morality of slavery in a desperate attempt to escape the threat of abolitionism from without and to minimize the danger of slave rebellion from within. As a last resort they sought both security and tranquillity through independence.

The historians of the repressible conflict thus failed to reconcile their case not only with the essential reality of a northern antislavery movement but with certain inescapable facts of southern slave society. Economic interests, racial beliefs, and fear of slave insurrections impelled Southerners to make demands and take actions that precipitated a series of sectional confrontations culminating in the secession crisis of 1860-61.[84] The Republican party of the 1850s was not an abolitionist party, as most Southerners seemed to think, and slavery in the southern states was never a clear issue in the politics of that decade. But the party was vaguely antislavery; its ranks contained an articulate minority of strong-minded abolitionists; and, for both racist and moral reasons, it was firmly committed to keeping slavery out of the territories. This is what gave substance to the southern perception of the Republican party as a threat to its peculiar institution. The interplay of these proslavery and antislavery forces, not the irresponsible blunders of northern or southern politicians, or economic conflict, or irreconcilable cultural differences, brought on the irrepressible conflict about which Seward spoke.

There still remains the question of the evitability or inevitability of the Civil War itself—a question that will probably continue to be, as it is now, unanswerable. It may well be that the country reached a point sometime in the 1850s when it would have been almost impossible to avoid a violent resolution of the sectional crisis. During that decade, northern antislavery and southern proslavery radicals became increasingly militant and prone to anticipate an ultimate resort to armed conflict; and the point of no return may have been reached in 1857 with the Dred Scott decision, the Kansas crisis, Douglas's break with the Buchanan administration, and the severe economic panic of that year. This, of course, is sheer speculation, for, as Seward would have reminded us, to make a case for an irrepressible conflict is not to prove the inevitability of war. But somehow the war came, and it seems no less tragic because it resulted from conditions and events more substantial than the irresponsible acts of a blundering generation. The irrepressible conflict of antebellum years made the war, if not inevitable, at least an understandable response to its stresses by men and women no more or less wise than we.

VIII

The Southern Road to Appomattox

Some years ago one of America's best political commentators made an observation about the problem of causation in history that every responsible historian would surely endorse:

> I hold a kind of Tolstoyan view of history and believe that it is hardly ever possible to determine the real truth about how we got from here to there. Since I find it extremely difficult to uncover my own motives, I hesitate to deal with those of other people, and I positively despair at the thought of ever being really sure about what has moved whole nations and whole generations of mankind. No explanation of the causes and origins of any war—of any large happening in history—can ever be for me much more than a plausible one, a reasonable hypothesis.[1]

This is a position to which I fully subscribe, and I believe that it is as valid for explanations of why a war was won or lost as for explanations of why a war began.

With this cautionary statement in mind, I am going to suggest one of the conditions, among several, that may help to explain why the South lost the Civil War. I think there is reason to believe that many Southerners—how many I cannot say, but enough to affect the outcome of the war—who outwardly appeared to support the Confederate cause had inward doubts about its validity, and that, in all probability, some, perhaps unconsciously, welcomed its defeat. Like all historical explanations, my hypothesis is not subject to definitive proof; but I think it can be established as circumstantially plausible, because it is a reasonable explanation for a certain amount of empirical evidence.

All interpretations of the defeat of the Confederacy fall into two broad categories: those that stress the South's physical handicaps, and those that stress human failings.[2] Explanations in the first category emphasize the overwhelming preponderance of northern manpower and economic resources. To some historians it is enough to note that the North had four times as many men of military age as the South, ten times as productive an industrial plant, three times as many miles of railroads in operation, and far greater supplies of raw materials. Moreover, the North had a large merchant marine and sufficient naval power to establish an effective blockade of southern ports, whereas the South had virtually no merchant marine and no navy at all. "The prime cause [of Confederate defeat] must have been economic," argued Richard N. Current. "Given the vast superiority of the North in men and materials, in instruments of production, in communication facilities, in business organization and skill—and assuming for the sake of the argument no more than rough equality in statecraft and generalship—the final outcome seems all but inevitable."[3]

And yet, as Current observed, "the victory is not always to the rich," for history provides some striking examples of wealthy nations losing to economically poorer adversaries. "In terms of economic logic," David M. Potter wrote, "it can perhaps be demonstrated that the Confederacy, hopelessly overmatched by almost every measure of strength, was doomed to defeat. But history not only shows that in war the lighter antagonist sometimes defeats the heavier, it also shows that what seems logically certain often fails to happen." Potter believed that for at least the first two years of the war the outcome was in doubt; therefore the analysis of Confederate defeat must "go beyond the *a priori* arguments of economic determinism," for "other countervailing factors" might possibly have offset northern economic superiority.[4] He thus introduced the second category of explanations for Confederate defeat: those that compare and evaluate the behavior of Northerners and Southerners under the stresses of war.[5]

The behavioral factor that Potter had in mind was political leadership. He suggested that superior Confederate leadership might have counterbalanced the North's economic power, but he found instead another area of decisive Confederate weakness. Potter emphasized Abraham Lincoln's brilliant record as a war leader and compared it with the dismal record of Jefferson Davis—a discrepancy "as real and as significant as the inequality in mileage between Union and Confederate railroad systems." Indeed, Potter believed that Lincoln contributed so much to the ultimate Union victory that "if the Union and the Confederacy had exchanged presidents with one another, the Confederacy might have won its independence." Moreover, because the South failed to develop a two-party system, no constructive leadership emerged from the opposition to Davis in Congress or in the state governments. Instead, the "petulant, short-sighted, narrow-gauge, negativistic, vindictive quality of the criticism of Davis made him seem, with all his shortcomings, a better man than most of those who assailed him."[6]

Potter argued the political failure of the Confederacy so convincingly that, for the purposes of my own argument, I need make only one additional point: It was odd that the South, with its long tradition of leadership in political affairs, should have thus given the appearance of political bankruptcy during the four years of the Civil War. Among the politicians who created the Confederate States of America were men of superior talent, and many of them had considerable legislative and administrative experience. One wonders what happened to them. A study of the political history of the Confederacy leaves one with the impression that the South was afflicted with what Roy F. Nichols described as "an undefined and stultifying force of some sort which inhibited effective statesmanship."[7] Political failure does help to explain Confederate defeat, but it also raises some questions that need to be answered.

The theme of political failure has several variations. According to one of them, the widespread and vigorous assertion of the constitutional doctrine of state rights during the war crisis made southern defeat certain. Frank L. Owsley maintained that "if the political system of the South had not broken down under the weight of an impracticable doctrine put into practice in the midst of a revolution, the South might have established its independence." He suggested that on the gravestone of the Confederacy should be carved these words: "Died of State Rights." Owsley provided ample illustrations of the extremes to which some Confederate politicians went in defense of the sovereignty of the states.[8]

Unquestionably, the state-rights doctrinaires helped to paralyze the hands of the Confederate government and thus grievously injured their own cause. But this explanation of Confederate defeat also raises questions, because before the war most southern politicians had not been consistent state-rights doctrinaires. Instead, like Northerners, they had shown a good deal of flexibility in their constitutional theories, and they had been willing to tolerate a relatively vigorous federal government as long as it heeded southern needs. They had not objected to a federally subsidized transcontinental railroad—along a southern route; they had not objected to federal appropriations for internal improvements—if the appropriations were for the improvement of transportation along southern rivers; and they showed no fear of creeping federal tyranny when they demanded effective federal action to recover fugitive slaves or to protect slavery in the territories. Indeed, some southern politicians seemed to show less constitutional flexibility in dealing with a government of their own creation than they had in dealing with the federal government before 1861.

David Donald offered another variation on the theme of Confederate political failure. He argued that the basic weakness of the Confederacy was that "the Southern people insisted upon retaining their democratic liberties in wartime. If they were fighting for freedom, they asked, why should they start abridging it? As soldiers, as critics of the government, and as voters they stuck to their democratic, individualistic rights." In the North civil rights were more severely compromised, the soldier was better disciplined, and regimentation was more readily accepted. Therefore, Donald concluded, "we should write on the tombstone of the Confederacy: 'Died of Democracy.' "⁹

Before the Civil War, needless to say, the South had not been notably more democratic than the North; and at some points Donald seemed to equate democracy with poor organization, political ineptitude, and chaos. But there is truth in his generalization, which raises still another question: Why was it that Northerners, who were every bit as democratic and almost as individualistic as Southerners, by and large were willing to tolerate more regimentation for the sake of their cause than Southerners appeared ready to tolerate for the sake of theirs? The question, of course, is one of degree, for many Northerners also resisted war measures such as conscription and encroachments on civil liberties.

Bell I. Wiley added a final touch to the behavioral approach to Confederate defeat. "Perhaps the most costly of the Confederacy's shortcomings," he suggested, "was the disharmony among its people. A cursory glance at the Confed-

eracy reveals numerous instances of bitter strife. . . . Behind
the battle of bullets waged with the invaders was an enormous
war of words and emotions among Confederates themselves
which began before secession and which eventually became so
intense that it sapped the South's vitality and hastened Northern victory." In a study of Confederate politics, Eric L. Mc-
Kitrick was also struck by the bickering "that seeped in from
everywhere to soften the very will of the Confederacy."[10]

Collectively, all these behavioral problems—the failure of
political leadership, the absurd lengths to which state rights
was carried, the reluctance of Southerners to accept the discipline that war demanded, and the internal conflicts among
the southern people—point to a Confederate weakness that
matched in importance its physical handicaps. This was a
weakness of morale. Assuming rough equality in military
training and similar military traditions, a country with inferior resources and manpower can hope to defeat a more
powerful adversary only if it enjoys decidedly superior
morale in its civilian population. High morale is the product
of passionate dedication to a cause, which creates a willingness
to endure hardships and to subordinate personal interests to
its success. This is what has sometimes enabled small states to
resist successfully the aggression of stronger neighbors, and
nationalist movements to succeed against colonial powers. In
such cases the fires of patriotism, fed by a genuine national
identity, burned fiercely, and the longing for political freedom produced a spirit of self-sacrifice. When the partisans of
a cause have no doubts about its validity, when they view the
consequences of defeat as unbearable, morale is likely to be
extremely high.

Such was not the case in the Confederacy, as numerous historians have observed. The collapse of the Confederacy,
Charles H. Wesley concluded, "was due in part to a lack of
resources, but more directly to the absence of a wholehearted
and sustained resistance, . . . without which no revolution

has been successful."[11] E. Merton Coulter, though admitting physical handicaps, insisted that "the Confederacy never fully utilized the human and material resources it had," because it "never succeeded in developing an *esprit de corps,* either in its civil or military organization." The reason for this, according to Coulter, was that the Confederacy "was not blessed with a 'one for all and all for one' patriotism with which future generations of sentimental romancers were to endow it." Coulter concluded succinctly: "The forces leading to defeat were many but they may be summed up in this one fact: The people did not will hard enough and long enough to win."[12]

The problem of morale to which I am referring here should not be confused with another persistent but separate Confederate problem: that of disloyalty among southern Unionists. Nor should it be confused with the defeatism and demoralization that grew out of military reverses, shortages of civilian supplies, and financial collapse during the closing stages of the war. In the Confederacy, weak morale was not simply the ultimate consequence of war weariness, for the problem was present at its birth. It was the product of uncertainty about the South's identity, of the peculiar circumstances that led to secession and the attempt at independence, and of widespread doubts and apprehensions about the validity of the Confederate cause. The problem was obscured for a time by the semihysteria that swept the Deep South in the months after Lincoln's election. Historically, it has been obscured to some extent by early military successes and by the undoubted courage and tenacity of some of the Confederacy's fighting forces. But the morale of an army often may have little to do with devotion to a cause, and it is not necessarily an accurate gauge of the morale of the civilian population. Among civilians the morale problem was always there and soon began to make itself felt, for the South was ill-equipped for a long war not only physically but spiritually and ideologically as well.

That Confederate morale was not high enough and dedica-

tion to the cause fierce enough to offset its physical handicaps
has sometimes been attributed to the failure of its leaders to
perform their duties as propagandists and morale builders.
Charles W. Ramsdell held the politicians responsible for failing to build an efficient propaganda organization or to portray some compelling issue for which the southern people
would have made great sacrifices.[13] Similarly, Bell I. Wiley
blamed both Jefferson Davis and the Confederate Congress
for not realizing "the necessity of winning the hearts and
minds of the people."[14] To Potter the prime responsibility for
the failure to dramatize the southern cause belonged to Davis.
One of his major shortcomings was his inability to "communi-
cate with the people of the Confederacy. He seemed to think
in abstractions and to speak in platitudes."[15]

   If Davis had a penchant for abstract and platitudinous discourse, most other Confederate politicians and publicists,
when upholding the Confederate cause, seemed to suffer from
the same defect. Yet the South had more than its share of able
speakers and editors, who exploited as best they could the
available issues: the menace of a ruthless northern invader, the
need to defend the constitutional principles of the Founding
Fathers, and the threat to southern civilization posed by
northern abolitionists and their doctrine of racial equality.
Significantly, however, only occasionally did they identify
the Confederacy with slavery. "Our new Government," Vice
President Alexander H. Stephens once boldly proclaimed, "is
founded upon . . . the great truth that the negro is not
equal to the white man; that slavery, subordination to the
superior race, is his natural and moral condition. This, our
new Government, is the first, in the history of the world,
based upon this great physical, philosophical and moral
truth." In his message to the Confederate Congress, April 29,
1861, President Davis declared that "the labor of African
slaves was and is indispensable" to the South's economic development. "With interests of such overwhelming magnitude

imperiled, the people of the Southern States were driven by the conduct of the North to the adoption of some course of action to avert the danger with which they were openly menaced." This rhetoric was hardly inspiring, but more important, to a nineteenth-century audience neither was the cause it supported. Confederate propagandists apparently found the defense of slavery a poor tool with which to build southern morale, and they usually laid stress on other issues.

The reluctance of southern propagandists candidly to identify the Confederacy with slavery helps to explain their sterile rhetoric and their dismal failure; for, in my opinion, slavery was the key factor that gave the antebellum South its distinct identity, and the supposed northern threat to slavery (and the supremacy of the white race) was the basic cause of secession. To understand why southern propagandists failed, one must, in addition to evaluating their skill and techniques, compare the issues at their disposal with those at the disposal of their antagonists. Northern propagandists exploited all the historic traditions associated with the federal Union; reaffirmed America's mission and manifest destiny; proclaimed that democracy and self-government were on trial; above all, especially after the Emancipation Proclamation, identified their cause with the principles of the Declaration of Independence. These were the themes that Lincoln developed in the letters, speeches, and state papers which we remember more than a century later. It is of the utmost significance that no southern leader, even if he had had Lincoln's skill with words, could have claimed for the Confederacy a set of war aims that fired the nineteenth-century imagination as did those described in the Gettysburg Address. One wonders what Lincoln could have done with the issues available to him in the South, what even Jefferson Davis might have done with those that every northern politician had available to him.

When southern propagandists found it expedient, for reasons of domestic policy as well as foreign, to soft-pedal the

could resist the appeal of American nationalism; few found a viable substitute in that most flimsy and ephemeral of dreams: southern nationalism.

This is not to say that the people of the Deep South were dragged out of the Union against their will. In all probability secession had the approval of the overwhelming majority, but most of them were driven to secession not by some mystical southern nationalism but by fear and anger, feeling that secession was not so much a positive good as a painful last resort. Potter's study of the secession movement left him with the impression "that the South did not want a separate destiny so much as it wanted recognition of the merits of southern society and security for the slave system, and that all the cultural ingredients of southern nationalism would have had very little weight if that recognition and that security had been forthcoming."[22] At his inauguration as provisional President, Jefferson Davis spoke of the "sincerity" with which Southerners had "labored to preserve the government of our fathers" and explained that they had turned finally to secession as "a necessity not a choice." A New Orleans editor believed that many left the Union "with feelings akin to those they would experience at witnessing some crushing national calamity." In January 1861, Mrs. Mary Jones of Georgia wrote that "An indescribable sadness weighs down my soul as I think of our once glorious but now dissolved Union! Our children's children—what will constitute their national pride and glory?" Yet, she added, "*We* have no alternative"— hardly a cry of exultation.[23] In fact, nearly all the public celebrations in the seceded states during the dismal winter of 1860-61 had about them a quality of forced gaiety, and much of the flamboyant oratory had a slightly hollow sound. Whatever was to be gained from independence, Southerners knew that some priceless things would inevitably be lost. They could hate the Yankees, but that was not quite the same as hating the Union.

They hated the Yankees for questioning their fidelity to American traditions and for denying them a share of the American dream; and they held the Yankees responsible for driving them out of the Union. As they departed, Southerners announced their determination to cherish more than Northerners the sacred heritage of the Founding Fathers. "They separated from the Union," wrote Hans Kohn, "not because they wished to assert themselves as un-American but because they believed themselves the better Americans, more faithful to the original idea."[24] In the Confederate Constitution, said Alexander H. Stephens, "all the essentials of the old Constitution, which have endeared it to the hearts of the American people, have been preserved and perpetuated." By 1861 it was too late for Southerners to escape this heritage, and rather than seeking to escape it they claimed it as their own. But in doing so they confessed rather pathetically the speciousness of southern nationalism.

This being the case, it may well be that for many Southerners secession was not in fact the ultimate goal. Roy F. Nichols suggested that even among the active secessionists "it may be doubted if all had the same final objective—namely, an independent republic, a confederacy of slave states." Nichols believed that some southern politicians were looking for a device that would enable them to negotiate for a better and stronger position in the old Union and that they thought of secession in these terms. "The real motive and object of many . . . was the creation of the Confederacy as a bargaining agency more effective than a minority group negotiating within the Union. As Thomas R. R. Cobb expressed it, better terms could be secured out of the Union than in it." John Bell of Tennessee described the secession movement as a stratagem to alarm the North, force it to "make such concessions as would be satisfactory and therefore the seceding states would return to the fold of the Union."[25] Robert M. T. Hunter of Virginia hoped that a union of the southern states would be the first step toward a new union of all the states, "with such guarantees of principle and such a new distribution of power as will make it as permanent as any system of government can be."[26] On December 5, 1860, the New Orleans *Bee* reported:

> Moderate men . . . are now forced painfully, reluctantly, with sorrow and anguish, to the conclusion that it is wholly impossible for the South tamely to tolerate the present, or indulge the slightest hope of an improvement in the future. They now see clearly that there are but two alternatives before the South, . . . either a final separation from the section which has oppressed and aggrieved her, or a new compact under which her rights will be amply secured. The one may take place, and still eventually prepare for the other.

Southerners who went out of the Union in anguish hoping for negotiations and peaceful reunion were bitterly disappointed by events. The Union did not negotiate with the Confederacy, and two months after its birth the Confederacy was involved in a war for which it was poorly equipped both physically and morally. Those who had expected reunion through negotiation found themselves trapped in a war they had not anticipated, fighting for an independence they had never sought; and in spite of their indignation at northern "aggression," they may well have turned now unconsciously to reunion through defeat. The game had to be played out, the war had to be fought—and the men who served in the Confederate armies displayed their share of gallantry—but a contestant suffering from a lack of national identity and a serious morale problem, as well as from inferior resources, was involved in a lost cause from the start. Defeat restored to Southerners their traditions, their long-held aspirations, and, as part of the federal Union, the only national identity they ever had. It is instructive to contrast the myth of a special southern national identity with the reality of, say, Polish nationalism, which survived more than a century of occupation, partition, and repression. After Appomattox the myth of southern nationalism died remarkably soon.[27] Commenting on the "swift restoration of American nationalism in the South" after 1865, Potter contended that "the readiness with which the South returned to the Union will defy explanation unless it is recognized that Southern loyalties to the Union were never really obliterated but rather were eclipsed by other loyalties with which, for a time, they conflicted."[28]

Defeat gave white Southerners another reward: a way to rid themselves of the moral burden of slavery. This is the second reason why I think that some of them, once they found themselves locked in combat with the North, failed to give the Confederacy their unqualified and wholehearted support. To suggest as I do that slavery gave the South such identity as it had, caused secession and war, and at the same time gave some Southerners, at least unconsciously, a reason for accepting defeat will, I admit, take some explaining.

Let me begin with what I believe to be a fact, namely, that a large number of white Southerners, however much they tried, could not persuade themselves that slavery was a positive good, defensible on Christian and ethical principles. In spite of their defense of the kind of slavery that existed among them and denial of its abuses, many of them, as their unpublished records eloquently testify, knew that their critics were essentially right. In saying this, I do not think I am judging nineteenth-century men and women by twentieth-century standards, for among the romanticists of the nineteenth century there was no greater moral good than individual liberty. Hence, the dimensions of the South's moral problem cannot be appreciated unless one understands that slavery was, by the South's own values, an abomination. The problem would not have been nearly as serious for many Southerners if abolitionist criticism, strident and abrasive though it often was, had not been a mere echo of their own consciences.[29]

In 1860, Robert M. T. Hunter observed that Southerners "no longer occupy a deprecatory attitude upon the question of negro slavery. . . . Whilst they by no means pretend that slavery is a good condition of things under any circumstances and in all countries, they do maintain that, under the relations that the two [races] stand to each other here, it is best for both that the inferior should be subjected to the superior." Hunter's statement was representative of the form that the southern defense of slavery usually took. Based primarily on race, it did not ordinarily endorse the general principle of slavery, only the principle of *black* slavery.[30] But even this limited defense created moral problems and internal doubts, because all southern churches long ago had recognized the humanity of black people. However inferior in talents they might have been, they were acknowledged to be the sons and daughters of Adam, with immortal souls, equal to whites in the sight of God. How flimsy, then, was the foundation on which the proslavery argument was built! To defend the South's peculiar institution in this limited way and under these compromising circumstances was to leave room for a great deal of moral anxiety and self-doubt.

No analysis of the Old South, wrote Professor Sellers, "that misses the inner turmoil of the ante-bellum Southerner can do justice to the central tragedy of the southern experience. . . . Southerners were at least subconsciously aware of the 'detestable paradox' of 'our every-day sentiments of liberty' while holding beings in slavery." The general misgivings about slavery "burrowed beneath the surface of the southern mind, where they kept gnawing away the shaky foundations on which Southerners sought to rebuld their morale and self-confidence as a slaveholding people."[31] Wilbur J. Cash insisted that the Old South "in its secret heart always carried a pow-

erful and uneasy sense of the essential rightness of the nineteenth century's position on slavery. . . . This Old South, in
short, was a society beset by the specters of defeat, of shame,
of guilt—a society driven by the need to bolster its morale,
to nerve its arm against waxing odds, to justify itself in its
own eyes and in those of the world."[32] In the Calvinist South,
Bell I. Wiley reminded us, "people were acutely aware of
sin and believed strongly that divine displeasure and punishment were normal consequences of wrong-doing." Hence, it
requires no "far-fetched psychology . . . to inspire the idea
that this spiritual turmoil about slavery . . . tended to make
Southerners ill at ease with themselves and more touchy in
their relations one with the other."[33]

To be sure, a basic purpose of the proslavery argument was
to soothe the troubled consciences of slaveholders. This is
evident in the frequency with which they recited the argument to themselves and to each other in diaries and letters.
But it did not seem to be enough. No people secure in their
conviction that slavery was indeed a positive good and unaware of any contradictions between theory and practice
would have quarreled with the outside world so aggressively
and reassured themselves so often as the slaveholders did.
"The problem for the South," William R. Taylor believed,
"was not that it lived by an entirely different set of values
and civic ideals but rather that it was forced either to live
with the values of the nation at large or—as a desperate solution—to invent others, others which had even less relevance
to the Southern situation. . . . More and more it became
difficult for Southerners to live in peace with themselves: to
accept the aspirations and the ideals of the nation and, at the
same time, accept the claims and rationalizations produced by
the South's special pleaders. Almost invariably they found
themselves confronted with contradictions of the most
troubling and disquieting kind."[34]

I do not mean to suggest that every slaveholder was guilt-ridden because of slavery. The private papers of many of them give no sign of such a moral crisis—only a nagging fear of slave insurrections and bitter resentment at outside meddling in the South's affairs. Countless slaveholders, in spite of the position of the churches on the Negro's humanity, looked upon him as subhuman, or at least so far inferior to whites as to be suited only for bondage, and some showed little sensitivity to the ugly aspects of slavery. On the other hand, many slaveholders were more or less tormented by the dilemma they were in. They could not, of their own volition, give up the advantages of slavery—a profitable labor system in which they had a $2 billion capital investment. They dreaded the adjustments they would have to make if they were to live in the same region with four million free Negroes, for their racial attitudes were much like those of other white Americans, North and South. Yet they knew that slavery betrayed the American tradition of individual liberty and natural rights and that the attack on it was in the main valid.

In their extremity sensitive Southerners joined their less sensitive neighbors in angry attacks on their tormentors, until, finally, driven by their inner tensions, they were ready to seek an escape from their problems by breaking up the Union, or at least by threatening to do so. Sellers argued persuasively that this moral crisis eventually converted Southerners into an "aggressive slavocracy." "The almost pathological violence of their reaction to northern criticism indicated that their misgivings about their moral position on slavery had become literally intolerable under the mounting abolitionist attack." Slavery was doomed, Sellers concluded, but Southerners were so caught in its contradictions "that they could neither deal with it rationally nor longer endure the tensions and anxieties it generated. Under these circumstances the Civil War or something very like it was unavoidable."[35]

Indeed, I believe that under these circumstances not only the Civil War but the outcome as we know it was, if not un-

avoidable, at least highly likely. Southerners, many of whom
were unsure of their goals and tormented by guilt about slavery, having founded a nation upon nothing more substantial
than anger and fear, were in no position to overcome the
North's physical advantages. Moveover, at least some of them
must have been troubled, at some conscious or unconscious
level, by the question of what precisely was to be gained
from winning the war—whether more in fact might be gained
from losing it. For it soon became evident that, in addition to
restoring the South to the Union, defeat would spell the doom
of slavery. Thus President Lincoln and the Union Congress
would do for the slaveholders what even the more sensitive
among them seemed unable to do for themselves—resolve once
and for all the conflict between their deeply held values and
their peculiar and archaic institution. "The Southern Confederacy was bound to fall," William P. Trent argued long ago,
"because it was founded, precisely as Alexander H. Stephens
had claimed, upon slavery as its cornerstone."[36]

What circumstantial evidence is there to suggest that
Southerners lost the Civil War in part because a significant
number of them unconsciously felt that they had less to gain
by winning than by losing? There is, first of all, the poor performance of some of the South's talented and experienced political leaders; the aggressive assertion of state rights even
though it was a sure road to defeat; and the internal bickering
and lack of individual commitment that would have made
possible the discipline essential to victory. Thomas B. Alexander and Richard E. Beringer, in their study of the Confederate Congress, found little evidence of passionate dedication to the southern cause; from the uninspiring record and
"helter-skelter operations" of that Congress they concluded
that, "in 1861, a country was created on paper before it was
a reality in the hearts of a sufficient number of its would-be
citizens."[37]

Equally significant was the behavior of Confederate civilians in areas occupied by Union military forces. One must be cautious in the use of historical analogies, but it is worth recalling the problems that plagued the German Nazis in the countries they occupied during the Second World War. Everywhere they met resistance from an organized underground that supplied information to Germany's enemies, committed acts of sabotage, and made life precarious for collaborators and German military personnel. At the same time, bands of partisans gathered in remote places to continue the war against the Nazis. The French had a similar experience in Algeria after the Second World War. The Algerian nationalists struggled with fanatical devotion to their cause; every village was a center of resistance, and no Frenchman was safe away from the protection of the French army. The country simply could not be pacified, and France, in spite of its great physical superiority, had to withdraw.

In the Confederate South, apart from border-state bushwhacking, there was only one example of underground resistance even remotely comparable to that demonstrated in Nazi-occupied Europe or French-occupied Algeria. This example was provided not by southern nationalists but by East Tennessee Unionists against the Confederacy itself. The counties of East Tennessee had been strongly opposed to secession, and so great was the disaffection that by the fall of 1861 some 11,000 Confederate infantry, cavalry, and artillery had occupied them. In response some 2000 Union partisans fled to Kentucky to begin training as an army of liberation, while others drilled in mountain fastnesses in preparation for the arrival of federal forces. Still other East Tennesseans organized an underground and engaged in such activities as cutting telegraph wires and burning bridges. The most strenuous Confederate efforts at pacification failed to suppress these dedicated Unionists, and East Tennessee remained a cancer in the vitals of the Confederacy.[38]

Nowhere in the South was there impressive resistance to

the federal occupation, even making allowance for the fact that most able-bodied men of military age were serving in the Confederate armies. In 1862 Middle Tennessee, West Tennessee, part of northern Mississippi, and New Orleans fell under federal military occupation, but no significant underground developed. In 1864 General Sherman marched through Georgia and maintained long lines of communication without the semblance of a partisan resistance to trouble him. In commenting on this remarkable phenomenon, Governor Zebulon Vance of North Carolina wrote: "With a base line of communication of 500 miles in Sherman's rear, through our own country, not a bridge has been burnt, a car thrown from its track, nor a man shot by our people whose country has been desolated! They seem everywhere to submit. . . . It shows what I have always believed, that the great *popular heart* is not now and never has been in this war!" The absence of civilian resistance was quite as remarkable when, early in 1865, Sherman's army turned northward from Savannah into South Carolina. In the spring, when the Confederate armies surrendered, there were no partisans to take refuge in the mountains for a last desperate defense of southern nationalism. The Confederate States of America expired quietly, and throughout the South most people were reconciled to its death with relative ease. Though Edmund Ruffin preferred death to surrender, soon after Appomattox his fellow-Virginians, George Fitzhugh and Edward A. Pollard, both ardent champions of the cause of southern cultural nationalism, had become equally ardent American patriots. We hear much of unreconstructed southern rebels, but the number of them was not very large; the great majority of Southerners made haste to swear allegiance to the Union. Even the postwar cult of the Lost Cause was always more of a literary than an action group, and the Cause was one to be cherished within the safe confines of the restored Union.

Finally, and to me most significant of all, was the readiness, if not always good grace, with which most Southerners accepted the abolition of slavery—a readiness that I do not think is explained entirely by the circumstances of defeat. Probably historians have given too much emphasis to the cases of recalcitrance on this matter in the months after Appomattox, when, actually, slavery collapsed with remarkably little resistance. Just a few years earlier it had been impossible publicly to oppose slavery in all but the border slave states, and southern politicians and publicists had aggressively asserted that black slavery was a positive good. Yet, soon after the Confederate surrender no Southerner except an occasional eccentric would publicly affirm the validity of the proslavery argument. Indeed, I believe that as early as the spring of 1866, if Southerners had been permitted to vote for or against the re-establishment of slavery, not one southern state would have mustered a favorable majority.

In 1862, while the war was still in progress, Herschel V. Johnson of Georgia expressed his belief that the days of slavery were numbered. "The first gun at Sumter tolled its funeral dirge. I have a sort of undefined notion that God . . . is permitting us by our own folly to work out the emancipation of our slaves." Two years later Fred A. Porcher of South Carolina asked privately: "Are we not fighting against the moral sense of the world? Can we hope to succeed in such a struggle?" Only two weeks after Appomattox, when a group of South Carolina aristocrats looked to the years ahead, though one of them could see only "poverty, no future, no hope," another found solace in the fact that at least there would be "no slaves, thank God!" In July another South Carolinian said more crudely: "It's a great relief to get rid of the horrid negroes." "Always I felt the moral guilt of it," recalled a Louisiana woman, "felt how impossible it must be for an owner of slaves to win his way into Heaven."[39]

Very soon, as a matter of fact, white Southerners were publicly expressing their satisfaction that the institution had

been abolished and asserting that the whites, though perhaps
not the blacks, were better off without it. Many were ready
now to give voice to the private doubts they had felt before
the war. They denied that slavery had anything to do with
the Confederate cause, thus decontaminating it and turning
it into something they could cherish. After Appomattox, Jefferson Davis claimed that slavery "was in no wise the cause of
the conflict," and Alexander H. Stephens argued that the war
"was not a contest between the advocates or opponents of
that Peculiar Institution." The speed with which white Southerners dissociated themselves from the cause of slavery is
striking evidence of how great a burden it had been to them.

The acceptance of emancipation, of course, did not commit Southerners to a policy of racial equality. Rather, they
assumed that the free Negroes would be an inferior caste, exposed to legal discrimination, denied political rights, and subjected to social segregation. They had every reason to assume
this, because these, by and large, were the policies of most of
the northern states toward their free Negro populations, and
because the racial attitudes of the great majority of Northerners were not much different from their own. White Southerners were understandably shocked, therefore, when Radical
Republicans, during the Reconstruction years, tried to impose
a different relationship between the races in the South—to
give Negroes legal equality, political rights, and, here and
there, even social equality. At that point Pollard suddenly discovered that the basic issue of the Civil War had not been
slavery but white supremacy.[40] Now for the first time white
Southerners organized a powerful partisan movement and
resisted Republican race policy more fiercely than the civilian
population had ever resisted the invading Union armies during the war. The difference, I think, was that in rejecting
innovations in race relations they felt surer of their moral
position, for they were convinced that Northerners were per-
petrating an outrage that Northerners themselves would not

have endured. As a result, the morale problem shifted to the other side; and the North, in spite of its great physical power, lacked the will to prevail. Unlike slavery, racial discrimination did not disturb many nineteenth-century white Americans, North or South. Accordingly, in a relatively short time, chiefly because of the unrelenting opposition of white Southerners, Radical Reconstruction collapsed.

The outcome of Reconstruction is significant: it shows what a people can do against overwhelming odds when their morale is high, when they believe in their cause, and when they are convinced that defeat means catastrophe. Historian Lawrence H. Gipson once asked: "How differently would the south have been answered in its appeal for help had the northern radicals . . . been able in 1860 to carry a constitutional amendment providing not only for the freedom of the slaves but also for their enfranchisement? Would not every man in the south have sprung to arms determined to fight to the bitter end? . . . Would there not have been created within the new government a degree of zeal that would have made the south literally unconquerable? But there was no such issue."[41] The fatal weakness of the Confederacy was that not enough of its people really thought that defeat would be a catastrophe; and, moreover, I believe that many of them unconsciously felt that the fruits of defeat would be less bitter than those of success.

Notes

I The Concept of a Perpetual Union

1. In addition to the numerous special studies of these constitutional crises, the evolution of the state-rights and secessionist arguments can be traced in Jesse T. Carpenter, *The South as a Conscious Minority, 1789-1861: A Study in Political Thought* (New York, 1930).

2. For background see Paul C. Nagel, *One Nation Indivisible: The Union in American Thought, 1776-1861* (New York, 1964), and Alpheus Thomas Mason, "The Nature of Our Federal Union Reconsidered," *Political Science Quarterly*, LXV (December 1950), pp. 502-21.

3. *Texas v. White*, 7 Wall. 700 (1869) at pp. 724-25.

4. Roy P. Basler, ed., *The Collected Works of Abraham Lincoln* (8 vols.: New Brunswick, N.J., 1953), IV, p. 265. Lincoln's historical case for a perpetual Union is amplified and affirmed in Curtis P. Nettels, "The Origin of the Union of the States," *Proceedings of the Massachusetts Historical Society*, LXII (1963), pp. 68-83.

5. Frank Moore, ed., *The Rebellion Record: A Diary of American Events* (12 vols.: New York, 1861-1868), I, pp. 3-4. For the secessionist argument see David M. Potter, *The Impending Crisis, 1848-1861* (New York, 1976), pp. 479-83.

6. One might argue that for a time in 1788 two Unions existed. The

first nine states to ratify formed a new Union, while the other four (New York, Virginia, North Carolina, and Rhode Island) remained in the old Union under the Articles of Confederation.

7. Jacob E. Cooke, ed., *The Federalist* (Cleveland, 1961), p. 298. Italics added.

8. Max Farrand, ed., *The Records of the Federal Convention of 1787* (4 vols.: New Haven, 1937), II, p. 561.

9. Jonathan Elliot, ed., *The Debates in the Several State Conventions on the Adoption of the Federal Constitution* (5 vols.: Philadelphia, 1861), IV, p. 203.

10. Merrill Jensen, ed., *The Documentary History of the Ratification of the Constitution* (2 vols.: Madison, Wis., 1976-), II, p. 394.

11. *Ibid.*, p. 86.

12. *Ibid.*, p. 89.

13. Farrand, *Records of the Federal Convention of 1787*, I, pp. 314-15.

14. Elliot, *Debates in the Several State Conventions*, IV, p. 308.

15. *Ibid.*, p. 230.

16. John Jay, "An Address to the People of the State of New-York on the Subject of the Constitution, Agreed upon at Philadelphia," in Paul Leicester Ford, ed., *Pamphlets on the Constitution of the United States, Published During Its Discussion by the People, 1787-1788* (Brooklyn, 1888), p. 83.

17. Farrand, *Records of the Federal Convention of 1787*, I, p. 335.

18. *Ibid.*, II, pp. 134-36; Charles C. Tansill, ed., *Documents Illustrative of the Formation of the Union of the American States* (Washington, 1927), pp. 964-66; Max Farrand, *The Framing of the Constitution of the United States* (New Haven, 1913), pp. 71-72, 127-28; [Andrew C. McLaughlin] "Sketch of Pinckney's Plan for a Constitution, 1787," *American Historical Review*, IX (July 1904), pp. 735-47.

19. Basler, *Collected Works of Abraham Lincoln*, IV, p. 265.

20. *Texas v. White*, 7 Wall. 700 (1869), at p. 725.

21. Samuel Eliot Morison, *The Life and Letters of Harrison Gray Otis: Federalist 1765-1848* (2 vols.: Boston, 1913), II, p. 188.

22. *New Orleans Bee*, January 22, 1861, quoted in Dwight L. Dumond, ed., *Southern Editorials on Secession* (New York, 1931), p. 410.

23. Alpheus Thomas Mason, *The States Rights Debate: Antifederalism and the Constitution* (Englewood Cliffs, N.J., 1964), p. 46.

24. Farrand, *Framing of the Constitution*, pp. 190-91.

25. Mason, *States Rights Debate*, p. 55. See also Alpheus Thomas Mason and Richard H. Leach, *In Quest of Freedom: American Political Thought and Practice* (Englewood Cliffs, N.J., 1959), pp. 110-14. Other constitutional historians who stress the ambiguity of the document include Homer Carey Hockett, *The Constitutional History of the United States* (2 vols.: New York, 1939), I, pp. 260-62, II, pp. 255-56; and Alfred H. Kelly and Winfred A. Harbison, *The American Constitution: Its Origins and Development* (New York, 1963), pp. 143-46, 212-13. "In summary," Kelly and Harbison conclude, "it is clear that the Convention did not make a decisive disposition of the locus of sovereignty in the new union." *Ibid.*, p. 143. For the more common view that the Constitution clearly establishes a perpetual union, see Edward S. Corwin, "National Power and State Interposition, 1787-1861," *Michigan Law Review*, X (May 1912), pp. 535-51; Andrew C. McLaughlin, *A Constitutional History of the United States* (New York, 1935), pp. 214-19, 438-39; Bernard Schwartz, *A Commentary on the Constitution of the United States: The Powers of Government* (New York, 1963), pp. 30-37; Edward Dumbauld, *The Constitution of the United States* (Norman, Okla., 1964), pp. 59-60; and Clinton Rossiter, *1787: The Grand Convention* (New York, 1966). According to Rossiter, "The Constitution . . . put the stamp of irrevocable legitimacy on the three great legacies of 1776: independence, republicanism, and union. From these three commitments there could now be no turning back . . ." *Ibid.*, pp. 261-62. Historically, of course, this statement is accurate, but I am unable to find such clarity in either the Constitution or the debates over ratification.

26. Basler, *Collected Works of Abraham Lincoln*, IV, pp. 264-65. Italics added.

27. *Letters and Other Writings of James Madison* (4 vols.: Philadelphia, 1867), I, p. 344.

28. Farrand, *Records of the Federal Convention of 1787*, I, pp. 122-23.

29. *Ibid.*, p. 467.

30. *Ibid.*, p. 136.

31. *Ibid.*, p. 165, II, p. 388.

32. *Ibid.*, I, p. 54. James Madison explained that his purpose in urging federal control of state militias and federal power to veto acts of state legislatures was to avoid the necessity of military coercion of a state. But after the Constitution failed to grant these powers, Madison's warning remained on the record: that the

alternative, coercion, might cause a state to dissolve its connection with the Union.

33. *Ibid.*, p. 596.
34. *Ibid.*, II, p. 221.
35. *Ibid.*, IV, p. 71.
36. *Ibid.*, II, p. 88.
37. Alpheus Thomas Mason, "The Federalist—A Split Personality," *American Historical Review*, LVII (April 1952), p. 627. See also Mason, "The Nature of Our Federal Union Reconsidered," pp. 502-21.
38. Cooke, *Federalist*, p. 12.
39. Elliot, *Debates in the Several State Conventions*. II, p. 35. See also *ibid.*, IV, pp. 59-60.
40. *Ibid.*, IV, p. 301.
41. *Ibid.*, pp. 187-88.
42. Ford, *Pamphlets on the Constitution*, p. 205.
43. Tansill, *Documents Illustrative of the Formation of the Union*, pp. 1009-59, 1018, 1027. The North Carolina convention proposed an additional amendment: "That Congress shall not declare any state to be in rebellion without the consent of at least two-thirds of all the members present of both houses." *Ibid.*, p. 1049.
44. Jensen, *Documentary History of the Ratification*, II, pp. 383, 478.
45. Harold C. Syrett and Jacob E. Cooke, eds., *The Papers of Alexander Hamilton* (24 vols.: New York, 1961-), V, pp. 147, 184-85. In his reply Madison added: "This idea of reserving [the] right to withdraw was started at Richmond, and considered as a conditional ratification which was itself considered as worse than a rejection." See also Irving Brant, *James Madison, Father of the Constitution, 1787-1800* (Indianapolis, 1950), pp. 225-27, 229-30.
46. Cooke, *Federalist*, pp. 254, 313. Mason stresses this aspect of Madison's contributions but, in my opinion, places too much responsibility on him alone for the ambiguity of *The Federalist*. Mason, "The Nature of Our Federal Union Reconsidered," pp. 512-19.
47. Elliot, *Debates in the Several State Conventions*, III, p. 94.
48. Tansill, *Documents Illustrative of the Formation of the Union*, pp. 979-88; Farrand, *Records of the Federal Convention of 1787*, I, p. 328.
49. Syrett and Cooke, *Papers of Alexander Hamilton*, IV, pp. 276-77.
50. Cooke, *Federalist*, pp. 73, 103.

51. *Ibid.*, p. 205. Thus, observes Mason, "Hamilton undercut the basis of [John] Marshall's jurisprudence" and enabled John Taylor to assert that the principles of state sovereignty "are forcibly sustained" in *The Federalist.* Mason, *States Rights Debate,* p. 196. At the New York ratifying convention, Hamilton apparently did read Madison's letter against conditional ratification, but without identifying the author. Syrett and Cooke, *Papers of Alexander Hamilton,* V, p. 193.

52. Cooke, *Federalist,* pp. 179-80.

53. Jensen, *Documentary History of the Ratification,* II, p. 376.

54. Paul Leicester Ford, ed., *Essays on the Constitution of the United States, Published during Its Discussion by the People, 1787-1788* (New York, 1892), p. 376.

55. John Bach McMaster and Frederick D. Stone, eds., *Pennsylvania and the Federal Constitution, 1787-1788* (Lancaster, Pa., 1888), p. 593.

56. Edward S. Corwin, *Court Over Constitution: A Study of Judicial Review as an Instrument of Popular Government* (Princeton, 1938), p. 247.

57. Ford, *Pamphlets on the Constitution,* p. 282. See also James C. Ballagh, ed., *The Letters of Richard Henry Lee* (3 vols.: New York, 1914), II, p. 472.

58. Jensen, *Documentary History of the Ratification,* II, p. 393.

59. McMaster and Stone, *Pennsylvania and the Federal Constitution,* p. 269.

60. Elliot, *Debates in the Several State Conventions,* I, p. 382.

61. Nagel, *One Nation Indivisible,* pp. 13-31, provides a good analysis of the concept of the Union as an experiment. The quote from John Randolph is on page 19.

62. Ford, *Pamphlets on the Constitution,* p. 269; Ballagh, *Letters of Richard Henry Lee,* II, p. 463.

63. William T. Hutchinson, "Unite to Divide; Divide to Unite: The Shaping of American Federalism," *Mississippi Valley Historical Review,* XLVI (June 1959), pp. 6-7.

64. Paul Leicester Ford, ed., *The Writings of Thomas Jefferson* (10 vols.: New York, 1892-1899), VI, p. 492; Syrett and Cooke, *Papers of Alexander Hamilton,* XII, p. 254.

65. Boston *Independent Chronicle and the Universal Advertiser,* August 20-23, 1798.

66. W. W. Henning, ed., *Statutes at Large of Virginia* (Philadelphia, 1823), XIII, pp. 237-38.

67. Syrett and Cooke, *Papers of Alexander Hamilton*, VII, p. 149.
68. James D. Richardson, ed., *A Compilation of the Messages and Papers of the Presidents* (10 vols.: Washington, 1899), I, pp. 213-24.
69. Elliot, *Debates in the Several State Conventions*, IV, pp. 537, 539; Frank Maloy Anderson, "Contemporary Opinion of the Virginia and Kentucky Resolutions," *American Historical Review*, V (October, December, 1899), pp. 45-63, 225-52.
70. [Henry Lee] *Plain Truth: Addressed to the People of Virginia* (Richmond, 1799), pp. 13, 22, 19-20.
71. Washington *National Intelligencer*, July 18, 1812.
72. Quoted in Nagel, *One Nation Indivisible*, p. 19.
73. Merrill D. Peterson, *Thomas Jefferson and the New Nation: A Biography* (New York, 1970), pp. 610, 623-24, 772, 1003.
74. Worthington C. Ford, ed., *Writings of John Quincy Adams* (7 vols.: New York, 1913), II, pp. 525-26.
75. Quoted in Albert J. Beveridge, *The Life of John Marshall* (4 vols.: Boston, 1919), IV, p. 145n. For a similar view see the letter of "Publius" in Richmond *Enquirer*, April 26, 1815.
76. Washington *National Intelligencer*, August 4, 1813.
77. *Ibid.*, April 28, 1814 (letter of "Hortensius"), December 2, 1814 (letter of "Aurora").
78. Richmond *Enquirer*, July 3, November 27, 1812; August 27, 1813; January 22, 1814.
79. *Ibid.*, November 1, 1814.
80. "Permanency of the American Union. Being Part of an Essay Delivered Before the Literary and Philosophical Society of Charleston in 1815," *Niles' Weekly Register*, XII (June 7, 1817), pp. 228-30.
81. *Annals of Congress*, 16 Cong., 1 Sess., p. 1106 (February 4, 1820); Lexington *Kentucky Reporter*, March 22, 1820.
82. *Annals of Congress* 16 Cong., 1 Sess., p. 209 (January 20, 1820); Charles Francis Adams, ed., *Memoirs of John Quincy Adams, Comprising Portions of His Diary from 1795 to 1848* (12 vols.: Philadelphia, 1874-1876), V, p. 12.
83. *Ibid.*, IV, pp. 525-26.
84. *Annals of Congress*, 16 Cong., 1 Sess., pp. 1294-98 (February 14, 1820).
85. *Ibid.*, p. 1436 (February 21, 1820).
86. As early as 1793, the Court under Chief Justice John Jay, in the case of *Chisholm* v. *Georgia*, traced the Union back to the Dec-

laration of Independence and affirmed that as to the purposes of the Union, the states are not sovereign. *Chisholm* v. *Georgia,* 2 Dallas 419 (1793).

87. *Fletcher* v. *Peck,* 6 Cranch 87 (1810) at p. 136.

88. *McCulloch* v. *Maryland,* 4 Wheaton 316 (1819) at p. 405.

89. *Gibbons* v. *Ogden,* 9 Wheaton 1 (1824) at p. 187.

90. *Cohens* v. *Virginia,* 6 Wheaton 264 (1821) at pp. 413-14, 389.

91. For the gradual evolution of the idea of the Union as an absolute good, see Nagel, *One Nation Indivisible,* pp. 104-44.

92. *Works of Daniel Webster* (6 vols.: Boston, 1851), III, pp. 248-347, 358.

93. *Register of Debates in Congress,* 21 Cong., 1 Sess., pp. 266, 270 (March 15, 1830).

94. John Quincy Adams, *An Oration to the Citizens of the Town of Quincy, on the Fourth of July, 1831* (Boston, 1831), pp. 7, 17-18, 35-36.

95. Joseph Story, *Commentaries on the Constitution of the United States* (2 vols.: Boston, 1833), I, pp. 146-270.

96. Gaillard P. Hunt, ed., *The Writings of James Madison* (9 vols.: New York, 1900-1910), IX, p. 471. The letter cited is one of Madison's most elaborate defenses against charges of inconsistency. For an account of Madison's role during the nullification crisis, see Irving Brant, *James Madison, Commander in Chief, 1812-1836* (Indianapolis, 1961), pp. 468-500.

97. Hunt, *Writings of James Madison,* IX, p. 587. Brant believes that Madison did not intend to justify nullification, but he is unsure what Madison did have in mind and admits that he "used language whose gravity suggested such power . . ." Brant, *James Madison, Father of the Constitution,* p. 463.

98. *Letters and Other Writings of James Madison,* IV, p. 293.

99. Hunt, *Writings of James Madison,* IX, p. 472.

100. *Ibid.,* pp. 383-403. This letter was published in the *North American Review,* XXXI (October 1830), pp. 537-46. See also Hunt, *Writings of James Madison,* IX, pp. 573-607.

101. Richardson, *Messages and Papers of the Presidents,* II, pp. 640-56. Quotations on pp. 648-50, 654-56. The proclamation was not notable for its originality, because the ideas in it had been stated by others, including Edward Livingston, during the nullification crisis. As early as 1824, Livingston had advanced nationalist arguments in support of federal aid for internal improvements, but he offered no argument for a perpetual union until his speech

in the Senate in 1830, cited above. See William B. Hatcher, *Edward Livingston: Jeffersonian Republican and Jacksonian Democrat* (Baton Rouge, 1940), pp. 305-06, 348-51, 382-86.

102. Calvin Colton, ed., *The Private Correspondence of Henry Clay* (Cincinnati, 1856), p. 313.

II *Rebels and Sambos: The Search for the Negro's Personality in Slavery*

1. Robert S. Starobin, *Blacks in Bondage: Letters of American Slaves* (New York, 1974).

2. John W. Blassingame, *Slave Testimony: Two Centuries of Letters, Speeches, Interviews, and Autobiographies* (Baton Rouge, 1977), is a valuable collection, but it hardly suggests that the sources are abundant.

3. Lawrence W. Levine, in *Black Culture and Black Consciousness* (New York, 1977), Chapters 1-2, explored the slave's culture and mind, cautiously but imaginatively, through slave songs and folklore.

4. The narratives were published in George P. Rawick, ed., *The American Slave: A Composite Autobiography* (19 vols.: Westport, Conn., 1972). See also Norman R. Yetman, "The Background of the Slave Narrative Collection," *American Quarterly*, XIX (Fall 1967), pp. 534-53, and Paul D. Escott, *Slavery Remembered* (Chapel Hill, 1979).

5. John W. Blassingame, in "Using the Testimony of Ex-Slaves: Approaches and Problems," *Journal of Southern History*, XLI (November 1975), pp. 473-92, made some acute observations on the limitations of the slave narratives, which he did not use in his book, *The Slave Community* (New York, 1972). He was decidedly less acute in his critique of the autobiographies, which he did use. For a critical comparison of the narratives and autobiographies see David Bailey, "A Divided Prism: Two Sources of Black Testimony on Slavery," *Journal of Southern History*, XLVI (August 1980).

6. This evidence has been exploited for various purposes by Vernon Lane Wharton, *The Negro in Mississippi, 1865-1890* (Chapel Hill, 1947); Benjamin Quarles, *The Negro in the Civil War* (Boston, 1953); Willie Lee Rose, *Rehearsal for Reconstruction* (Indianapolis, 1964); Joel R. Williamson, *After Slavery: The Negro in South Carolina during Reconstruction, 1861-1877* (Chapel Hill,

1965); Eugene D. Genovese, *Roll, Jordan, Roll: The World the Slaves Made* (New York, 1974); Herbert G. Gutman, *The Black Family in Slavery and Freedom, 1750-1925* (New York, 1976); and, unusually effectively, by Leon F. Litwack, *Been in the Storm So Long: The Aftermath of Slavery* (New York, 1979).

7. For an excellent example of the kind of precise information regarding slave behavior available in white sources, see Charles B. Dew, "Disciplining Slave Ironworkers in the Antebellum South: Coercion, Conciliation, and Accommodation," *American Historical Review*, LXXIX (April 1974), pp. 398-418.

8. Herbert Aptheker, *American Negro Slave Revolts* (New York, 1943).

9. Stanley M. Elkins, *Slavery: A Problem in American Institutional and Intellectual Life* (2d ed., Chicago, 1968), Chapter 3.

10. Aptheker, *Slave Revolts*, p. 374.

11. Elkins, *Slavery*, p. 82.

12. Aptheker, *Slave Revolts*, p. 162.

13. *Ibid.*, pp. 325-36.

14. Elkins, *Slavery*, pp. 84-86, 88-89.

15. *Ibid.*, pp. 81-82, 84, 134-37.

16. *Ibid.*, pp. 130, 242.

17. Sullivan defined personality as "the relatively enduring pattern of recurrent interpersonal situations which characterize a human life." *The Interpersonal Theory of Psychiatry* (New York, 1953), p. 111. Similarly, but somewhat more clearly, Mordechai Rotenberg and Theodore R. Sarbin wrote: "The self arises out of the actor's interbehaving with significant others, and their evaluations of his role behavior form or modify the self." "Impact of Differentially Significant Others on Role Involvement: An Experiment with Prison Social Types," *Journal of Abnormal Psychology*, LXXVII (April 1971), p. 97.

18. "A role is a cluster of traits (or pattern of behavior) which serves as the culturally normal or modal solution to recurrent, usually social problems peculiar to a particular status or position in society." David C. McClelland, *Personality* (New York, 1951), p. 293. See also Eugene L. and Ruth E. Hartley, *Fundamentals of Social Psychology* (New York, 1952), pp. 485-86.

19. Elkins, *Slavery*, pp. 86-87, 137-38.

20. *Ibid.*, pp. 104, 225.

21. *Ibid.*, pp. 128-30.

22. Ann Lane, ed., *The Debate over Slavery: Stanley Elkins and His*

Critics (Urbana, Ill., 1971). In his response, except for one important point mentioned in note 39 below, Elkins conceded very little to his critics. Therefore, since he has neither changed his position significantly nor added any supporting empirical evidence, my comments on his use of analogy, his use of personality theory, and his view of the life of plantation slaves are as relevant to the new essay as to the old.

23. It is unlikely that Elkins thought of his analogy as more than an explanation. Yet he created a small ambiguity by labeling one of the sections of Appendix A (p. 225) *"Analogy as evidence."*

24. Winthrop D. Jordan has called my attention to an important question about when Sambo first began to appear prominently in southern plantation literature. He was not the typical slave depicted in the seventeenth and eighteenth centuries. In those earlier years the slave was more often thought of as a dangerous element in the population—a threat to the peace and safety of the English colonies. Of course, it is possible that the Negro's personality had changed by the nineteenth century, when Sambo first became important in southern literature; but there may have been a connection between the appearance of Sambo and the growing moral attack on slavery. Sambo was always one of the proslavery writers' major arguments for keeping the Negro in bondage.

25. Elkins, *Slavery*, p. 224.

26. *Ibid.*, pp. 131-32. It hardly needs to be said that Elkins did not endorse the racist implications of these statements. He used them merely to illustrate the Sambo character that slavery allegedly forced on the Negro in the South. Still, it is worth noting that, except for the racist overtones, his description of the plantation slave was almost identical with that found in the writings of Ulrich B. Phillips.

27. McClelland, *Personality*, p. 70.

28. Genovese, "Rebelliousness and Docility in the Negro Slave: A Critique of the Elkins Thesis," *Civil War History*, XIII (December 1967), p. 314.

29. *Ibid.*, esp. pp. 295-98. See also David B. Davis, *The Problem of Slavery in Western Culture* (Ithaca, 1966), esp. Chapter 8; Carl N. Degler, *Neither Black nor White: Slavery and Race Relations in Brazil and the United States* (New York, 1971); Marvin Harris, *Patterns of Race in the Americas* (New York, 1964), pp. 65-78.

30. Elkins, *Slavery*, p. 229.

31. Bruno Bettelheim, *The Informed Heart* (Glencoe, Ill., 1960), p. 138. For statements of the crucial differences between slavery and the concentration camps see Genovese, "Rebelliousness and Docility in the Negro Slave," pp. 308-309; and Earle E. Thorpe, "Chattel Slavery and Concentration Camps," *Negro History Bulletin*, XXV (May 1962), p. 173.

32. The literature on the camps indicates that there was resistance, but such behavior was not taken into account in Elkins's essay. See especially Eugen Kogen, *The Theory and Practice of Hell* (New York, 1950). See also Genovese, "Rebelliousness and Docility in the Negro Slave," pp. 312-13: Thorpe, "Chattel Slavery and Concentration Camps," p. 175.

33. Since psychologists cannot agree on a definition of personality, the literature gives the historian plenty of latitude. One psychologist compiled a list of almost fifty definitions of personality. Calvin S. Hall and Gardner Lindzey, *Theories of Personality* (New York, 1957), pp. 7-10. Though I am not here considering the personality theories that Elkins did not use, I do question whether he was justified in making so little use of Freud, especially Freud's emphasis on the molding of the child's superego through experiences with the parents. Elkins explained why he thought that Freud is not very useful in understanding the impact of the concentration camps on personality, but he never explained adequately why he thought that Freudian concepts would not help us to understand the personality of the slave. While on the subject of what Elkins has neglected, I must note his failure to use the decidedly relevant writings of Erik H. Erikson on the problem of identity.

34. McClelland, *Personality*, p. 296. See also Hartley and Hartley, *Fundamentals of Social Psychology*, pp. 509-11. However, it is important to note that those who related roles to personality were usually writing about children and the role the parents prescribe. In the case of the slave child, it was the mother or the father or a slave nurse, not the master, who taught the child a role in his early years. The master's direct involvement in child training did not usually begin until the child was old enough to perform some chores—say, at the age of seven or eight. By that time a large part of the child's personality had been formed. In the early formative years the master was not so much the one who prescribed a role as he was an object whom the child was taught to cope with in one way or another.

35. Ralph Linton, *The Cultural Background of Personality* (New York, 1945), p. 26.

36. Erving Goffman, *The Presentation of Self in Everyday Life* (New York, 1959), p. 77.

37. Theodore R. Sarbin and Vernon L. Allen, "Role Theory," in Gardner Lindzey and Elliot Aronson, eds., *The Handbook of Social Psychology* (2d ed., 5 vols.: Reading, Mass., 1968-69), I, esp. pp. 550-57.

38. Elkins, *Slavery*, pp. 86n, 125, 227-28.

39. *Ibid.*, pp. 132n-33n. In his recent essay Elkins claimed that his statement about "a broad belt of indeterminacy between 'mere acting' and the 'true self' " expressed the position he had taken in the original essay. Lane, ed., *The Debate over Slavery*, p. 359. However, in my opinion, this claim represented a shift in his basic position rather than an accurate statement of his original point of view.

40. McClelland, *Personality*, pp. 316-18; Hartley and Hartley, *Fundamentals of Social Psychology*, pp. 521-32; Sarbin and Allen, "Role Theory," pp. 540-44.

41. Erving Goffman, *Encounters: Two Studies in the Sociology of Interaction* (Indianapolis, 1961), pp. 89-90, 107-108.

42. Harry Stack Sullivan, *Conceptions of Modern Psychiatry* (Washington, 1947), p. 18. Speaking of the child and his relations with his parents, Sullivan noted the child's "realistic appreciation of a necessity and a human development of devices to meet the necessity . . . that marvelous human thing, great adaptive possibilities applied successfully to a situation." *Ibid.*, pp. 19-20.

43. *Ibid.*, pp. 13, 21-22.

44. *Ibid.*, p. 22.

45. George M. Fredrickson and Christopher Lasch, "Resistance to Slavery," *Civil War History*, XIII (December 1967), pp. 315-29; Willie Lee Rose, "Childhood in Bondage," unpublished paper read at the annual meeting of the Organization of American Historians, Los Angeles, April 1970; John W. Blassingame, *The Slave Community*; Genovese, *Roll, Jordan, Roll*; Leslie H. Owens, *This Species of Property* (New York, 1976); Levine, *Black Culture and Black Consciousness*. I have suggested other possibilities in Chapters 3 and 8 of *The Peculiar Institution: Slavery in the Ante-Bellum South* (New York, 1956).

46. My study of slavery also called attention to these pressures: "Ideally [slavery] was the relationship of parent and child.

". . . The system was in its essence a process of infantilization . . ." Stampp, *Peculiar Institution*, p. 327.

47. Elkins, *Slavery*, pp. 134-35. I suspect that the ability of these petty administrators to escape the full impact of the terror and brutality of the camps was even more crucial to their psychological balance.

48. In her unpublished paper, "Childhood in Bondage," Willie Lee Rose argued that historians have underestimated the importance of the slave family, especially the role of the father in raising children. See also Genovese, *Roll, Jordan, Roll,* pp. 450-523; Gutman, *The Black Family in Slavery and Freedom,* Part One.

49. In cases where the father lived apart on another plantation, I have counted the children as living with the mother alone, as we would today when parents are separated or divorced. A few slave children lived with the father alone or with neither parent.

50. See Albert J. Raboteau, *Slave Religion: The "Invisible Institution" in the Antebellum South* (New York, 1978), esp. Chapter 8.

51. Goffman, *Encounters*, p. 90.

52. In discussing the problem that boys without fathers have in learning the male role, Eugene and Ruth Hartley noted that the situation changes quickly when such boys find other opportunities to observe this role: "They learn from their playmates and from adult males with whom they come into repeated contact." *Fundamentals of Social Psychology,* p. 504.

53. *Southern Cultivator,* IX (1851), p. 85.

54. Goffman, *Encounters*, pp. 90-91.

55. Fredrickson and Lasch, in "Resistance to Slavery," pp. 322-25, suggested that slaves developed their own standards of fair play through their varying experiences with different masters and overseers.

56. "*Role,* a term borrowed directly from the theater, is a metaphor intended to denote that conduct adheres to certain 'parts' (or positions) rather than to the players who read or recite them." Sarbin and Allen, "Role Theory," pp. 489, 547-50.

57. Thorpe, "Chattel Slavery and Concentration Camps," pp. 174-75. This is an excellent example of one kind of role conflict—the kind that results when an authority figure holds "simultaneous contradictory expectations for one role." Sarbin and Allen, "Role Theory," p. 540.

58. Genovese, "Rebelliousness and Docility in the Negro Slave," pp. 310-11.

59. *Ibid.,* p. 312.

60. *De Bow's Review*, XXV (July 1858), p. 51.
61. Davis, *Problem of Slavery*, p. 238.
62. See Fredrickson and Lasch, "Resistance to Slavery," pp. 325-27, and their sources for behavior in total institutions, especially Erving Goffman, *Asylums: Essays on the Social Situation of Mental Patients and Other Inmates* (Garden City, N.Y., 1961).
63. For persuasive explanations of why there were relatively few insurrections in the antebellum South, see Carl N. Degler, "Slavery in Brazil and the United States: An Essay in Comparative History," *American Historical Review*, LXXV (April 1970), pp. 1013-16; Eugene D. Genovese, "The Legacy of Slavery and the Roots of Black Nationalism," *Studies on the Left*, VI (November-December 1966), pp. 4-6. I believe that a major factor contributing to the larger number of insurrections in Brazil was the imbalance of the sexes on the plantations, whereas most southern slaves lived in family groups. The presence of a large number of young men without women and the absence of the stabilizing influence of the family on Brazilian plantations were bound to create a condition highly conducive to rebellions.
64. See Raymond A. and Alice H. Bauer, "Day to Day Resistance to Slavery," *Journal of Negro History*, XXVII (October 1942), pp. 388-419; Stampp, *Peculiar Institution*, Chapter 3.
65. Genovese, "The Legacy of Slavery," pp. 7-11; Fredrickson and Lasch, "Resistance to Slavery," pp. 317, 326.
66. Sarbin and Allen noted the great qualitative differences in role performance among individuals: "One person may enact a role convincingly and skillfully, while another may be inept." "Role Theory," p. 515.
67. *Ibid.*, pp. 492-96. Hartley and Hartley, *Fundamentals of Social Psychology*, p. 493.
68. Sarbin and Allen, "Role Theory," pp. 491, 496-97, 535; Hartley and Hartley, *Fundamentals of Social Psychology*, p. 498.
69. Elkins, *Slavery*, p. 133n.
70. Fredrickson and Lasch, "Resistance to Slavery," pp. 320-23.
71. John Dollard, *Caste and Class in a Southern Town* (3d ed., Garden City, N.Y., 1957), pp. 257-59.
72. See, for example, Lawrence W. Levine, "The Concept of the New Negro and the Realities of Black Culture," in Nathan I. Huggins, Martin Kilson, and Daniel M. Fox, eds., *Key Issues in the Afro-American Experience* (2 vols.: New York, 1971), II, pp. 125-47.
73. *Farmer's Register*, V (May 1837), p. 32. For an excellent analysis

of "Quashee," the Jamaican counterpart of Sambo, and of the degree to which he was a conscious role-player, see Orlando Patterson, *The Sociology of Slavery: An Analysis of the Origins, Development and Structure of Negro Slave Society in Jamaica* (London, 1967), pp. 174-81.

74. Sarbin and Allen, "Role Theory," p. 524.

75. One must, of course, ask whether runaways were not exceptional slaves with special psychic problems. I do not think that this was the case, because many kinds of slaves ran away for a variety of reasons.

76. *Time*, XCVI (August 24, 1970), p. 42. See also Sarbin and Allen, "Role Theory," p. 527.

III   Time on the Cross: *A Humanistic Perspective*

1. Robert W. Fogel and Stanley L. Engerman, *Time on the Cross*, Vol. I: *The Economics of American Negro Slavery;* Vol. II: *Evidence and Methods—A Supplement* (Boston, 1974). Hereafter cited as FE, I, and FE, II.

2. Edward H. Carr, *What Is History?* (New York, 1962), p. 5.

3. Marc Bloch, *The Historian's Craft* (New York, 1953), pp. 43-44.

4. Eugene D. Genovese, *Roll, Jordan, Roll: The World the Slaves Made* (New York, 1974), p. 676.

5. Lee Benson, *Toward the Scientific Study of History* (New York, 1972), pp. 307-26.

6. Douglass C. North, *Growth and Welfare in the American Past* (Englewood Cliffs, N.J., 1966), pp. v-vi.

7. FE, I, pp. 4, 7-8.

8. *Ibid.,* pp. 3-4, 8.

9. *Ibid.,* pp. 8-9.

10. *Ibid.,* pp. 258-64.

11. *Ibid.,* p. 6.

12. *Ibid.,* pp. 9-11.

13. *Ibid.,* pp. 9-11.

14. *Ibid.,* pp. 108-109.

15. Ulrich B. Phillips, *American Negro Slavery* (New York, 1918). See also Phillips, *Life and Labor in the Old South* (Boston, 1929).

16. Peter Passell, "An Economic Analysis of that Peculiarly Economic Institution," *New York Times Book Review*, April 28, 1974, p. 4.

17. Thomas Fleming, "The 'Real' Uncle Tom," *Reader's Digest* (March 1975), pp. 124-28.

18. Other historical conferences on the book included one at the

University of South Carolina, Columbia, in November 1974, and
a session at the annual convention of the American Historical
Association in Chicago in December 1974.

19. C. Vann Woodward, "The Jolly Institution," *New York Review
of Books*, May 2, 1974, pp. 3-6.

20. Paul A. David, Herbert G. Gutman, Richard Sutch, Peter Temin,
and Gavin Wright, *Reckoning with Slavery* (New York, 1976).

21. Carl Bridenbaugh, "The Great Mutation," *American Historical
Review*, LXVIII (January 1963), p. 326.

22. For example, in fourteen pages of printed text (pp. 109-26) devoted to food, shelter, clothing, and medical care, Fogel and
Engerman resorted to vague, impressionistic quantitative measurements 63 times, or 4.5 times per page. They used the quantitative
term "usually" 14 times, "many" 10 times, "most" 6 times, "generally" 6 times, "some" 5 times, and "much," "occasionally," "frequently," "sometimes," "often," "few," "virtually all," "time after
time," "not uncommon," and "quite common" one to four times
each. These impressionistic measurements were not always used
with care, for they wrote "some" or "many" on occasions when
they would have been more accurate to write "a few" or "hardly
any."

23. For illustrations, see especially David *et al., Reckoning with
Slavery*, Chapters 2-4.

24. Charlotte Erickson, "Quantitative History," *American Historical
Review*, LXXX (April 1975), pp. 359-60.

25. FE, I, p. 226.

26. *Ibid.*, pp. 4-6.

27. See David *et al., Reckoning with Slavery*, Chapters 5, 7.

28. Robert Starobin, *Industrial Slavery in the Old South* (New York,
1970).

29. Richard A. Easterlin, "Interregional Differences in Per Capita
Income, Population, and Total Income, 1840-1950," *Trends in the
American Economy in the Nineteenth Century*, National Bureau
of Economic Research, Studies in Income and Wealth, Vol.
XXIV (Princeton, 1960), pp. 73-140. For a criticism of Fogel and
Engerman's interpretation of Easterlin's findings, see David *et al.,
Reckoning with Slavery*, Chapter 7.

30. *Ibid., passim.*

31. FE, I, p. 215.

32. In another passage, Fogel and Engerman assigned equal responsibility to antislavery and proslavery writers for the false stereotype: "[N]either side ever called the alleged natural incompetence

implausible suggestion (I, p. 134) that, rather than having sexual relations with his own slave women, a wealthy planter could have maintained a mistress in town, "where his relationship could have been . . . more discreet."

54. *Ibid.*, pp. 41, 43, II, p. 42.
55. *Ibid.*, I, p. 215.
56. David *et al.*, *Reckoning with Slavery*, Chapter I.
57. FE, I, p. 40.
58. Passell, "An Economic Analysis of that Peculiarly Economic Institution," p. 4. I do not mean to suggest that quantification results inevitably in an unnuanced and dehumanized history. Properly used, it should improve our comprehension of the great variety of human experience. I am suggesting only that this shortcoming was characteristic of *Time on the Cross*.
59. FE, I, p. 134.

IV   Race, Slavery, and the Republican Party of the 1850s

1. V. O. Key, "A Theory of Critical Elections," *Journal of Politics*, XVII (February 1955), pp. 3-18. Though our interpretations differ in some respects, I have profited from reading William Gienapp's unpublished seminar paper, "The Republican Party before the Civil War" (Berkeley, 1971), and his unpublished dissertation, "The Origin of the Republican Party" (Berkeley, 1979). The first is a perceptive historiographical and methodological critique; the second is a major study based on exhaustive research in both literary and statistical sources.
2. Michael F. Holt, "The Politics of Impatience: The Origins of Know Nothingism," *Journal of American* History, LX (September 1973), pp. 309-31; *id.*, *The Political Crisis of the 1850s* (New York, 1978), pp. 155-88; Eric Foner, *Free Soil, Free Labor, Free Men* (New York, 1970), pp. 226-60. It is important to note that many antislavery Republicans strongly disapproved of nativism and opposed the coalitions favored by more conservative members of the party.
3. Even after the Civil War anti-Catholic sentiment was strong among Republican voters. For example, on May 19, 1865, the Rev. S. A. Bronson wrote to Representative John Sherman of Ohio predicting that the next major political controversy would be "between Protestants and Romanists. . . . Now an effort will be

made for the political ascendency of Romanism in the whole
country. . . . It is very clear to my mind that the African has
been bro't here . . . and now set free that the colored race may
by their enfranchisement, be a Protestant barrier to the Roman-
ising tendencies of foreign immigrants. We are yet doubtless to
owe our salvation as a free people to the aid of negro voters. So
wonderful are the ways of God."

4. Leon F. Litwack, *North of Slavery* (Chicago, 1961); George M.
Fredrickson, *The Black Image in the White Mind* (New York:
1971); William H. and Jane H. Pease, "Antislavery Ambivalence:
Immediatism, Expediency, Race," *American Quarterly*, XVII
(Winter 1965), pp. 682-95.

5. Eugene H. Berwanger, *The Frontier Against Slavery* (Urbana,
1967). See also Chaplain W. Morrison, *Democratic Politics and
Sectionalism: The Wilmot Proviso Controversy* (Chapel Hill,
1967); Frederick J. Blue, *The Free Soilers: Third Party Politics,
1848-54* (Urbana, 1973); Eric Foner, "Politics and Prejudice: The
Free Soil Party and the Negro, 1849-1852," *Journal of Negro
History*, L (October 1965), pp. 232-56.

6. C. Vann Woodward, "The Northern Crusade Against Slavery,"
in *American Counterpoint* (Boston, 1971), p. 147.

7. *Ibid.*, p. 154.

8. Berwanger, *The Frontier Against Slavery*, pp. 137, 140; Woodward, "The Northern Crusade Against Slavery," pp. 147-48.
Though there was some truth in Woodward's statement, it nevertheless strikes me as a considerable exaggeration. The Republican
party was a more complex body than this statement suggested.
Moreover, none of the congressional measures against slavery
adopted during the Civil War was passed in the name of white
supremacy. Nor did Lincoln justify his Emancipation Proclamation in those terms. Finally, in the congressional debates over the
Thirteenth Amendment, the opposition, not the supporters of the
Amendment, spoke in behalf of white supremacy.

9. Eric Foner, *Free Soil, Free Labor, Free Men* (New York, 1970),
pp. 261-300; Richard H. Sewell, *Ballots for Freedom: Antislavery
Politics in the United States, 1837-1860* (New York, 1976), pp.
321-36; George M. Fredrickson, "A Man but Not a Brother:
Abraham Lincoln and Racial Equality," *Journal of Southern His-
tory*, XLI (February 1975), pp. 39-58. See also Hans L. Trefousse,
The Radical Republicans: Lincoln's Vanguard for Racial Justice
(New York, 1969), esp. Chapters 2-3.

10. Woodward, "The Northern Crusade Against Slavery," p. 154.
11. David M. Potter, "Why the Republicans Rejected both Compromise and Secession," in George H. Knoles, ed., *The Crisis of the Union, 1860-1861* (Baton Rouge, 1965), pp. 92-93.
12. Foner, *Free Soil, Free Labor, Free Men*, pp. 303-304. It was significant, moveover, that in spite of all the talk of colonization among conservative Republicans, in neither 1856 nor 1860 did the national platform contain a plank supporting it.
13. Sewell, *Ballots for Freedom*, p. 198.
14. Don E. Fehrenbacher, "Only His Stepchildren: Lincoln and the Negro," in George M. Fredrickson, ed., *A Nation Divided* (Minneapolis, 1975), p. 46.
15. Allan Nevins and Milton Halsey Thomas, eds., *The Diary of George Templeton Strong* (4 vols.: New York, 1952), II, pp. 22, 174, 273-74, 281, 305.
16. Sewell, *Ballots for Freedom*, p. 292. For Sewell's case for the Republican party as primarily an antislavery party in the late 1850s, see pp. 292-320.
17. For the text of the debates see Robert W. Johannsen, ed., *The Lincoln-Douglas Debates of 1858* (New York, 1965). The best critical appraisal is Harry V. Jaffa, *Crisis of the House Divided* (New York, 1959).
18. For the political aspects of Lincoln's racial position see Fehrenbacher, "Only His Stepchildren," pp. 46-47.
19. For a thoughtful discussion of this question see Jaffa, *Crisis of the House Divided*, pp. 28-37, 308-29, 363-86. For an argument that on "the broad racial problem" Lincoln and Douglas "thought alike," see James G. Randall, "The Civil War Restudied," *Journal of Southern History*, VI (November 1940), p. 451.
20. As Fehrenbacher has observed, this statement "is fast becoming the most quoted passage in all of Lincoln's writings, outstripping even the Gettysburg Address and the Second Inaugural." "Only His Stepchildren," p. 41.
21. Given the history of race relations in the century after Lincoln's death, the despair of many black leaders, and the tenacity of the segregationists, Lincoln's pessimism may strike the modern reader as something more than the rationalizing of a racist.
22. Avoiding the slavery issue was as crucial to Douglas's political career as avoiding the race issue was to Lincoln's. That Douglas was no defender of slavery Jaffa amply demonstrates in *Crisis of the House Divided*, pp. 41-62.

23. It is safe to assume that these left-wing Republicans were the voters who favored Negro suffrage in various elections in the northern states, and who had earlier opposed Negro exclusion laws in Indiana and Illinois. For evidence of support for Negro rights in the Republican party see Foner, *Free Soil, Free Labor, Free Men*, pp. 281-90; Robert R. Dykstra and Harlan Hahn, "Northern Voters and Negro Suffrage: The Case of Iowa, 1868," *Public Opinion Quarterly*, XXXII (Summer 1968), pp. 202-15; Phyllis F. Field, "Republicans and Black Suffrage in New York State: The Grass Roots Response," *Civil War History*, XXI (June 1975), pp. 136-47; Michael J. McManus, "Wisconsin Republicans and Negro Suffrage: Attitudes and Behavior, 1857," *Civil War History*, XXV (March 1979), pp. 36-54.

24. Sewell, *Ballots for Freedom*, p. 336.

V The Republican National Convention of 1860

1. Charles W. Johnson, ed., *Proceedings of the First Three Republican National Conventions of 1856, 1860 and 1864* (Minneapolis, 1893), p. 83 (hereafter cited as *Proceedings*). For general accounts of the Republican National Convention of 1860, see Murat Halstead, *Caucuses of 1860: A History of the National Conventions of the Current Presidential Campaign* (Columbus, Ohio, 1860), pp. 120-54; Reinhard H. Luthin, *The First Lincoln Campaign* (Cambridge, Mass., 1944), pp. 136-67; William E. Baringer, *Lincoln's Rise to Power* (Boston, 1937), pp. 188-300; P. Orman Ray, *The Convention that Nominated Lincoln* (Chicago, 1916); Emerson D. Fite, *The Presidential Campaign of 1860* (New York, 1911), pp. 117-31; Allan Nevins, *The Emergence of Lincoln* (2 vols.: New York, 1950), II, pp. 229-60; Don E. Fehrenbacher, "The Republican Decision at Chicago," in Norman A. Graebner, ed., *Politics and the Crisis of 1860* (Urbana, 1960), pp. 32-60.

2. For insights into American political practices in the 1840s, see Robert Gray Gunderson, *The Log Cabin Campaign* (Lexington, Ky., 1957). For the 1850s, see Roy F. Nichols, *The Disruption of American Democracy* (New York, 1948). See also Joel R. Silby, *The Transformation of American Politics, 1840-1860* (Englewood Cliffs, N.J., 1967).

3. Halstead, *Caucuses of 1860*, p. 121; Ray, *The Convention that Nominated Lincoln*, pp. 5-9; John Tweedy, *A History of the Republican National Conventions from 1856 to 1908* (Danbury, Conn., 1910), pp. 38-39; John G. Nicolay and John Hay,

Abraham Lincoln, A History (10 vols.: New York, 1890), II, p. 265.

4. Halstead, *Caucuses of 1860*, pp. 140-41; Frederick Bancroft and William A. Dunning, eds., *The Reminiscences of Carl Schurz* (3 vols.: New York, 1907-1908), II, pp. 176-77; Glyndon G. Van Deusen, *Thurlow Weed: Wizard of the Lobby* (New York, 1947), pp. 245-47, 250.

5. Luthin, *First Lincoln Campaign*, pp. 136-38; Fite, *Presidential Campaign of 1860*, p. 123; William E. Smith, *The Francis Preston Blair Family in Politics* (2 vols.: New York, 1933), I, pp. 474-75.

6. Halstead, *Caucuses of 1860*, p. 121.

7. *Ibid.*, pp. 122, 131-32, 140-41.

8. *Proceedings*, p. 169.

9. *Ibid.*, pp. 91, 97-100.

10. *Ibid.*, p. 130.

11. Halstead, *Caucuses of 1860*, pp. 133-34.

12. *Proceedings*, pp. 127-28, 167.

13. Halstead, *Caucuses of 1860*, p. 129. D. D. Pratt of Indiana served as reading clerk. A Chicago *Tribune* reporter described him as a man "endowed with lungs of brass and clarion vocal powers, the one never tiring and the other superior to all competing sounds." Quoted in Ray, *Convention that Nominated Lincoln*, p. 21.

14. For Republican ideology, see Eric Foner, *Free Soil, Free Labor, Free Men: The Ideology of the Republican Party before the Civil War* (New York, 1970).

15. *Proceedings*, p. 108.

16. Halstead, *Caucuses of 1860*, p. 131.

17. *Proceedings*, pp. 84-86.

18. *Ibid.*, pp. 101-102.

19. *Ibid.*, p. 102; Halstead, *Caucuses of 1860*, p. 129.

20. *Proceedings*, pp. 83-85, 101-102.

21. *Ibid.*, pp. 101-102, 103-104.

22. See, for example, speech of Charles Lee Armour of Maryland, *ibid.*, p. 113.

23. *Ibid.*, pp. 118-19.

24. *Ibid.*, pp. 85-86, 127-28.

25. *Ibid.*, pp. 159, 165.

26. Halstead, *Caucuses of 1860*, p. 134.

27. *Proceedings*, p. 157.

28. *Ibid.*, pp. 83-86; address signed by F. P. Blair, Horace Greeley, John D. Defrees, and others, in New York *Times*, May 15, 1860.

29. *Proceedings*, p. 157.

30. *Ibid.*, pp. 83-86.
31. *Ibid.*, p. 157.
32. *Ibid.*, p. 119.
33. *Ibid.*, pp. 83-84, 159.
34. *Ibid.*, p. 85.
35. *Ibid.*, p. 86.
36. Jeter A. Isely, *Horace Greeley and the Republican Party* (Princeton, 1947), p. 266.
37. *Proceedings*, p. 133.
38. *Ibid.*, pp. 133-37; Tweedy, *History of the Republican National Conventions*, pp. 43-44.
39. Halstead, *Caucuses of 1860*, pp. 135-36.
40. *Proceedings*, pp. 140-43.
41. Halstead, *Caucuses of 1860*, pp. 137-38; Nicolay and Hay, *Lincoln*, II, p. 269.
42. Roy P. Basler, ed., *The Complete Works of Abraham Lincoln* (8 vols.: New Brunswick, N.J., 1953), IV, pp. 34, 47; Halstead, *Caucuses of 1860*, p. 153.
43. *Proceedings*, pp. 109-30.
44. Bancroft and Dunning, eds., *Reminiscences of Carl Schurz*, II, p. 176; Thurlow Weed Barnes, ed., *Memoir of Thurlow Weed* (Boston, 1884), p. 262; Van Deusen, *Thurlow Weed*, pp. 247-49, 251; Luthin, *First Lincoln Campaign*, p. 141. As late as 11:40 p.m. on May 17, the night before the balloting, Greeley reported that Seward would be nominated. New York *Semi-Weekly Tribune*, May 18, 1860.
45. New York *Times*, May 25, 1860; Luthin, *First Lincoln Campaign*, p. 154.
46. New York *Times*, May 25, 1860; Isely, *Horace Greeley and the Republican Party*, pp. 276-86; Barnes, ed., *Memoir of Thurlow Weed*, pp. 273-76.
47. Norman B. Judd to Lyman Trumbull, April 2, 1860, Lyman Trumbull Papers, Library of Congress; Baringer, *Lincoln's Rise to Power*, pp. 184-87; James G. Randall, *Lincoln the President* (4 vols.: New York, 1945-55), I, p. 169. For Lincoln's efforts in his own behalf, see Luthin, *First Lincoln Campaign*, pp. 86-87; Basler, *Complete Works of Abraham Lincoln*, IV, pp. 31-32, 36, 44, 45-46, 47.
48. Luthin, *First Lincoln Campaign*, pp. 146-47, 154-55; Randall, *Lincoln the President*, I, p. 153; Lee F. Crippen, *Simon Cameron: Ante-Bellum Years* (Oxford, Ohio, 1942), pp. 207-13.

49. Kenneth M. Stampp, *Indiana Politics during the Civil War* (Indianapolis, 1949), pp. 38-39; Luthin, *First Lincoln Campaign*, pp. 142-43, 158-59; Crippen, *Simon Cameron*, pp. 214-16; Smith, *Blair Family*, I, pp. 476-77; Thomas J. McCormack, ed., *Memoirs of Gustave Koerner* (2 vols.: Cedar Rapids, 1909), II, pp. 87-89.

50. Halstead, *Caucuses of 1860*, pp. 141-43.

51. Charles Roll, "Indiana's Part in the Nomination of Abraham Lincoln for President in 1860," *Indiana Magazine of History*, XXV (March 1929), pp. 1-13; Stampp, *Indiana Politics*, p. 39; Luthin, *First Lincoln Campaign*, pp. 141-42; Ovando J. Holister, *Life of Schuyler Colfax* (New York, 1886), p. 147n.

52. Fite, *Presidential Campaign of 1860*, pp. 130-31; Luthin, *First Lincoln Campaign*, pp. 160-61; Nicolay and Hay, *Lincoln*, II, p. 270; Koerner, *Memoirs*, II, p. 85; Baringer, *Lincoln Rise to Power*, pp. 267-68.

53. *Proceedings*, pp. 148-49; Halstead, *Caucuses of 1860*, pp. 144-45.

54. Halstead, *Caucuses of 1860*, pp. 149-50; *Proceedings*, p. 153; Chicago *Tribune*, in Ray, *Convention that Nominated Lincoln*, p. 34.

55. Van Deusen, *Thurlow Weed*, pp. 253-54; Luthin, *The First Lincoln Campaign*, p. 166. For Weed's account of the nomination of Lincoln, see his letter to Seward, edited by Glyndon G. Van Deusen in *Mississippi Valley Historical Review*, XXXIV (June 1947), pp. 101-104. In the afternoon, after Lincoln's nomination, Senator Hannibal Hamlin of Maine was nominated for the vice-presidency.

56. Baringer, *Lincoln's Rise to Power*, pp. 222-23.

57. Letter from "Howard" in New York *Times*, May 21, 1860.

58. *Ibid.*, May 19, 1860.

59. *Proceedings*, pp. 163, 165.

60. Halstead, *Caucuses of 1860*, p. 153.

VI *Lincoln and the Secession Crisis*

1. Paul M. Angle, ed., *Herndon's Life of Lincoln* (New York, 1930), p. xxxix.

2. *Ibid.*, pp. 387, 408; New York *Herald*, February 27, 1861. Herndon quoted Davis as saying in 1866: "I know it was the general impression in Washington that I knew all about Lincoln's plans and ideas, but the truth is, I knew nothing. He never confided to me anything of his purposes."

3. Charles W. Ramsdell, "Lincoln and Fort Sumter," *Journal of*

Southern History, III (August 1937), pp. 259-88. See also John
S. Tilley, *Lincoln Takes Command* (Chapel Hill, 1941); Clement
Eaton, *A History of the Southern Confederacy* (New York,
1954), Chapter 21.

4. James G. Randall, "When War Came in 1861," in *Lincoln the Liberal Statesman* (New York, 1947), pp. 88-117. See also *id., Lincoln the President* (4 vols.: New York, 1945-1955), I, pp. 342-50.

5. David M. Potter, *Lincoln and His Party in the Secession Crisis* (New Haven, 1942).

6. Roy P. Basler, ed., *The Collected Works of Abraham Lincoln* (8 vols.: New Brunswick, N.J., 1953), IV, pp. 264-65.

7. *Ibid.,* pp. 151, 153-54, 183.

8. *Ibid.,* pp. 151, 154.

9. Horace White, *Life of Lyman Trumbull* (New York, 1913), p. 111.

10. Basler, ed., *Collected Works of Abraham Lincoln,* IV, pp. 175-76.

11. *Ibid.,* pp. 149-50, 172.

12. Howard K. Beale, ed., *The Diary of Edward Bates, 1859-1866,* American Historical Association, *Annual Report,* 1930, IV (Washington, 1933), pp. 157-58; Indianapolis *Indiana American,* November 21, 1860.

13. Basler, ed., *Complete Works of Abraham Lincoln,* IV, pp. 149-50, 154, 172.

14. Letter of "J. W." in Worcester *Spy,* December 29, 1860; Thurlow Weed Barnes, ed., *Memoir of Thurlow Weed* (Boston, 1884), pp. 312-13; Indianapolis *Daily Journal,* December 25, 1860.

15. Herndon noted that in November Lincoln, like most of the northern people, was reluctant to believe that the South was in earnest. This attitude soon changed, and before his departure for Washington, "Mr. Lincoln had on several occasions referred in my presence to the gravity of the national questions that stared him in the face." Angle, ed., *Herndon's Lincoln,* pp. 382, 408.

16. New York *Herald,* February 1, 1861.

17. Ida M. Tarbell, *Life of Abraham Lincoln* (4 vols.: New York, 1900), I, pp. 405-407.

18. Basler, ed., *Complete Works of Abraham Lincoln,* III, p. 502.

19. John G. Nicolay personal memorandum in John G. Nicolay and John Hay, *Abraham Lincoln: A History* (10 vols.: New York, 1890), III, pp. 247-48. On December 17, Lincoln wrote Weed that "it is the duty of the President . . . to run the machine as it is." Basler, ed., *Complete Works of Abraham Lincoln,* IV, p. 154.

20. *Ibid.*, pp. 157-60, 162, 164-65.
21. *Ibid.*, p. 195.
22. New York *Tribune*, February 18, 1861; New York *Herald*, February 13, 14, 1861. See also New York *Evening Post*, February 12, 13, 1861.
23. Basler, ed., *Complete Works of Abraham Lincoln*, IV, p. 237.
24. For the revisions and text see *ibid.*, pp. 249-71.
25. Philadelphia *Pennsylvanian*, quoted in New York *Evening Post*, March 5, 1861.
26. Boston *Daily Advertiser*, March 9, 1861.
27. *Ibid.*, December 24, 1860. This is the precise distinction that President James Buchanan made when he denied the right of coercion but proclaimed it to be his duty to enforce the laws. James D. Richardson, ed., *A Compilation of the Messages and Papers of the Presidents, 1789-1897* (10 vols.: Washington, 1896-1899), V, pp. 626-37. Lincoln made the same distinction in his Indianapolis address on February 11. Yet, whatever constitutional distinction exists between coercing a sovereign state and using force to maintain federal authority, the practical result is the same.
28. Springfield *Republican*, December 19, 1860.
29. New York *Evening Post*, December 10, 1860.
30. The Rev. C. S. Henry to Senator ———, *ibid.*, January 30, 1861.
31. Basler, ed., *Complete Works of Abraham Lincoln*, IV, pp. 195, 237, 240, 245.
32. *Ibid.*, pp. 204, 211.
33. *Ibid.*, p. 194.
34. *Ibid.*, pp. 266, 271. In the first draft the following words concluded the paragraph quoted above: "*You* can forbear the *assault* upon it; *I* can *not* shrink from the *defense* of it. With *you*, and not with *me*, is the solemn question of 'Shall it be peace, or a sword?' " *Ibid.*, p. 261.
35. Springfield *Republican*, March 6, 1861; Boston *Journal*, March 12, 1861.
36. For detailed accounts of the development of the Fort Sumter crisis, see Kenneth M. Stampp, *And the War Came: The North and the Secession Crisis, 1860-1861* (Baton Rouge, 1950), Chapter 13; Allan Nevins, *The War for the Union* (4 vols.: New York, 1959-71), I, Chapter 3; Richard N. Current, *Lincoln and the First Shot* (Philadelphia and New York, 1963); Stephen B. Oates, *With Malice Toward None* (New York, 1977), pp. 195-227.
37. For arguments that military necessity required the evacuation of Sumter, see Basler, ed., *Complete Works of Abraham Lincoln*, IV,

pp. 279, 286. There is evidence, not altogether reliable, that Lincoln may have proposed the abandonment of Fort Sumter to a delegation of Virginia Unionists if they "would break up their convention, without any row or nonsense." See Potter, *Lincoln and His Party in the Secession Crisis*, pp. 353-58; Nevins, *War for the Union*, I, pp. 46-47, 64; Current, *Lincoln and the First Shot*, pp. 34-35, 94-96. Whether Lincoln seriously expected the Virginians to accept the offer cannot be ascertained. In any event, he could hardly have avoided developing his defensive policy in other directions.

38. Basler, ed., *Complete Works of Abraham Lincoln*, IV, p. 280.
39. *Ibid.*, pp. 424-25. In a sense, Lincoln thus made it clear that he held the prevention of "our national destruction" above peace.
40. *Ibid.*, pp. 316-17.
41. In his message to Congress on July 4, Lincoln mentioned only the letter sent to Anderson by messenger on April 6, but that copy never reached Fort Sumter. The copy sent by mail on April 4 reached Anderson on April 7, and he wrote a reply to it the following day. *War of the Rebellion: A Compilation of the Official Records of the Union and Confederate Armies* (129 vols.: Washington, 1880-1901), Ser. I, Vol. I, p. 294. Lincoln's private secretaries insisted that the letter to Anderson of April 4 "was immediately sent by mail to Sumter." Nicolay and Hay, *Lincoln*, IV, pp. 27-29.
42. New York *Courier and Enquirer*, December 14, 1860.
43. Cleveland *Plain Dealer*, quoted in New York *World*, March 22, 1861. On April 8, the Republican New York *Evening Post* confessed: "Since Mr. Lincoln came into power there has been with some a disposition to censure his seeming inactivity, and to complain that his Administration, thus far, has been only a continuation of the disgraceful policy of his predecessor."
44. For the influence of the tariff issue on the New York merchants, see Philip S. Foner, *Business and Slavery: The New York merchants and the Irrepressible Conflict* (Chapel Hill, 1941), pp. 275ff.
45. Washington Correspondence in New York *Evening Post*, March 29, 1861.
46. Basler, ed., *Collected Works of Abraham Lincoln*, IV, p. 323.
47. *Ibid.*, p. 316.
48. *Ibid.*, p. 330.
49. New Haven *Journal and Courier*, quoted in New York *Tribune*, April 15, 1861; Boston *Daily Advertiser*, April 15, 1861; Provi-

dence *Journal,* quoted in Boston *Evening Transcript,* April 13, 1861.

50. Albany *Argus,* quoted in Boston *Post,* April 6, 1861; New York *Morning Express,* April 11, 1861; Utica *Observer,* quoted in New York *Tribune,* April 13, 1861; Washington Correspondence of New York *Journal of Commerce,* quoted in New York *Morning Express,* April 15, 1861.

51. Nicolay and Hay, *Lincoln,* IV, pp. 44-45, 70.

52. Basler, ed., *Collected Works of Abraham Lincoln,* IV, p. 351.

53. Theodore C. Pease and James G. Randall, eds., *The Diary of Orville Hickman Browning* (2 vols.: Springfield, Ill., 1925-33), I, pp. 475-76.

54. Nicolay and Hay, *Lincoln,* IV, pp. 33, 44-45. John G. Nicolay, *The Outbreak of Rebellion* (New York, 1881), pp. 55, 74.

55. Nicolay and Hay, *Lincoln,* IV, p. 62.

56. See the preface to the paperback edition of Potter, *Lincoln and His Party in the Secession Crisis* (New Haven, 1962), pp. xxxi-xxxii. I should emphasize again that this essay does not accuse Lincoln of "scheming to bring on a war."

57. Basler, ed., *Collected Works of Abraham Lincoln,* IV, p. 332.

58. *Ibid.,* p. 345.

59. Current, *Lincoln and the First Shot,* pp. 199-201. Grady McWhiney, "The Confederacy's First Shot," in *Southerners and Other Americans* (New York, 1973), pp. 72-82, argued that Jefferson Davis "would have liked to do precisely what Ramsdell claimed Lincoln did—maneuver the enemy into firing the first shot . . ."

60. Pease and Randall, eds., *Browning Diary,* I, p. 453.

61. Boston *Post,* December 5, 1860.

62. Springfield (Mass.) *Republican,* April 17, 1861.

VII   *The Irrepressible Conflict*

1. Henry Wilson, *History of the Rise and Fall of the Slave Power in America* (3 vols.: Boston, 1872-77); James Schouler, *History of the United States of America under the Constitution* (7 vols.: New York, 1880-1913). For general historiographical studies of Civil War causation see Howard K. Beale, "What Historians Have Said about the Causes of the Civil War," in *Theory and Practice in Historical Study,* Social Science Research Council Bulletin No. 54 (New York, 1946), pp. 55-102; Thomas J. Pressly,

Americans Interpret Their Civil War (Princeton, 1954); Don E. Fehrenbacher, "Disunion and Reunion," in John Higham, ed., *The Reconstruction of American History* (London, 1962), pp. 98-118; David M. Potter, *The South and the Sectional Conflict* (Baton Rouge, 1968), pp. 88-147.

2 James Ford Rhodes, *Lectures on the American Civil War* (New York, 1913), pp. 2-16, 76-77. These ideas are fully developed in the first three volumes of Rhodes's *History of the United States from the Compromise of 1850* (7 vols.: New York, 1893-1906).

3. Edward Channing, *The United States of America, 1765-1865* (New York, 1896), p. 261; and *A History of the United States* (6 vols.: New York, 1905-1925), VI, p. 3.

4. Arthur C. Cole, *The Irrepressible Conflict, 1850-1865* (New York, 1934), pp. 406-407.

5. Arthur M. Schlesinger, Jr., *The Age of Jackson* (Boston, 1945), p. 432.

6. Allan Nevins, *Ordeal of the Union* (4 vols.: New York, 1947-50), II, pp. 553-54, IV, p. 468.

7. Eugene D. Genovese, *The Political Economy of Slavery* (New York, 1965), pp. 30-31, 34-36. See also Genovese, *The World the Slaveholders Made* (New York, 1969).

8. Eric Foner, *Free Soil, Free Labor, Free Men* (New York, 1970), pp. 71-72.

9. Algie M. Simons, *Class Struggles in America* (Chicago, 1906), pp. 32-36.

10. Charles A. and Mary R. Beard, *The Rise of American Civilization* (2 vols.: New York, 1927), II, pp. 36-42.

11. *Ibid.*, pp. 3-10.

12. C. Vann Woodward, *Reunion and Reaction* (Boston, 1951), "Acknowledgements." Beard's economic determinism attracted a number of southern historians seeking an interpretation that did not stress the moral issue of slavery. See Thomas N. Bonner, "Civil War Historians and the 'Needless War' Doctrine," *Journal of the History of Ideas* XVII (April 1956), pp. 196-97.

13. Nevins, *Ordeal of the Union*, IV, p. 465. For a recent economic interpretation of Civil War causation, see Gavin Wright, *The Political Economy of the Cotton South: Households, Markets, and Wealth in the Nineteenth Century* (New York, 1978), Chapter 5.

14. Avery Craven, *The Coming of the Civil War* (New York, 1942), p. viii. For a critique of revisionism see Bonner, "Civil War Historians and the 'Needless War' Doctrine," pp. 193-216. See also

the brief but perceptive critiques in Fehrenbacher, "Disunion and Reunion," pp. 111-14, and Potter, *The South and the Sectional Conflict*, pp. 92-103.

15. There seemed to be an increased appreciation for the revisionist point of view among history graduate students during the years of the Vietnam War. For a variation of revisionism from a "New Left" perspective see John S. Rosenberg, "Toward a New Civil War Revisionism," *The American Scholar*, XXXVIII (Spring 1969), pp. 250-72.

16. Ulrich B. Phillips, *American Negro Slavery* (New York, 1918), pp. 291-92, 339, 341-42.

17. Frank L. Owsley, "The Irrepressible Conflict," in *I'll Take My Stand*, by Twelve Southerners (New York, 1930), pp. 69, 76.

18. James G. Randall, *The Civil War and Reconstruction* (New York, 1937), pp. 48, 66, 73, 132.

19. Craven, *Coming of the Civil War*, pp. 1, 36-37, 73-74, 76-77, 85, 93.

20. David M. Potter, *Lincoln and His Party in the Secession Crisis* (New Haven, 1942), Preface to the 1962 paperback edition, pp. xviii-xxiii.

21. Charles W. Ramsdell, "The Natural Limits of Slavery Expansion," *Mississippi Valley Historical Review*, XVI (September 1929), pp. 151-71.

22. Henry H. Simms, *A Decade of Sectional Controversy* (Chapel Hill, 1942), p. 146. See also David M. Potter, *The Impending Crisis, 1848-1861* (New York, 1976), p. 454.

23. Ulrich B. Phillips, "Conservatism and Progress in the Cotton Belt," *South Atlantic Quarterly*, III (January 1904), p. 8.

24. Owsley, "The Irrepressible Conflict," pp. 82-83.

25. James G. Randall, *Lincoln the President* (4 vols.: New York, 1945-55), I, p. 86.

26. Craven, *Coming of the Civil War*, p. 161.

27. Charles W. Ramsdell, "The Changing Interpretations of the Civil War," *Journal of Southern History*, III (February 1937), p. 23.

28. Ramsdell, "The Natural Limits of Slavery Expansion," p. 171.

29. [James Buchanan], *Mr. Buchanan's Administration on the Eve of the Rebellion* (New York, 1866), pp. 9-14, 64.

30. Mary Scrugham, *The Peaceable Americans of 1860-1861: A Study in Public Opinion* (New York, 1921), pp. 124-25.

31. Ramsdell, "The Natural Limits of Slavery Expansion," pp. 163, 167.

32. George Fort Milton, *The Eve of Conflict: Stephen A. Douglas and the Needless War* (Boston and New York, 1934), pp. 1-2, 117, 155. For a similar view see Gerald W. Johnson, *The Secession of the Southern States* (New York, 1933).

33. Simms, *Decade of Sectional Controversy*, p. viii.

34. James G. Randall, "A Blundering Generation," in *Lincoln the Liberal Statesman* (New York, 1947), pp. 49-52; *id.*, *Civil War and Reconstruction*, p. iii; *id.*, "The Civil War Restudied," *Journal of Southern History*, VI (November 1940), p. 446.

35. Craven, *Coming of the Civil War*, p. 2; *id.*, *The Repressible Conflict* (Baton Rouge, 1939), pp. 5, 63-64; *id.*, "Coming of the War between the States: An Interpretation," *Journal of Southern History*, II (August 1936), pp. 303-22. For another major study of the sectional crisis of the 1850s with decidedly revisionist overtones, see Roy F. Nichols, *The Disruption of American Democracy* (New York, 1948).

36. Craven's revised revisionism appears somewhat repetitiously in "The Civil War and the Democratic Process," *Abraham Lincoln Quarterly*, IV (June 1947), pp. 269-92; "The 1840's and the Democratic Process," *Journal of Southern History*, XVI (May 1950), pp. 161-76; *The Growth of Southern Nationalism, 1848-1861* (Baton Rouge, 1950), esp. pp. 391-401; *Civil War in the Making* (Baton Rouge, 1951); and "Why the Southern States Seceded," in George H. Knoles, ed., *The Crisis of the Union, 1860-61* (Baton Rouge, 1965), pp. 60-79.

37. David Donald, *An Excess of Democracy: The American Civil War and the Social Process* (Oxford, England, 1960).

38. For an evaluation of recent interpretive trends see Eric Foner, "The Causes of the American Civil War: Recent Interpretations and New Directions," *Civil War History*, XX (September 1974), pp. 197-214. Richard D. Brown, *Modernization: The Transformation of American Life, 1600-1865* (New York, 1976), Chapter 6, develops the thesis that the "strains of modernization" and their uneven impact on North and South caused the Civil War.

39. For a recent exposition of the slavery-cultural interpretation see William J. Cooper, Jr., *The South and the Politics of Slavery, 1828-1856* (Baton Rouge, 1978).

40. Ludwell H. Johnson, *Division and Reunion: America 1848-1877* (New York, 1978), pp. 22-23, 56-57, 61-62.

41. Michael F. Holt, *The Political Crisis of the 1850s* (New York, 1978), pp. 3, 11, 147-48, 152-53, 184-85.

42. Craven, *Coming of the Civil War*, pp. vii-viii.

43. *Ibid.*, 117.

44. Randall, "A Blundering Generation," pp. 40, 44; *id.*, *Lincoln the President*, I, p. 76.

45. Arthur Schlesinger, Jr., "The Causes of the Civil War: A Note on Historical Sentimentalism," *Partisan Review*, XVI (October 1949), pp. 969-81; Pressly, *Americans Interpret Their Civil War*, p. 274.

46. Harry V. Jaffa, *Crisis of the House Divided* (New York, 1959), pp. 27, 395-96, 408-409.

47. Fehrenbacher, "Disunion and Reunion," pp. 105-111.

48. Bernard DeVoto, "The Easy Chair," *Harper's Magazine* (February, March, 1946), pp. 123-26, 234-37; Beale, "What Historians Have Said about the Causes of the Civil War," p. 89. See also Fehrenbacher, "Disunion and Reunion," p. 112; Potter, *The South and the Sectional Conflict*, pp. 96-97.

49. Bonner, "Civil War Historians and the 'Needless War' Doctrine," p. 214.

50. Pressly, *Americans Interpret Their Civil War*, pp. 257, 261, 270-72.

51. Beale, "What Historians Have Said about the Causes of the Civil War," p. 83.

52. Scrugham, *The Peaceable Americans*, pp. 124-25.

53. Randall, *Lincoln the Liberal Statesman*, pp. 151-74.

54. Compare *ibid.*, p. 64, with the original version in *Mississippi Valley Historical Review*, XXVII (June 1940), p. 27.

55. Randall, "Lincoln the Liberal Statesman," pp. 41-44.

56. Fehrenbacher, "Disunion and Reunion," p. 113.

57. Bonner, "Civil War Historians and the 'Needless War' Doctrine," pp. 197, 201, 205-206, 215, 216.

58. Pressly, *Americans Interpret Their Civil War*, pp. 231-53, 260, 283-84.

59. Randall was born in Indiana but lived in Virginia for many years and married a Virginia woman.

60. Craven, *Coming of the Civil War*, pp. vii-viii, 17. Craven's footnotes and bibliography indicate that this book was written largely from southern manuscript and newspaper sources.

61. Phillips, "Conservatism and Progress in the Cotton Belt," pp. 3-4.

62. Simms, *A Decade of Sectional Conflict*, p. viii.

63. Chauncey S. Boucher, "*In Re* That Aggressive Slavocracy," *Mississippi Valley Historical Review*, VIII (June-September 1921), pp. 13-79.

64. Craven, *The Repressible Conflict*, pp. 27-66; id., *Coming of the Civil War*, p. 162.
65. Frank L. Owsley, "The Fundamental Cause of the Civil War: Egocentric Sectionalism," *Journal of Southern History*, VII (February 1941), pp. 3-18.
66. Craven, *Coming of the Civil War*, p. 176.
67. Mr. *Buchanan's Administration on the Eve of the Rebellion*, p. 64.
68. Ramsdell, "Changing Interpretations of the Civil War," p. 27.
69. E. Merton Coulter, *The South during Reconstruction, 1865-1877* (Baton Rouge, 1947), p. 1. For a recent statement of the Ramsdell thesis see Clement Eaton, *Jefferson Davis* (New York, 1977), p. 111.
70. Nor, it should be added, were the attacks of some of their critics.
71. For a perceptive critique of revisionist evaluations of abolitionists, see Martin Duberman, "The Northern Response to Slavery," in Duberman, ed., *The Antislavery Vanguard* (Princeton, 1965), pp. 395-413.
72. See, for example, James Brewer Stewart, *Holy Warriors: The Abolitionists and American Slavery* (New York, 1976), pp. 33-41. Stewart's excellent study is in no sense a traditional revisionist work.
73. See especially David Brion Davis, *The Problem of Slavery in Western Culture* (Ithaca, New York, 1966), and *The Problem of Slavery in the Age of the Revolution, 1770-1822* (Ithaca, New York, 1975).
74. Leon F. Litwack, *North of Slavery* (Chicago, 1961), pp. 216-30; William H. and Jane H. Pease, "Antislavery Ambivalence: Immediatism, Expediency, Race," *American Quarterly*, XVII (Winter 1965), pp. 682-95; C. Vann Woodward, *American Counterpoint* (New York, 1964), pp. 140-62. The indictment of abolitionists as racists is carried to absurd lengths in Robert W. Fogel and Stanley Engerman, *Time on the Cross* (2 vols.: Boston, 1974), I, p. 215.
75. Duberman, "The Northern Response to Slavery," p. 408.
76. See Robert McColley, *Slavery and Jeffersonian Virginia* (Urbana, 1964).
77. For northern racist opposition to slavery expansion, see Eugene H. Berwanger, *The Frontier against Slavery* (Urbana, 1967); Eric Foner, "Politics and Prejudice: The Free Soil Party and the Negro, 1849-1852," *Journal of Negro History*, L (October 1965), pp. 232-56; Woodward, *American Counterpoint*, pp. 140-62.

78. The decline of freedom of thought in the Old South is traced and analyzed in Clement Eaton, *Freedom of Thought in the Old South* (Durham, 1960).

79. For abolitionist exploitation of southern violations of civil liberties, see Russell B. Nye, *Fettered Freedom* (East Lansing, Michigan, 1949).

80. For my argument against the existence of a distinctive southern culture and national identity, see below, Chapter 8.

81. See especially George M. Fredrickson, *The Black Image in the White Mind* (New York, 1971), pp. 43-70; Potter, *Impending Crisis*, pp. 452-56, 458-61; *id.*, *The South and the Sectional Conflict* (Baton Rouge, 1968), pp. 78-83; Stephen A. Channing, *Crisis of Fear: Secession in South Carolina* (New York, 1970), pp. 17-62, 92-93, 264-73; James M. McPherson, "Slavery and Race," *Perspectives in American History* (Cambridge, Mass., 1969), III, pp. 460-73.

82. Ulrich B. Phillips, "The Central Theme of Southern History," *American Historical Review*, XXXIV (October 1928), pp. 30-43.

83. See Chapter 8 below, and Charles Grier Sellers, Jr., "The Travail of Slavery," in Sellers, ed., *The Southerner as American* (New York, 1966), pp. 40-71.

84. Cooper, in *The South and the Politics of Slavery, 1828-1856*, found that "slavery remained constantly at the center of the political debate in the South" and "dominated all other public questions," and that southern politicians "insisted that party policy on slavery-related questions conform to their needs." In explaining this phenomenon Cooper argued that, to Southerners, defending slavery meant "guaranteeing control over their own destiny" and upholding their "sense of honor and equality." (Pp. xii-xiii, 370-71.) This is an accurate description of much proslavery rhetoric, but the rhetoric tended to euphemize the practical interests and deep fears that troubled the South.

VIII   *The Southern Road to Appomattox*

1. Richard H. Rovere in *The New Yorker*, October 28, 1967, p. 87.

2. For an evaluation of early interpretations of Confederate defeat, see Robert D. Little, "Southern Historians and the Downfall of the Confederacy," *Alabama Review*, III (October 1950), pp. 245-62; IV (January 1951), pp. 38-54.

3. David Donald, ed., *Why the North Won the Civil War* (Baton

Rouge, 1960), p. 19. See also John C. Schwab, *The Confederate States of America, 1861-1865: A Financial and Industrial History of the South during the Civil War* (New York, 1901).

4. Donald, ed., *Why the North Won the Civil War*, pp. 19-20, 92-93.

5. Physical factors, such as manpower, railroads, and resources, can be argued more easily with empirical evidence than behavioral factors; but it does not follow that the former are therefore more readily proved as historical causes than the latter. In neither case does the evidence establish a cause-effect relationship outside the historian's mind, and in both cases it is easy for the historian to fall into the logical fallacy of *post hoc, ergo propter hoc*. Both physical and behavioral explanations can be only reasonable hypotheses, and it is as valid to explore one as the other.

6. Donald, ed., *Why the North Won the Civil War*, pp. 91-114. Eric McKitrick developed more fully Potter's thesis that the Confederacy suffered from the lack of a two-party system. William N. Chambers and Walter D. Burnhan, eds., *The American Party System: Stages of Political Development* (New York, 1967), pp. 117-51. For another critical assessment of Jefferson Davis see Nathaniel W. Stephenson, "A Theory of Jefferson Davis," *American Historical Review*, XXI (October 1915), pp. 73-90.

7. Roy F. Nichols, unpublished paper delivered at the annual meeting of the American Historical Association, New York, December, 1960.

8. Frank L. Owsley, *State Rights in the Confederacy* (Chicago, 1925).

9. Donald, ed., *Why the North Won the Civil War*, pp. 77-90.

10. Bell I. Wiley, *The Road to Appomattox* (Memphis, 1956), p. 78; Chambers and Burnham, eds., *The American Party System*, p. 142.

11. Charles H. Wesley, *The Collapse of the Confederacy* (Washington, D.C., 1937), p. 168.

12. E. Merton Coulter, *The Confederate States of America, 1861-1865* (Baton Rouge, 1950), pp. 374, 566. See also Lawrence H. Gipson, "The Collapse of the Confederacy," *Mississippi Valley Historical Review*, IV (March 1918), pp. 437-58; Frank L. Owsley, "Defeatism in the Confederacy," *North Carolina Historical Review*, III (July 1926), pp. 446-51.

13. See J. Cutler Andrew, "The Confederate Press and Public Morale," *Journal of Southern History*, XXXII (November 1966), pp. 445-46, for a summary of Ramsdell's unpublished paper read before the annual meeting of the American Historical Association,

December 1924. See also James W. Silver, "Propaganda in the Confederacy," *ibid.*, XI (November 1945), pp. 487-501.

14. Wiley, *The Road to Appomattox*, p. 106.

15. Donald, ed., *Why the North Won the Civil War*, p. 104.

16. Nichols, unpublished paper.

17. For critical evaluations of the roots of nationalism see Hans Kohn, *The Idea of Nationalism* (New York, 1951); David M. Potter, *The South and the Sectional Conflict* (Baton Rouge, 1968), pp. 34-59.

18. For a vigorous dissent from the interpretation of southern culture presented here, see Eugene D. Genovese, *The World the Slaveholders Made* (New York, 1969). See also Rollin G. Osterweis, *Romanticism and Nationalism in the Old South* (New Haven, 1949).

19. Potter, *The South and the Sectional Conflict*, pp. 68-69; *id.*, *The Impending Crisis, 1848-1861* (New York, 1976), p. 469. See also Carl N. Degler, *Place over Time: The Continuity of Southern Distinctiveness* (Baton Rouge, 1977), pp. 67-97.

20. Charles G. Sellers, Jr., ed., *The Southerner as American* (Chapel Hill, 1960), pp. 40-41.

21. Potter, *The South and the Sectional Conflict*, p. 70. See also Hans Kohn, *American Nationalism: An Interpretive Essay* (New York, 1957), pp. 114, 117.

22. Potter, *The Impending Crisis*, p. 469.

23. Robert Manson Meyers, ed., *The Children of Pride* (New Haven, 1972), p. 641.

24. Kohn, *American Nationalism*, p. 117.

25. Roy F. Nichols, *Blueprint for Leviathan: American Style* (New York, 1963), pp. 143-47, 160-63, 239-41.

26. William S. Hitchcock, "Southern Moderates and Secession: Senator Robert M. T. Hunter's Call for Union," *Journal of American History*, LIX (March 1973), p. 876.

27. The myth of antebellum southern nationalism should not be confused with the twentieth-century concept of regionalism, which is apparent not only in the United States but in most other countries. That the South had distinct regional characteristics is undeniable, but these characteristics never have given the South anything remotely resembling a national identity.

28. Potter, *The South and the Sectional Conflict*, pp. 76-78. See also Paul H. Buck, *The Road to Reunion, 1865-1900* (Boston, 1937).

29. Genovese, in *The World the Slaveholders Made*, rejected the idea

that a significant number of white Southerners had feelings of guilt about slavery and attributes this notion "to the currently fashionable disease, guiltomania." In his view the slaveholders constituted a confident ruling class whose defense of slavery as a positive good signalized its "maturation." Far from a rationalization, the positive-good theory "represented the formulation of a world view that authentically reflected the position, aspirations, and ethos of the slaveholders as a class." Genovese stresses the defense of slavery as a matter of class more than of race.

30. Even as extreme a defender of slavery as George Fitzhugh, when he applied his doctrine specifically to the South, based his argument principally upon race.

31. Sellers, ed., *The Southerner as American*, pp. 40, 44, 47.

32. W. J. Cash, *The Mind of the South* (New York, 1941), pp. 60-61.

33. Wiley, *The Road to Appomattox*, pp. 102-105. See also Lawrence H. Gipson, "The Collapse of the Confederacy," *Mississippi Valley Historical Review*, IV (March 1918), pp. 437-38, 441-43; C. Vann Woodward, *The Burden of Southern History* (Baton Rouge, 1960), pp. 20-21.

34. William R. Taylor, *Cavalier and Yankee* (New York, 1961), pp. 17-18.

35. Sellers, ed., *The Southerner as American*, pp. 67-71.

36. William P. Trent, *Southern Statesmen of the Old Regime* (Boston, 1897), pp. 291-92.

37. Thomas B. Alexander and Richard E. Beringer, *The Anatomy of the Confederate Congress: A Study of the Influences of Member Characteristics on Legislative Voting Behavior, 1861-1865* (Nashville, 1972), pp. 339-40.

38. E. Merton Coulter, *William G. Brownlow* (Chapel Hill, 1937), pp. 154-77.

39. Wiley, *The Road to Appomattox*, pp. 102-105.

40. Jack P. Maddex, Jr., "Pollard's *The Lost Cause Regained*: A Mask for Southern Accommodation," *Journal of Southern History*, XL (November 1974), pp. 595-612.

41. Gipson, "Collapse of the Confederacy," p. 443.

Index

DATE DUE